Possessed

BRUCE HOOD

Possessed

Why We Want More Than We Need

ALLEN LANE
an imprint of
PENGUIN BOOKS

ALLEN LANE

UK | USA | Canada | Ireland | Australia
India | New Zealand | South Africa

Allen Lane is part of the Penguin Random House group of companies
whose addresses can be found at global.penguinrandomhouse.com

Penguin
Random House
UK

First published 2019
001

Copyright © Bruce Hood, 2019

The moral right of the author has been asserted

Set in 10.5/14 pt Sabon LT Std
Typeset by Jouve (UK), Milton Keynes
Printed and bound in Great Britain by Clays Ltd, Elcograf S.p.A.

A CIP catalogue record for this book is available from the British Library

ISBN: 978-0-241-40995-4

For my lawyer brother, Ross; someone who has made a career out of ownership but, in spite of this, remains one of the most generous human beings I have known.

Contents

Prologue

If the whole of Earth's existence were a 24-hour clock, then our species, *Homo sapiens*, which evolved around 300,000 years ago, would appear at about 5 seconds to midnight. Each of our individual lives represents an even more infinitesimal time in the life of the universe. That you are even here at all is a miracle. The likelihood of any of us being born is almost zero when you think about all the other countless eggs and sperm that never met, and all the individuals who could have potentially existed, compared to those of us who were actually born. If you are reading this, then you have also probably been given certain opportunities in life that are denied to many. Education and access to books are not shared with all of humanity. We are very fortunate to be here, even for such a short time. And yet, how do we typically spend this precious moment of existence? In the relentless pursuit of ownership, mostly, and defending what is ours from those who seek to take it away.

We are so lucky to exist in the first place, and yet many of us who live in affluent societies pursue lifestyles that have the goal of accumulating as much stuff as possible, in the belief that this is our purpose in life. After our basic needs and comforts are met, however, acquiring more stuff is rarely fulfilling; yet there is an insatiable desire to own more. Humans are not content to just exist within the physical universe, but rather we feel the compulsion to claim as much ownership over it as possible, because we believe the more we possess, the better we will be. We come into existence for the duration of a lifetime, our physical bodies made from the particles of stardust from a distant cosmic explosion, and then spend much of that life staking our claim over parts of the universe! Not only is this a gross miscalc-ulation of our importance, but the pursuit is ultimately pointless.

During our time on this planet, we fight for property, fence it off, covet it and feel that the goals of life come down to everything we can claim ownership over, only to die and return to dust and never know what becomes of the stuff we worked so hard to get. We spend our lives building sandcastles with turrets and moats to defend from intruders, only for them to be washed away by the waves of time. We are not ignorant. We know we are not immortal and can't take stuff with us, but the pursuit of possessions is an all-consuming drive that gives many of us our purpose in life.

We are defined by what we own, and the psychological power of ownership is so strong that individuals will risk their lives to keep their possessions. The prospect of death should be a sobering reminder of the ultimate futility of ownership. Yet in 1859, 450 passengers on the *Royal Charter*, returning from the Australian goldmines to Liver-pool, drowned when it was shipwrecked off the north coast of Wales. Many were weighed down by the gold they would not abandon so close to home. History and mythology are littered with tales of mat-erialistic folly, from the legend of King Midas with his golden touch, unable to appreciate his wealth, to the reality of recurrent boom–bust economic cycles of the modern era where ordinary lives are shattered by financial institutions gambling with the global economy. It's not just gamblers who have an addiction to wealth accumulation; so does the majority of mankind.

Our lives are controlled by the accumulation of possessions, and with each new generation we discard most of what was left to us and set out to acquire our own new stuff. It is not enough to own, but rather we pursue more stuff, because in doing so we are satisfying the urge to acquire. Possessions are associated with individuals and each of us wants to carve out our own piece of the universe by what we own. Twenty years ago, my wife, Kim, and I inherited the worldly possessions of her parents, who had both died fairly young. These are household items that her parents had cherished. We still use a few items, but most are stored away in the attic. We should get rid of them, but Kim cannot bring her-self to do so because it would represent removing the last physical trace of her parents.

All of us leave behind evidence of ourselves through what we owned. Much of the appeal of memorabilia and antiques is this connection with the past. I like to visit auction houses and second-hand shops to marvel at the sorts of possessions that filled up people's lives. Everything was once owned by someone who may have thought it was the most desirable thing to have. They may have worked hard for it, felt the joy of owning it or even risked their lives to get it. Maybe a medal for bravery, a collection of toy cars, or a silver-backed mirror – all these items could have had some special significance for the previous owner. How would you feel knowing that personal stuff you cherish will be discarded eventually, or sold to someone who has no idea who you are? Not everyone would be bothered, and some of us are clearly more obsessed by materialism than others, but ownership reveals something profound about what motivates us as a species. The word 'motivate' is apt here as it comes from the word 'emotion'. Why do we feel the need to own? And why does ownership produce such emotional capital?

The rich have more wealth and can buy more stuff than the poor, but possessions represent more than simply economic status. Rather, we have an emotional relationship with many of the things we own or aspire to own. We think that happiness comes from getting what we want, but very often what we want does not make us happy. The psychologist Dan Gilbert calls this 'miswanting' and it is a common human affliction.[1] We are just not very good at predicting how much joy and satisfaction that acquiring things will bring us. This is particularly true for ownership and, indeed, much consumer advertising works by selling us the promise that we will be happier owning particular products.

Take the pride and joy for many people in the West: the first car that they own. Many will work hard to attain one, feel pride in acquiring it and will defend it vigorously. It becomes part of their identity. Every year, owners are seriously, even fatally injured trying to prevent the theft of their vehicles which are leased or insured. It's not the money at stake but rather the ownership. When someone threatens to take our stuff we behave unreasonably, as if the threat is directed at us personally. This can lead to an unhealthy relationship with our possessions. Car owners have been known to stand in front of speeding vehicles[2] or cling to the bonnets of their stolen property[3] in a futile attempt to keep their possession, and yet, in the cold light of day, few rational individuals would endanger their lives for the value of a car. But, equally, we can become easily dissatisfied with our cars and feel the pressure to upgrade when we see our neighbour's new car in their driveway. Ownership fuels competition. In this one-upmanship race we cannot all be winners as there is always someone ahead of us and there must be those behind us.

Then there are the long-term consequences of ownership. Many of us buy and consume more than we need in the full knowledge that we are acting irresponsibly towards future generations because of the limited resources we are using up, the expended energy and increased carbon emissions that are changing the climate. The vast number of people on the planet and their activity are contributing to global warming, and it is their consumption patterns that are the most significant factor.[4] Individually, we do not feel personally responsible. We justify our actions as insignificant in comparison to the 7 billion others and question why we should curtail our behaviour when everyone else is helping themselves. Even though individually we would readily die for our children today, ownership is such a motivating drive that we are not readily going to change our wanton consumerism for the next generation.

In 2011, according to the Worldwatch Institute, which produces the annual 'State of the World' report on human behaviour:

> By virtually any measure – household expenditures, number of consumers, extraction of raw materials – consumption of goods and services has risen steadily in industrial nations for decades, and it is growing rapidly in many developing countries . . . If the consumption aspirations of the wealthiest of nations cannot be satiated, the prospects for corralling consumption everywhere before it strips and degrades our planet beyond recognition would appear to be bleak.[5]

It goes on to report that for each category of consumption the evidence presented is overwhelming, but there is one simple calculation worth focusing on. Currently, the planet has 1.9 hectares of biologically productive land per person to supply resources and absorb wastes, yet the average person on Earth already uses 2.3 hectares' worth. These 'ecological footprints' range from the 9.7 hectares claimed by the average American to the 0.47 hectares used by the average Mozambican. The situation can only worsen with the world's population predicted to rise continually, with 83 million being added each year. How can we also address such growing inequality?

If ownership evokes inequality between the haves and have-nots, then even the most ardent capitalist can see that things have got out of hand. Less than 1 per cent of the world's population own over half of the world's wealth, stoking the fires of unrest, rebellion, uprising, revolution and wars. China and India have a combined population of over 2.75 billion people. Most are poor. How can developed countries morally defend their privileged position of wealth by denying the same level of prosperity to other countries? Then there are the consequences of conflict. Wars are fought on many grounds, but they all share the same conflict over ownership. The current refugee crisis in Europe has triggered xenophobia and fear of loss of ownership, with a corresponding shift to right-wing protectionism. Today's politics is replete with the language of ownership and control, whether it is President Trump campaigning to build a wall to keep migrants out of the US or the UK exiting the European Union to halt the influx of immigrant workers and refugees.

Why this book now? Why should we be concerned that ownership is the root cause of conflict? Fighting over resources is not new and the data tells us that the world is actually a much better place to live today than in the past. In virtually all the key dimensions of human well-being life is much better than it was only a few hundred years ago, and yet most of us think the world is going to hell in a handcart in a phenomenon known as *declinism* – the belief that the past was much better than the present.

Various polls in the last few years reveal that most citizens in prosperous countries overwhelmingly believe that the world is getting worse, though it is notable that this pessimism is not shared with citizens of developing countries who are experiencing increased economic growth.[6] Again, declinism is a distorted perspective that plays into the hands of right-wing politicians who stoke the fires of nationalism and protectionism. The reasons for declinism are many, from various biases in human cognition (including rose-tinted nostalgia and the tendency to pay greater attention to future dangers, especially if you are already wealthy) to the well-known adage that bad news is more newsworthy than optimism. Declinism explains why extreme actions and politicians seem warranted when you hold unreasonable fears for the future.

In contrast to this wall of pessimism, psychologist Steven Pinker is fiercely optimistic and thinks that doom-mongers are stirring up unwarranted panic.[7] The world is getting better by all measures of progress, from violence, health and wealth – even if these have all been achieved at a cost of increased consumption of natural resources. The healthier, wealthier lives that more and more of us expect means that life is getting better; but for how long, and what about the environmental consequences of unbridled consumerism? No worries, Pinker argues. As soon as we approach a crisis point, history tells us that humans have the ingenuity and intellect to overcome adversity and will always have the capacity to pivot to address environmental challenges. I hope he is right, but surely it is more prudent to address behaviours that we know are creating environmental problems now rather than put faith in future solutions.

One unequivocal crisis that is with us already – and not about to be solved easily or quickly – is climate change. Here there is universal agreement among the experts that things will change significantly in the future and may get much worse for life on the planet. However, both extreme pessimism and optimism on this issue are equally dangerous. The problem with pessimism is that it generates a sense of 'what's the point?' fatalism that it is futile to try to change, thereby undermining any efforts to find a solution. On the other hand, unbridled optimism that relies on the hope that future science and technology will solve all the problems is equally irresponsible, in that it ignores the urgent need to address and change current behaviours.

No doubt, science and future technologies *will* overcome many of the problems generated by the current over-consumption by an increasing world population, but with better education we can change our ways to avoid ecological disaster. The more affluent and educated people are, the more they become concerned over environmental issues. For example, since dramatic images of sea-life choking on discarded plastic in our oceans appeared in the BBC *Blue Planet II* documentary in 2018, there have been high-profile campaigns in the UK and abroad to reduce the amount of plastic packaging and wastage – symptoms of the throwaway consumer economy. Although a drop in the ocean, plastic straws have all but disappeared from bars and restaurants across the UK. It might be a minor gesture, but one that demonstrates that people and businesses respond quickly when faced with a bad-news story. These gestures can lead to movements. In the same way that the cumulative lack of responsibility in caring for our environment can generate problems, as we examine in later chapters, solutions can also emerge if individuals collectively raise concerns. The Extinction Rebellion protest that disrupted London during the unseasonably hot spring of 2019 was noteworthy in that it included children and adults from all walks of life with no history of civil unrest. It was less to do with anarchy and more to do with anxiety and frustration at the lack of progress to halt climate change. Campaigns for better futures from educated, healthy, wealthy people based on concerns over declinism have arisen precisely because people are less optimistic that things will get better on their own or that technological progress will find solutions. In the case of climate change and environmental concerns, manufacturers are now reacting by investing in alternatives because consumers are demanding it. In January 2019, one of the world's largest chemical conglomerates, Dow, announced that it was committing $1 billion to lead a global alliance of companies to end plastic waste, with a further goal of another $1.5 billion of investment.

As the world's population grows, we can expect greater demands for energy to improve the quality of life, but consumerism for the sake of ownership is a human preoccupation that we should abandon as unnecessary. In the same way that the demand for furs and ivory in the West was curtailed by concerned conservationists over the last thirty years, humans can change their behaviour when it comes to consumerism. What better way to do that than to lift the lid on ownership to reveal what really motivates us to own things that we don't really need?

Possessed is the first book to explore how the psychology of ownership has shaped our species and continues to control us today. 'To own' is such a common term in our everyday language that we barely notice it, and yet it is one of the most powerful concepts in the human mind. Ownership is interwoven into human behaviour in profound ways – what we do, where we go, how we describe ourselves and others, who we help and who we punish. The very fabric of civilization is founded on the concept of ownership, and without it our societies would collapse. How did this dependency on ownership come about? How do each of us learn to yield or wield the power of ownership? Why are we compelled to own more and more? How does ownership shape our 'own' identities? When you start to ask these sorts of questions, the familiar concept we are all used to begins to look decidedly strange. It is no longer a legal state, an economic position, a political weapon or a convenient way to demarcate possession. Rather, it is one of the defining features of what it is to be human and how we all conceive of ourselves.

We come into the world with nothing and leave with nothing, but in between, in our brief moment on life's stage, we strut and fret over possession as if our existence is defined by what we can own. For many of us, our lives are controlled by this relentless pursuit, even though we do so at the risk to ourselves, our children and, ultimately, the future of the planet. If we are going to change, then we need to understand what ownership is, where it comes from, the motivation it generates and how to be just as happy without it.

We think that happiness will come from owning things but, if anything, it often leads to more misery. Few people can look back on a life preoccupied with the accumulation of wealth and honestly conclude, 'That was a life worth living.' We are so caught up in the chase that we rarely truly appreciate the achievements, or the costs – for the individual, for the species, or for the planet. When you take into consideration all the effort, all the competition, all the disappointment, all the injustices and, ultimately, all the damage we have wreaked in the pursuit of material wealth, it does seem such a wasted life to be constantly striving to own. And yet we can't seem to stop ourselves. We are possessed – but it is a demon we can exorcise if we understand *why* we need to own.

I

Do We Really Own Anything?

FINDERS KEEPERS

Shannon Whisnant wanted to be famous. He dreamed of being a somebody. He used to fantasize about having his own TV show and becoming a celebrity and, following a bizarre ownership dispute, he did.

In 2007, Shannon bought a meat smoker grill at an auction in Maiden, Catawba County in North Carolina. A storage unit company was legally selling off the contents of lock-ups where owners had fallen behind in their rental payments. Shannon, a local trader, paid a couple of dollars for the grill but soon discovered that he had bought more than he had bargained for. After opening the grill, he made a grisly discovery – a human left foot. Whose foot was it? Was it the remains of a grave robbery or some unreported murder? Following a 911 phone call, the Catawba County police confiscated the foot to begin their investigations. Soon everyone was talking about the foot. Shannon thought there was money to be made in people's morbid curiosity, so he called the police to demand his foot back. Meanwhile, the police had discovered that the foot had not come from someone deceased, but rather from a man named John Wood, who was well and truly alive and living in South Carolina.

Three years earlier, John had been in an aeroplane crash that had tragically killed his father and left him with severe injuries, requiring the amputation of his foot. John wanted to keep his foot as a memorial to his father, so he requested it from the hospital and, remarkably, they complied. Unusual behaviour, but then at the time John had a severe drink and drugs problem. Eventually he lost his home and so he put his belongings, including his foot and the grill, in a lock-up before moving to South Carolina. When his mother refused to keep up with the storage rental payments, the contents were auctioned off. That's how John's foot came into the possession of Shannon Whisnant.

When John Wood returned to reclaim his limb, Shannon protested that he was the rightful owner. The two men met in a car park in Maiden where Shannon tried to persuade John to agree to joint custody of the foot. Eventually, the dispute was settled in court, where it was ruled that the foot should be returned to John but that Shannon was entitled to $5,000 compensation as he had a legitimate claim of ownership over the foot.

The story, featured in a 2015 documentary film, *Finders Keepers*, is intriguing because it challenges our natural assumptions about ownership.[1] What could be more obvious than the uncontested ownership of your own body? We are appalled that someone would claim ownership over another's body part. The unwelcome touching of another person's body, let alone claiming ownership over it, is not acceptable to most people. This is something that even pre-schoolers are sensitive to; four-year-olds think that you need permission to touch someone else's hand or foot.[2] With age, that appreciation of personal ownership gives a person the right to treat his or her body as they wish: as independent adults, tattooing, piercing, modifying or allowing others to touch their body, are simply ways for people to exercise their ownership.

Contrary to intuition and common wisdom, however, you do not necessarily own your body. If you did, then you would be perfectly entitled to do with it as you wish. But this depends on where you live. Take tattooing, for example. It is illegal and restricted in many countries. When I was a Harvard professor in the 1990s, tattooing was still illegal in Massachusetts and considered a 'crime against the person'. If you wanted to get inked you had to travel across to Rhode Island, until the law was finally changed in 2000. When it comes to buying or selling your body, or even just parts of it, in many countries, the law prevents you. For example, it is currently illegal to sell one of your kidneys in the US and the UK, but it's perfectly legal to do so in Australia and Singapore where live organ donors can profit from the sale of their organs.[3]

The most extreme personal act against our body is suicide. Though largely decriminalized, suicide is still illegal in many countries. Assisted suicide and euthanasia, even when a patient is terminally ill and miserable, are against the law in the UK. In ancient Rome, suicide was considered an acceptable, even noble act among its citizens, but it was illegal for slaves and soldiers because these individuals were considered property of the slaveowners and the state and so suicide was considered theft. As theft was a capital crime, attempted suicide by these individuals was technically, but ironically, punishable by death.

Destruction of property is still part of the modern definition of ownership in many jurisdictions. It operates in the Anglo-American legal systems and originates from Roman law – *jus abutendi*, the right to destroy property or treat it as you wish. In his book *Playing Darts with a Rembrandt*,[4] Illinois law professor Joseph Sax points out that if an art collector wants to play darts with his Rembrandt portrait, no one should stop him because of *jus abutendi* rights. The logic behind the law was that if destruction is recognized as the most extreme legitimate act, then the owner who is entitled to destroy his property is necessarily entitled to all the other rights over his property as well.

Most of us would not knowingly destroy a masterpiece but there are examples, such as the Rockefeller family who commissioned the renowned Mexican artist Diego Rivera to paint a mural at their Manhattan office complex in 1932, only to have the artwork chiselled off the walls because they did not like the political message it portrayed. Then there was the Taliban, who blew up two giant statues of the Buddha in Afghanistan in 2001 as the world looked on in horror at this cultural vandalism. The magnificent statues, dating back to the sixth century, were carved out of the solid rock of a cliff and recognized as a world heritage site. The Taliban justified the destruction as removing idolatry but, as the occupying force in the country, they were also making a point about ownership, asserting their right to do as they wish with property they had seized.

Even if you are dead, issues of body ownership are still contested. When the British broadcaster Alistair Cooke, famous for his *Letter from America* radio show, died, his daughter chose to have him cremated by a cut-price funeral home she selected from the yellow pages. She received his ashes in a cardboard box, assuming that these were all the last mortal remains of her father. What she did not know was that his body had already been plundered by an unscrupulous bio-medical tissue company who paid the funeral home to retrieve the celebrated broadcaster's leg bones. These were worth $7,000 on the human tissue market: a market where no one owns the remains of the deceased, but companies can earn up to $100,000 for 'processing' a body to recover tissue. This is all perfectly legal and necessary for biomedical procedures. Harvesting body parts is worth over $1 billion annually in the US, even though not one cent goes back to the families of the deceased.[5]

We may be appalled by these cases of wanton destruction and apparent theft, but our intuitions are often out of kilter with the law. One recent study took ten actual 'finders keepers' cases from the legal archives and then submitted them as thought experiments to see how members of the public would adjudicate.[6] Each of these was an example of somebody finding some item of value on another's property but, rather than defaulting to finders keepers, people used a wide variety of criteria to make their decisions, which often conflicted with the actual ruling of the courts. Some people thought that if a landowner does not know about an object then the finder is entitled to it, whereas others thought that landowners owned every object on their land even if they did not know it was there. Then there were distinctions between finding objects in public versus private spaces, underneath or on top of the ground, and whether an item was originally lost or mislaid. Each of these distinctions generated different attitudes to ownership. Clearly, when it comes to ownership, people have differing opinions.

WHAT IS PROPERTY?

It might seem straightforward but defining property can be tricky. Explicit rules regarding property can be traced back about 4,000 years, to the first known written code of law that contained – among other things – rules regarding lost and stolen property. Plato and Aristotle began a philosophical debate about how to best regulate ownership and possession of things. Their discussions would continue into Roman law, medieval laws and the considerations of Enlightenment thinkers such as Thomas Hobbes, who argued that without state interventions regulating property ownership, bitter disputes would be common, and life in peace and harmony impossible.[7]

Nearly every subsequent modern law textbook begins with the question 'What is property?' but it is never answered. In fact, the question is unanswerable because the meaning of property constantly changes. Consider the definition of property based on the work of English philosopher John Locke, who in 1698 argued that, as we own ourselves, we own property that we create, shape, or produce through our labour: 'Whatsoever then he removes out of the State of Nature hath provided, and left it in, he hath mixed his Labour with, and joined to it something that is his own, and thereby makes it his Property.'[8] In other words, we can claim possession of property through the work we put into it either in the form of our labours or through the value we place upon items through investing our money in them by purchase. Locke argued that purchasing is simply another form of creating an object because wealth stems from the fruits of our labour. But this straightforward transaction requires mutual agreement about what is property and capable of being owned in the first place. Nomadic peoples such as the Scandinavian Sami considered you could only own what you could carry, whereas the North American indigenous peoples believed that the only thing you could own was your soul, as it was the only thing that could be taken into the next world.

These differing cultural understandings of property have produced some odd exchanges. In 1626, Dutch explorer Peter Minuit purchased the island of Manhattan from the Delaware tribe of the Lenape people for around $24 worth of goods. There is no bill of sale signed by the various parties, other than a brief mention in a letter to the Dutch West India company that simply states: 'They have purchased the Island of Manhattes from the savages for the value of 60 guilders.' At the time, Manhattan (from the Lenape *manna-hata*, 'hilly island') was rich farming land surrounded by water and perfect for establishing a colony. It may have seemed like a bargain but the Lenape had no real concept of the transaction so it could never be a fair deal. It was common practice to exchange goods for safe passage or to occupy lands, but the notion of land ownership in perpetuity was alien to the indigenous peoples. Both parties probably left the meeting with different thoughts about what had taken place. Heather Crowshoe-Hirsch, a modern Skinnipiikani-speaking descendant of one of the First Nation tribes, explains: 'The use of the term "property" is inadequate as that which is transferred does not, technically speaking, belong to anyone. The possession of these items is "Creator-given" and as such, cannot be owned or deemed property as such.'[9] The indigenous peoples of North America did not recognize the concept of ownership of land, which is why they were probably bemused by the offers to hand over possession owned by the gods. No one can sell what they do not own in the first place. Indeed, it is questionable whether a legal sale ever took place.

Ownership also varies from one jurisdiction to the next; for example, it is illegal to own a hedgehog in New York City, but not across the Hudson River in the neighbouring state of New Jersey.[10] In some US states you cannot resell concert tickets above the face value even though you own the ticket. The resale of medical prescriptions is prohibited, even for innocent items such as spectacles or contact lenses, because it is considered in the same category as drug dealing. You never really own software for your computer but rather just license it, which means you can't legally sell it on. The situation gets even more complex when you cross the border of another country; there is a whole legal area known as 'Conflict of Laws' which attempts to resolve differing legal systems. Most countries consider their neighbours' systems to be illogical. If they did not, then we would all have the same international laws of ownership. Currently they do not exist. The right to property is recognized in Article 17 of the Universal Declaration of Human Rights, but there are no universal laws on what is property or what you can do with it.

What can be owned has also changed over time. Take the now-abhorrent notion of owning another person. Until fairly recently in history, in many countries, people could be legally owned as slaves. One of the objectives of war was not only to take control of lands and resources but also to enslave people who were valuable for the labour they could provide. Some of the greatest wonders of the ancient world were built by foreign slaves, such as the Great Pyramid of Giza, which required 100,000 slaves toiling for thirty years to complete.

Slavery raises not just moral concerns but logical inconsistencies in ownership as well. For example, Locke's concept of property established through labour was enshrined in the US constitution as an incentive for homesteaders and pioneers to transform the land through their efforts. By working the land to forge a new nation, they were granted the legal rights of ownership through the toil of their efforts. Indigenous peoples were moved out of their territories into reservations so that their ancestral land could be handed over to homesteaders to develop. This was often conducted in chaotic land grabs or land runs. It must have been an incredible sight when, at noon on 16 September 1893, 100,000 homesteaders rushed forward with their horses and wagons to stake their claims (by driving stakes into the ground) for the best spots on 6 million acres of former Cherokee grazing land in the state of Oklahoma. This was all perfectly legal as the Cherokee had been compensated with a paltry sum for their ancestral lands.

When it came to slaves, however, the new nation was faced with a major contradiction between the constitution and Locke's concept of property. If slaves worked the land, then they should become owners, according to Locke. Even though 'all men were created equal', according to the Declaration of Independence of 1776, slaves were considered property to be bought and sold. And as property, they should not be able to own independently of their masters.

To reconcile the conflict, slaves were deemed not to have free will. They were, in effect, considered lacking the capacity to think for themselves. In one famous test case in the nineteenth century, a black slave named Luke was put on trial in Florida for the malicious destruction of property when he shot donkeys that had strayed on to his master's property.[11] Initially, the court sentenced Luke to prison, but an appeal ruled him innocent because he had been ordered to shoot the animals by his master. To punish him would have amounted to acknowledging that Luke had free will. Ironically, in order to uphold the slave code, the court ruled that it was wrong to imprison Luke. Slaves were considered chattels and, as such, had 'no volition to disobey a master' any more than an animal did.

In addition to classifying slaves as animals with no free will, the slaveowners argued that they did not actually own the slaves themselves, but rather their productivity. As the Southern law professor Francis Lieber wrote in 1857, 'Properly speaking ... the slave himself is not property but his labour is. Property involves the idea of a free disposal over the thing owned ... we possess no such right over the slave and have never claimed it.'[12] In other words, any action of the slave was owned by his master but, in turn, the master was accountable for the actions of his slave. The laws relating to slavery were not directed at the slaves (because they had no free will anyway) but rather the owners who were responsible for their property. An elaborate example of this principle is provided when in 1827, the State of Louisiana judged that a small sum of money found by a slave, but unbeknown by his master, which was then stolen from the slave, counted as theft from the master.

Today slavery is recognized as illegal in every country, but that has not stopped the lucrative trade in human ownership. Globalization has generated considerable wealth in the West by exploiting cheap labour in other countries, but this has created the conditions where the poorest are forced to survive on less. According to various bodies, including the UN International Labour Organization[13] and the Global Slavery Index,[14] over 40 million people are currently enslaved worldwide. The quality of life that we enjoy in the West is achieved through the inadvertent misery we cause by demanding cheaper and cheaper products. For example, much of the tea and chocolate we consume is produced by workers in conditions that amount to slavery. We regularly enjoy the benefits of cheap labour when we buy products from countries such as China and India, two of the five worst-offending nations that account for 58 per cent of all modern slavery. Many workers become the migrants who pay traffickers to get them to the West, even though they then risk getting trapped in a cycle of abuse and indentured labour.

Unlike the slave trade of the previous centuries, modern-day slaves are 'free' to leave their workplace, but the threat of punishment and grinding poverty leaves labourers with no option but to keep working in sweatshops making the everyday things we consume. Consider the Apple iPhone, 'Designed in California. Assembled in China' and one of the most popular devices in the world. However, what many iPhone owners are probably unaware of is that these sleek, must-have trophies of designer consumerism are assembled in sprawling Chinese factories that have long been criticized for exploitation, stress, bullying and high rates of worker suicides.[15] In 2012, 150 workers at an iPhone factory gathered on a rooftop and threatened to jump, until they were talked down with the promise of improved working conditions. In other sweatshops across the world, it is estimated around a quarter of these modern slaves are children, generating $150 billion each year in illicit profits for traffickers. Most of them are female.[16] All of them are considered property to be traded.

YOU'RE MINE

PAUL: Holly, I'm in love with you.
HOLLY: So what?
PAUL: So what? So plenty. I love you. You belong to me.
HOLLY: No. People don't belong to people.
PAUL: Of course they do.
HOLLY: Nobody's going to put me in a cage.

Breakfast at Tiffany's, dir. Blake Edwards (1961)

Over the centuries, in addition to slaves and indigenous peoples, the other major subjugated group have been wives. Up until the nineteenth century, marriages were exercises in ownership rights as wives were considered the property of their husbands, described in English common law by the term 'coverture'. A wife was under the authority ('cover') of her husband and she was not entitled to ownership rights independently. Legally, husband and wife were considered one person as far as the law was concerned, and that one person was the husband.

The reasons for marriage have changed as well. Contrary to romantic Western views, love and marriage do not go together like a horse and carriage, or at least, that was never the intention. As the historian Stephanie Coontz points out, until the late eighteenth century, marriage was regarded as far too vital an economic and political issue to be left to the free choices of the individuals involved, let alone to be based on something so transitory or ephemeral as love.[17] Indeed, marrying for love was considered a serious threat to the social order as it placed the marital relationship above the priorities of parents, family and God.

For centuries, marriage had done much of the work of markets, governments and social-security systems. It controlled the distribution of wealth through inheritance, enabling provision for the extended family members in an uncertain future. At the top end of the scale, society marriages were used to set up political, economic and military alliances. Even though Shakespeare wrote of love extensively in his plays, it was often in conflict with family obligations as epitomized in his romantic tragedy *Romeo and Juliet*. It would have been regarded as foolish to marry for love alone, especially when the stakes were high. Rather, the primary directive was the stability and transfer of wealth, not happiness ever after. Marital bliss was an added bonus only, if it all worked out.

The higher the stakes, the more the couple's relatives had a say in the process of marriage. In many cultures, if the husband died before the wife, she would be expected to marry another man from her husband's family so as to retain the continuity of inherited wealth. Then there was the initial price of marriage. Probably the most common form of this is the dowry system, where the family of the bride pays a sum to the husband's family to allow their daughter to marry their son.

In the West, where the dowry system was abandoned centuries ago, it is still the custom when it comes to paying for the wedding. When I got married, I had naively assumed that my in-laws had bankrolled the event because, at the time, I was a poor graduate student and they wanted to impress their friends and acquaintances by putting on a big bash. In fact, their display of generosity was also a legacy from the old dowry system. Today, many people still adhere to the tradition that the bride's family hosts and pays for the wedding.

Why would families pay the cost of a dowry to marry off their daughters? For the simple reason that in most societies marriage was essential for recognition as an adult for both sexes. In the Middle Ages, an Englishman was expected to marry when he achieved some degree of financial independence in order to establish a household. This is the origin of the word 'husband'. Prior to that, he was a man of no substance.

A woman needed to marry in order to be socially accepted. An unmarried woman was regarded with suspicion and generally ostracized. It is ironic, then, that in marriage a woman lost her ownership rights to property or even the right to speak for herself in a court of law. Any property she brought to the marriage came under her husband's control. Any major decisions beyond the day-to-day running of the household required the permission of her husband. Only by the end of the nineteenth century did this situation change significantly with the gradual introduction of the Married Women's Property Act in the UK between 1870 and 1893. Certain aspects of coverture survived as late as the 1960s in some US states, and in the UK it was not until 1980 that a married woman could apply for a mortgage in her own name. Even the country's first female prime minister, Margaret Thatcher, was not entitled to take out a mortgage when she came into power in 1979. Today, there are still many societies that discriminate against women. According to a 2016 World Bank report, thirty nations still designate men as head of the household, while women in nineteen countries are legally obliged to obey their husbands.[18]

Marriage was a strategic way of sharing resources to ensure the long-term prosperity of the family. The husband was responsible for his property, which included his wife, children and servants, and could be called to account on their behalf in a court of law. He was expected to control them like an owner. The term 'wedlock' conveys the notion of this committed ownership. Only in the eighteenth and nineteenth centuries, with the rise of the Romantic movement in Western culture, did love really enter into the equation that is considered a prerequisite for a successful marriage today.

Although most modern Westerners are appalled at the notion of arranged marriages, we should not forget that this is a minority view; most societies today still operate with some form of the practice. Contrary to Western prejudices, arranged marriages do not necessarily mean forced marriages, where the potential partners have no say in the final decision. Very often there is a considerable amount of research, matchmaking and introductions done on behalf of the couple who end up agreeing to any potential match.

Even if we believe we have abandoned arranged marriages in the West, a quick consideration of the socio-economic circumstances that bring people together reveals that families still play a major role. In one way or another, families pay for the schooling, college, neighbourhood and the eventual profession that their child enters, which all contribute to Mr Right meeting Ms Right (or whatever combination that emerges). It may not feel arranged, but people are more likely to marry someone they meet on a regular basis.[19] To some extent, all this is changing as digital communications make it easier to find and change partners, as evidenced by the popularity of dating apps among the 'Tinderella' generation.

The wider landscape is also changing. Marriages are not inevitable, and there are traditional societies that have no such institution, such as the Mosuo tribe of China. Then there are the various combinations of multiple wives (polygamy), multiple husbands (polyandry) and the recent trend for multiple lovers out of wedlock (polyamory). There are many reasons for these varieties of cohabitation in the West, but one important factor is the rise of the welfare state that has provided support to the individual, reducing the need for co-dependency through marriage. It was not so long ago that bearing children out of wedlock was relatively rare and considered shameful, whereas today, half of all UK children are born outside marriage. The rise in single parenting is due to the decline in marriage, with half as many marriages taking place today in the West compared to the 1960s. And around half of marriages now end in divorce. In Europe, the divorce rate has doubled over the same period.[20]

Divorce is largely focused on property and ownership, but divorce lawyers are a fairly recent phenomenon. In the past, divorce was so difficult and complicated that it was rarely enacted.[21] Moreover, the husband stood to gain everything. Before a divorce law was finally enacted in 1857, the number of divorces in English history stood at a mere 324. Only four of those cases were initiated by the wives. Compare that to the 107,000 divorces in England in 2016 alone, which represents a rate of around four out of every ten marriages. By contrast India, with its predominant system of arranged marriages, has a divorce rate of only 1 in 100. However, as the Indian economy grows and provides more social support for individuals, it remains to be seen whether this shift towards Western values will threaten traditional marriage.

Not only is divorce a source of much misery, it is one of ownership inequality that is stacked firmly against the divorced wife, who is more likely to be financially worse off. A large-scale study of marital splits estimated that divorced men, especially fathers, are around a third wealthier following divorce.[22] Regardless of whether she has children, the average divorced woman's income falls by more than a fifth and remains low for many years. Even though ownership does not usually bring individuals together in marriage, as it did in the past, it certainly plays a major role in the separation of couples today.

PARENTAL POSSESSION

Ownership also binds families together. There are varying perceptions of obligation to the family but, across the world, children all start off as the responsibility of their parents. This is a form of ownership in that parents have control over their children. However, that relationship is reciprocal. We belong to the family and the family belongs to us. When we no longer want a child to be part of the family because they have shamed us, then we disown them and, in turn, if they no longer want anything to do with the family, they disown the family.

From the parent's perspective, there is an expectation of exclusive access to their child, just like property. Parents rarely talk about owning their children, but testimony collected during the 2001 Redfern Report into the UK's Alder Hey scandal was full of references to ownership that many identified with.[23] Between 1988 and 1995, organs and tissue samples from children who had died were collected and stored at the Alder Hey Children's Hospital in Liverpool without the full consent of their parents. As we have already established, this was not illegal as there can be no ownership of a corpse. It was also fairly standard practice in pathology at the time to retain human tissue for research purposes. When this practice came to light, however, parents were outraged. In the report, one parent commented, 'It feels like bodysnatching. The hospital stole something from me', with another stating: 'Alder Hey stole 90 per cent of my child.'

The grieving parents' demands for the return of the body parts were couched in terms of ownership: returning what was rightfully theirs and the right to decide what would then happen to their children's remains. It is clear from their commentary that the parents felt they had a right to their children's body parts, whether this consisted of whole excised organs, tissue slides, or small segments of tissue encased in paraffin blocks. One of the most remarkable things about the Redfern Report was that there was little consideration given to the legal standing of ownership of the deceased; instead it focused on making a set of recommendations to address the parents' concerns by putting in place procedures to prevent the practice happening again.

Public opinion and the law remain at odds when it comes to looking after our children. For most parents, it is unacceptable that others, including the state, could take control over their child, even when it is in the child's best interest. In 2018, Alder Hey hospital would once again come under critical public scrutiny when the parents of Alfie Evans, a terminally ill toddler, battled doctors over the decision to remove his life support. The parents took their case to the High Court, Court of Appeal, Supreme Court and European Court of Human Rights but were unsuccessful. Many protesters who supported the parents thought this was a simple case of the state controlling the life of a toddler – or, as Brexiteer Nigel Farage complained in an interview with Fox News, 'Are our children now owned by the state?'[24] Legally, however, parents in most Western countries do not own their children, and have not since the nineteenth century. Rather, parents are guardians who are expected to look after the best interests of the child – the same criterion that courts apply in such cases.

It is a little-known fact that this parental ownership works both ways: adult children are legally obliged to look after their elderly parents if they become dependent on others, though few destitute parents have ever enforced the 'filial support laws' that exist in the US and the UK. However, this might be set to change; nursing homes in the US have begun to sue children on behalf of infirm parents to recover the cost of their care. In 2012, a Pennsylvanian nursing home successfully sued a son for $92,000 to pay for his mother's care and the number of similar cases is on the increase.[25] As the post-war baby boomers approach their senior years and people are living longer than ever before, the state is ill-prepared to look after its elderly and will be seeking to recover those costs of care from the children.

In many cultures, parents can give their children away and, in some instances, effectively sell them. In India, despite the fact that the dowry system has been outlawed for the past forty years, many families of the groom still expect payment from the bride's family in order to marry their sons. They want a return on their investment. Having only girls can therefore spell economic disaster for poor families. Often dowry disputes lead to violence; sometimes wives are tortured to extract more money, or simply killed so that their husband can remarry to obtain another dowry. There is even an official statistic specifically for it. Section 304B of the Indian Penal Code accounts for dowry deaths and registered over 24,000 such deaths in the three years between 2012 and 2015.[26] Those that are not killed are often scarred for life in acid attacks. (Arranged marriages might produce low divorce rates, but the persistence of the traditional dowry system in India is still a source of much misery for women.)

Another despicable abuse of parental ownership is the trafficking and sale of children, especially daughters, into the sex trade, which is still prevalent in many poorer parts of the world such as rural Thailand. There it is commonplace for daughters working in the infamous Bangkok brothels to support their entire family. It is not considered an honourable way to make a living but poverty overrides moral judgement in these situations. Agents scour the countryside offering the promise of employment opportunities in the 'recreation or entertainment business' with cash loans to poor families, which have to be paid off.

Before we cast judgement on these families, however, we should remember that the industrial revolution in nineteenth-century Europe was largely supported by children working in terrible conditions. Children were a source of income in hard times, something that will be familiar to anyone who has read Charles Dickens. There was even a 'stubborn son' law enacted in New England in 1646 that entitled parents to have their sons executed if they were disobedient.[27] Prior to modern social-care systems, children were an investment. They were expected to earn their keep and, when the parents and grandparents needed care and assistance, it was usually the family's daughters who were expected to look after them. It is only in modern times in wealthy Western societies that we have shifted the burden of supporting families from the individual to the state's healthcare and social-support systems. What we must not forget is that throughout the world this societal support is the exception, not the rule. This is why children are considered vital resources in many developing countries and are still traded as commodities.

Our reliance on children is likely to become more pronounced with the so-called demographic time bomb in countries that have falling birth rates. As the population ages, the elderly become increasingly dependent on the young to look after them. An ageing population means higher costs for government, a shortfall in pensions, reduced social-security funds, a shortage of people to care for the very aged, a shortage of young workers and, ultimately, a slow-down in the economy. This recession produces a spiralling cycle of decline, and as the economy shrinks people have fewer children, thereby exacerbating the problem further.

This shortfall in live births is particularly worrying for increasingly secularized societies with declining populations. Compared to secular societies, religious societies have fertility rates two or three times as high as the population-replacement level.[28] This difference explains why the demographic time bomb is particularly bad for countries in the West, where a combination of the decline in births, increased life expectancy and the high cost of social care are a perfect storm for economic disaster. We have become so used to social support from our governments that many from the political right believe that the state has gone too far and must return the responsibility to look after family members to the families themselves – to look after their own.

POLITICAL OWNERSHIP

As someone of Scottish descent from the MacFarlane clan, I was amused to discover that the motto for my clan is, 'This I'll defend.' I am not sure what my ancestral fellow clansmen were promising to defend but I expect that it was land they believed they owned. In many ways, the political unrest and conflicts that are currently sweeping the globe reflect this sentiment of fear of loss. Many people today feel an acute sense of threat from others competing for resources, taking over their lands and control of their lives. To give an extreme example, suicide terrorism is often associated with individuals who feel dispossessed because their lands have been illegally taken. In his analysis of over 188 suicide attacks between 1980 and 2001 around the world, from Sri Lanka to the Middle East, Robert Pape, an American political scientist, concluded that the dominant purpose for these actions was to coerce foreign governments to withdraw from occupying territories that the terrorists regarded as homelands they owned.[29]

The recent political unrest spreading across Western democracies is also a fight over national identity and ownership in the face of a perceived threat from outsiders. Both Brexit's 'taking back control' and Trump's 'America first' campaigns were blatant displays of nationalism in the face of perceived attack from foreigners. The campaign language was all about possession: my country, my job, my way of life.

Why are we now witnessing the rise of populists such as Donald Trump in the US and Matteo Salvini in Italy? And why did we not see this wave coming? In retrospect, what might seem surprising is the extent of incredulity that someone like Trump could ever win the presidential election. How could people vote for such a xenophobic, misogynistic, polarizing person with no political experience, who lacked any integrity and espoused paranoid conspiracy theories about his rivals and the media and who traded insults on Twitter with anyone who dared to criticize him? He might not be statesman-like, but Trump is a self-professed man of the people. His resemblance to the Italian dictator Mussolini, another famous populist, is more than just physical.[30] They both represent a shift in politics to the extreme right, and similar populist movements have taken place across many Western democracies. According to a 2018 BBC report, far-right political parties have made significant gains in elections across Europe in recent years.[31] Remarkably, viewing these political upheavals through the lens of ownership provides an intriguing explanation for this phenomenon.

One common assumption is that Trump rose to power because of economic hardship experienced by his core voters. It is true that inequality in the Midwest Rust Belt, where Trump enjoys the strongest support, has increased as traditional industries in the region have been devastated by technological innovation and competition from cheaper foreign imports. In the past few decades, increased globalization has spurred these economic shifts. It is ironic, then, that the poor voted for someone who comes from the wealthiest 1 per cent of society who have all benefitted from globalization at the expense of domestic workers.

According to the economic hardship perspective, this inequality, rising economic insecurity and social deprivation among the left-behinds has fuelled resentment of the political establishment in not being represented or in control of their destiny. It is certainly true that much of Trump's voter base includes this sector of society, but economic hardship alone does not explain why populism has also gained wide support across Europe as well. Nor does it explain why populist support is generally stronger among the older generation, males, the less educated and the religious.

The explanation comes down to fear. Most people aren't authoritarian, but they can easily become so. One reason is uncertainty for the future, which makes people more inclined towards the obedience and authority appeal of the far right. In their analysis of the current political environment, psychologists Karen Stenner and Jonathan Haidt concluded that a third of adults across Europe and the US were predisposed to authoritarianism, while 37 per cent were non-authoritarian and 29 per cent were neutral.[32] However, when we feel we are under threat or perceive that our moral values are being eroded, we shut down our openness and prefer individuals with power. For example, following the 9/11 terrorist attacks, national surveys found no change in attitudes to civil liberties among US citizens who already scored high on measures of authoritarianism. Rather, the perceived threat led to increased support for more aggressive and restrictive policies among those who had previously been more liberal.[33] Those who sit on the fence when it comes to politics are easily pushed over to the right when they are frightened.

This shift in response to threat is argued to be one of the main reasons why the majority of otherwise liberal Germans supported the rise of the Nazis, as a backlash against the economic hardship they faced after the First World War.[34] The reason people react like this is that they cannot easily cope with uncertainty. Across a wide range of studies of both humans and non-humans, conditions of uncertainty produce psychological and physiological stress. This uncertainty triggers the so-called 'fight or flight' response, an evolutionary preparation for action that, if not resolved one way or the other, produces chronic anxiety. In times of uncertainty, we seek reassurance from leaders who articulate a strong, resolute vision to compensate for our own weakness. This partly explains the support for individuals like Trump. 'Often mistaken but never in doubt' is considered a virtue in such climates. This hypothesis received support in a study of 140,000 voters, across sixty-nine countries over the past two decades, which revealed that those experiencing the greatest economic hardship voted for populist candidates unless they reported a strong personal sense of control.[35] However, economics still does not explain why Trump also received the support of rich, white males for whom hardship was not a primary concern.

Ronald Inglehart, a political scientist, argues that, in addition to economic inequality, we are witnessing the effects of a reaction against post-materialism that began in the 1970s.[36] For much of human history there has been constant conflict and economic uncertainty, which leads to frugal and cautious behaviour. Following the end of the Second World War, industrialized countries, especially the US, experienced a sustained economic boom that lasted from 1945 to the recession in the early 1970s, a period commonly known as the Golden Age of Capitalism. When Trump talks about 'making America great again', he is referring to this period of prosperity. The majority of the workforce during this time was made up of individuals born between 1925 and 1945 who are known as the silent generation because, having experienced the austerity of the war years as well as the insecurity of the post-war years linked to the threat of nuclear Armageddon, they were more cautious than their parents.

As the major wage earners in the workforce during this period, the silent generation invested in material possessions and provision for stability through investments and financial planning. However, the generation that followed did not share the same values. By the 1960s, the children of the silent generation were rebelling against their parents' values. These were the teenagers and twenty-something baby boomers who represented the counterculture. Many of them became political activists, resisting authority, control or convention. As a consequence there was an intergenerational shift from those who survived years of uncertainty to those who grew up taking their security for granted. This was a post-materialist movement that was less materialistic, less conformist, less authoritarian, more secular and more sexually diverse, and which valued human rights, equality and self-expression over the establishment. This counterculture of the 1960s railed against the establishment, but eventually the frenzied activism was replaced by a period of relative calm in the 1970s when the world recession hit. Inglehart contends, however, that during this period of apparent inactivity, a 'silent revolution' backlash was brewing among the older generation, who saw these social changes in the younger generation as a threat to their traditional materialist values.

According to Stenner and Haidt, things changed too fast for the older generation, as 'Western liberal democracies have now exceeded many people's capacity to tolerate them'.[37] Among this group, progressive change is perceived as moral decline. Moreover, as we noted in the Prologue, declinism – the tendency to view the past more favourably through rose-tinted nostalgia and fear for the future – is also more prevalent in older generations. For example, the market research company YouGov reported that most UK citizens they surveyed in 2012 thought that since the Queen's coronation in 1953 Britain had changed for the worse, with the greatest proportion endorsing this negative view among the over sixties.[38] However, when the pollsters asked whether the quality of life for the average person had improved, respondents overwhelmingly agreed that it had. People can objectively recognize better healthcare, better education and a better quality of life but this does not translate into an appreciation that things are getting better overall. When asked whether the world was getting better in a second poll in 2016, only 11 per cent thought the future would be better, with 58 per cent saying that it was getting worse.[39] Again, the older participants were, the more pessimistic their responses. As the witty columnist Franklin P. Addams noted, 'Nothing is more responsible for the good old days than a bad memory.'

A silent revolution would explain why older members of society voted for populist politicians. In their analysis of the shifting political landscape, Inglehart and his colleague Pippa Norris discovered that the economic hardship account could not explain all the data they analysed from the demographics of voters for 268 political parties in 31 European countries.[40] Rather, there was more consistent evidence for a cultural backlash against post-materialism and the changing social values that engendered:

> We believe that these are the groups most likely to feel that they have become strangers from the predominant values in their own country, left behind by progressive tides of cultural change which they do not share. Older white men with traditional values – who formed the cultural majority in Western societies during the 1950s and 1960s – have seen their predominance and privilege eroded. The silent revolution of the 1970s appears to have spawned an angry and resentful counter-revolutionary backlash today.[41]

If populism reflects deep resentment of big business, banking, multi-nationals, the media, government, intellectual elites, scientific experts and the privileged rich, then it is somewhat ironic that much of this list resonates with the anti-establishment attitudes of the post-materialist movement. The similarity of grievances, however, makes more sense when the issues are considered from the perspective of ownership. Each generation wants to take back control of the values they hold most dear from the current generation who seem to be squandering them.

CAN YOU OWN AN IDEA?

We usually think of property as material possessions but, increasingly, our understanding of property reflects an appreciation that immaterial things can also be owned. With the rapid expansion of digital technology into everyday life over the last twenty years, consumers are increasingly aware of how easy it is to create and own information that forms the basis of original ideas such as songs, images and stories. These used to be stored on physical media such as vinyl, film and paper but now they are patterns of noughts and ones stored as computer code. In the past pirates stole physical things, but now simply downloading or copying a file of code can be theft of intellectual property.

Intellectual property has been legally protected – and disputed – for hundreds of years. In one of the first documented cases of copyright infringement, dating back to the sixth century, an Irish missionary,

St Columba, copied a religious text belonging to St Finnian, who demanded the copy back. Finnian petitioned and received the support of King Diarmait, who ruled, 'To every cow belongs her calf, therefore to every book belongs its copy.' However, Columba was undeterred and argued that no one could own the word of God. With the support of the O'Neill clan, the dispute escalated and resulted in the battle of Cúl Dreimhne (also known as the Battle of the Book) in *c.*560 CE and the loss of 3,000 lives.

Today, intellectual property disputes are less bloody but much more common. In 2017, the US Patent and Trademark Office issued 347,642 patents, most to protect intellectual property. We not only recognize the legal ownership of intellectual property, but we despise those who plagiarize others' ideas. Often the complaint is financial, but for many claimants it is also a matter of pride and principle. For example, consider one of the greatest scientific discoveries of all time, the structure of DNA. Teams of scientists from the universities of Cambridge (Watson and Crick), London (Franklin and Wilson) and the California Institute of Technology (Pauling) raced against each other to be the first to discover the double helix. Rather than working together, they competed to claim the prize at the cost of personal conflicts and dubious professional conduct. Scientists are notoriously sensitive about who can claim the right of discovery even when there is no financial gain involved. The venom directed at those who take credit for someone else's ideas conveys the extent to which plagiarism is considered a despicable act.

Even children intuitively understand the basics of intellectual property from around six years of age, as they tend to dislike 'copycats'. They prefer those who draw their own pictures, compared to those who copy, and value original ideas over effort.[42] In one study, a group of six-year-olds was asked to value pictures where either an adult or the child provided the idea of what to draw, or where they simply provided the labour. Irrespective of who actually drew the picture, they preferred those pictures with original concepts.[43] Even when the output has no material content, young children have a concept of intellectual ownership. When they are told that Steven hears Zack talking about a mathematics problem he is trying to solve, and provides Zack with the answer, children reason that Steven is the owner of the solution. If Tim overhears Steven explaining the answer to Zack and tells other members of the class, six-year-olds think Tim has stolen the idea. Likewise, if one child comes up with a story, then it is not acceptable for another child to change the ending.[44]

Despite this concern for the ownership of ideas from an early age, there really is no such thing as an original idea. Take a moment and try to think of one. You can't logically, because all ideas are preceded by earlier ideas that have come from someone else. Like the ancestral lands of the North American indigenous peoples, there has always been someone there before you. Somehow intellectual property lawyers must establish that the idea you claim ownership over is sufficiently different to any pre-existing ideas, and that really comes down to a judgement call. Even if there is a pre-existing idea, it has to be recognized as such in order to be judged as the original.

Figments of the imagination can be property too. Not only do people spend around $165 billion on video games, but some are prepared to spend considerable amounts of money acquiring virtual property. The current record is for a virtual property, 'Club Neverdie', located on a virtual asteroid, in a virtual universe, that sold for $635,000 in 2010. Before you question who in their right mind would pay that amount for something that does not exist in reality, the club was earning an average of $200,000 per year for its owner, Jon Jacobs, from players who bought virtual goods and services. According to *Forbes* magazine, Jacobs bought the virtual asteroid back in 2005 for $100,000, after taking out a mortgage on his real-life house.[45]

What about our digital property? If someone takes your picture in the street, do they own your image? Like selling body parts, it depends on where in the world you are. In many countries photography in public places is considered acceptable, whereas in other countries you require the permission or consent of the person being photographed. You can look at other people, but you can't record that experience as a photograph.

Probably the most surprising (and, for many, the most worrying) development in intellectual property concerns ownership of personal data. In 2014, Facebook was criticized for conducting an experiment on 700,000 unsuspecting users where the company manipulated the content of the news feed to present either happier or sadder stories.[46]

When positive stories were reduced, Facebook users produced fewer positive posts and more negative posts; when negative stories were reduced, the opposite pattern occurred. Even though the effect was very small, the researchers concluded that, given Facebook's scale, this would have corresponded to hundreds of thousands of emotional expressions per day.

The concern was that people's choices were being covertly manipulated and controlled by others. In 2016, the personal information of 50 million Facebook users was stolen by a data analysis company, Cambridge Analytica, in order to influence the outcome of the Brexit vote in the UK and to propel Donald Trump into power in the US – or at least that was the claim.[47] Here the property of value was the list of users and their friends that enabled targeted marketing strategies, which were believed to influence voting by 'psychographic' manipulation. Despite the media frenzy surrounding Cambridge Analytica and the paranoia of psychographics, there is very little scientific evidence that people's choices could be so easily controlled.[48] Much like the myth of subliminal messages, where it was claimed that cinema audiences bought more popcorn or soda when a brief image of the item was inserted into a frame in the movie without them noticing,[49] there is no good evidence that either consumers' or voters' choices can be swayed by such subterfuge.[50]

It is not so much that we are being manipulated by advertising that offends (because most of us realize when it is happening), but rather we become indignant when we think our personal data has been taken and used without our consent – a violation of ownership. In truth, we have been giving it away for years. Digital companies who provide us with 'free' services, in the forms of platforms, games and all the other amazing software that is readily available today, make money out of the personal data we give them. And we willingly consent to this. When you sign up for some online service or download an app on to your smartphone, then it is highly likely that, buried within those 'Terms and Conditions' that you need to assent to in order to access the service, there will be a series of statements allowing the service providers to harvest, process and store your personal data. How the data will be used has to be described, but very few of us have the time, inclination or legal knowledge to decode the pages and pages of legal jargon – so we simply tick the box saying that we accept the terms and conditions. This data can be used or sold on to other companies that analyse how people vary and how they behave. Such data is extremely valuable because it enables companies to discover patterns and trends that can be used to shape commercial strategies. In the past, this market research was very expensive and limited as it required individuals to conduct the sampling and surveys, but with digital technology it is trivially easy, if somewhat overwhelming in the sheer volume of data we provide. That's one of the reasons why digital companies can become so valuable, even though they do not charge for their services. If a service is free, then you and your personal data are the product.

Every time we use our smartphones, we can be tracked in terms of what we do, where we go and who we speak to. There are laws that are meant to protect us, but if we tick the consent box then these companies are acting perfectly legally. In fact, not many of us seem to care that much, at least not until our attention is drawn to the fact that these companies are in the business of data mining. Recently, it has become a legal right to take back ownership of your personal data by having it removed or deleted, so that you can be effectively 'invisible' online, but aside from the hassle, in doing so you will lose out on the conveniences and benefits these companies provide. It's the price we pay to be part of the digital generation.

A MERE CONCEPT

I opened this book by focusing on bodies, values, ideas and information because they are so personal, and seemingly obviously owned. But ownership is a convention that varies over time and across civilizations. Disputes over ownership may be resolved using legal and moral systems established thousands of years ago, but more often we need lawyers, since ownership can be interpreted in different ways. It also seems likely that there will be continuing need to revise the laws of ownership as societies change. The problem of establishing ownership was pointed out by the English moral philosopher Jeremy Bentham, when he wrote, 'There is no image, no painting, no visible trait, which can express the relation that constitutes property. It is not material, it is metaphysical; it is a mere conception of the mind.'[51] In other words, ownership does not exist in Nature but rather is constructed in the human mind. As such, it is a concept – a thought – but, nevertheless, a very powerful one. Ownership controls just about every aspect of our daily lives: what we can claim rights over; what we can and cannot do with property; and where or where not we can go. Without ownership, our lives would be chaotic and unstructured, which is why it is at the core of our legal systems and the basis for the norms of social behaviour that most of us abide by. When we ignore ownership, or fail to recognize it, we are acting antisocially and, in some cases, illegally.

Ownership not only shapes society by its rules and legislation, it controls us psychologically as well. Legal ownership is a product of society; hence the rights that come with ownership are specified and protected by the legal system. But there is more to ownership than the law. We pursue possessions even though we do not necessarily need them. There is something deep in our minds, as if we are emotionally compelled to possess. This is psychological ownership, an emotional experience generated by the satisfaction of ownership which does not always correspond with legal ownership. We may legally own something but not care about it. In contrast, we can care about things we do not legally own, and yet feel we do. It is purely a state of mind.

In writing about psychological ownership, Jon Pierce and his colleagues described a common phenomenon in the workplace to illustrate how it can easily arise.[52] Truck drivers employed at a mine did not feel ownership over the trucks they operated until a new company policy was implemented that assigned each driver to a particular truck. Prior to that, the drivers had not looked after the trucks they drove. After the trucks were allocated, however, they gradually began to refer to their truck as 'my' truck, to clean its interior and to attend to mechanical maintenance. One driver even named his truck and spent his own money to have this name painted on the doors. It was his. Similarly, racing drivers do not own the team sportscars they drive, but they nevertheless come to experience a deep sense of ownership over their particular car.

We can all relate to this. Consider how many things you do not legally own but think of as yours. If we rent a car, then we are not particularly attached to it, but a leased car is usually a different story. Even though we do not technically own a leased car (the finance company owns the property), we readily perceive personal ownership and treat it with much more care. The same is true for the majority of properties bought on mortgages: we do not legally own them until we have settled the debt but still regard such houses as 'ours'. And many people feel ownership of their rental properties, especially if they have lived there for a long time, which is why it can be difficult for developers to evict people even though they don't own their homes. You might regard this as a technicality, if you have a mortgage, because you will own your property outright in the future. However, that reasoning does not capture the deep psychological connection we have to our possessions. Repossession is not simply an economic hardship, but an assault on our sense of self.

In order to understand why, we need to explore this powerful psychological dimension of ownership. For many of us, our lives are controlled by this relentless pursuit of ownership. Where does the urge come from? In the next chapter we consider this question from a biological perspective.

2

Non-humans Possess, But Only Humans Can Own

THE RACE FOR LIFE

Two long-distance runners are crossing the Serengeti when they stop for a break and decide to take off their shoes. At that point they see that a ferocious lion has spotted them and is starting to charge towards them. One of the runners starts to quickly put on his shoes. The other runner gasps, 'There's no point trying to out-run that lion, she is much faster than a human.' Whereupon the other replies, 'I don't have to out-run the lion; I only have to out-run you!' This old joke captures the essence of natural selection, the process of evolution that explains the diversity of life on Earth as a competition to survive and reproduce. The fight for survival is not only against the elements but also against your competitors. You simply have to outperform your rivals.

Humans are competitive by nature. In 1898, the psychologist Norman Triplett noticed that cyclists' performance times were faster when they competed against each other rather than against the clock. In what is considered the first ever social-psychology experiment, he measured how fast children reeled in their fishing lines in a game where either they were alone or in competition against another child.[1] Just like the athletes, the children were faster competing against each other. Triplett called this the 'competitive instinct' and it appears to be a fundamental behaviour found across the animal kingdom. The most obvious competitive situation is feeding time. When you next see your kids scoffing down their food at the dinner table, don't scold them for being animals. Feeding frenzies have been observed in every species, from armadillos to zebras, when there are many mouths to feed.

Even though we rarely fight over food in civilized society, we are

constantly comparing ourselves to others, and many of us will recognize those instances when we have felt competitive with our in-laws,
our friends or colleagues. A study of 5,000 British adults revealed
that irrespective of how much money workers were earning, they
were more dissatisfied if they thought a fellow worker, doing the
same job, was earning more than them.[2] The problem is that we are
not very accurate in our perceptions. Another survey, of over 71,000
employees, revealed that nearly two-thirds of individuals who were
paid the market rate for their job believed that they were underpaid,
compared to only 6 per cent who thought they were overpaid.[3] And
among individuals who were actually paid above the market rate for
their job, only one in five thought they were overpaid. A third thought
they deserved more. Not only are we competitive but we feel under-
valued and assume that others are doing better than us.

One obvious way we compare ourselves is through what we own.
The desire to have more is motivated by the relative difference in
ownership between ourselves and those we regard as our closest
rivals. As the American satirist H. L. Mencken once joked, wealth is
any income that is at least $100 more annually than the income of
your wife's sister's husband.[4] It may have been a quip, but studies
show that this sibling rivalry is true. Women with husbands who earn
less than their sister's husband are more likely to take on work themselves in order to bring in more money so that they have a higher
relative family income than that of their sister.[5]

Ownership is clearly competitive but there are two schools of thought
when it comes to understanding its origins. Evolutionary accounts
argue that ownership is a legacy of the competitive instinct where having exclusive access to valuable resources gives you the upper hand in
the struggle to survive and reproduce. This could be simple possession
where access is important. The other school of thought argues that
ownership is different from possession in that it is cultural and emerges
when communities settled to develop political and legal systems. Here
the competition is primarily social. For humans, both positions must
be correct to some extent, and both can be seen as strategies for survival. However, as we will see, possession is common in the animal
kingdom, whereas ownership is only found in human societies.

To take possession comes from the Latin, *possidere*, which literally means 'to sit or put one's weight or foot over'. When dogs place their paw on humans, we usually interpret it as a sign of affection, but it is actually a mark of dominance. Their wolf genes are still showing the signs of the hierarchy of the pack. Possession gives you control, which gives you the competitive edge. The problem is attaining that control and maintaining it once you have it. Direct physical competition leads to potentially costly conflicts, which is why certain behavioural strategies emerge as a way of reducing such costs by avoiding confrontation.

One such strategy is known as the 'first possession rule', resulting in an advantage when defending resources. You might call it the 'first dibs' rule. It's considered innate because even the simplest animals instinctively operate with the first possession rule without any need to learn it. Unlike strategies based on brain or brawn, successful possession in these circumstances is less related to the mental or physical attributes of competitors (though it is true that the fastest, strongest and smartest are the most likely to take possession first) but can still emerge as a stable strategy to avoid conflict for less well-endowed competitors. For one thing, first possessors are more willing to defend their property. A number of species will respect first possession even when the possessor is more diminutive and could be overcome. Crickets will take on larger challengers when first possession is established, whereas larger competitors tend to back off from smaller crickets in possession.[6]

Deferring to the first possession rule is observed throughout the animal kingdom. Consider the butterfly. Male butterflies are aggressive and will fight to claim possession of a sunny spot which is desirable for attracting mates. They are assertive in defending a resource they discover first but are deferential when they arrive upon it late. For first possession to become stable, however, both parties need to know when to be assertive and when to be deferential. An animal that does not defend its territory will be easily overrun by usurpers, whereas an aggressive competitor will compete for resources which are fiercely defended. Knowing when to back off or stand your ground requires some observable criterion of that condition being met. If there is some ambiguity, then both parties may feel entitled to claim possession and fight accordingly, which is why speckled wood butterflies will engage in battle for ten times longer if two have touched down on the spot at the same time – they both thought they saw it first.[7]

The primacy of first possession is also one of the fundamental principles of legal systems across the globe.[8] It is such an important factor in determining legal ownership that it has given rise to the common adage that 'possession is nine-tenths of the law'. Even though there is no such universal equation, this does convey the general legal principle that the individual in possession is presumed to be the rightful owner and that the onus is on any challenger to demonstrate that their claim is stronger.

THE MANUFACTURING MIND

Many animals possess food, territory and mates, but humans are unique in that we also make artefacts that we treasure and pass on to our relatives. Transfer of these material possessions depends on establishing the concept of ownership, because you cannot take or give away what is not yours in the first place.

We have been making things since before we became *Homo sapiens*. The earliest tools (stone hammers, anvils and knives), discovered in Kenya,[9] date to around 3.3 million years ago and were made by our early hominid ancestors long before modern humans appeared on the scene about 300,000 years ago. We are not the only animal that makes tools, but we are the only one that holds on to them. The only other creature known to retain a tool is the sea otter, which keeps a small pebble for cracking open shellfish.[10] Compare that to our ancestors who not only produced a vast array of tools but other artefacts that they valued and became emotionally attached to. Wild animals are not known to hold on to possessions unless they are food, territory or mates.

Not only did early humans manufacture possessions but they traded them. We know that for at least 40,000 years during the Upper Palaeolithic era humans have engaged in barter and trade, as artefacts from this period have been found in geographical locations that are considerable distances from their original source. Shells from Mediterranean shores ended up hundreds of miles away in various locations across Northern Europe.[11] The most likely explanation is that they were traded by travellers. Bartering is a hallmark of human behaviour that is not commonly seen in other species. It not only requires communication to negotiate with another, but the ability to work out the relative value of items. Both monkeys and apes can be taught to barter, but this requires extensive training. Moreover, once trained to exchange with an experimenter, they do not trade with each other and the behaviour disappears if it is not enforced.[12] In other words, trading is not in their nature.

In our research, we have looked at barter in a variety of great apes. My colleague Patricia Kanngiesser, a developmental psychologist, demonstrated that chimpanzees, bonobos, gorillas and orangutans who have been trained to exchange goods all prefer to keep food once it is in their possession and are reluctant to barter with an experimenter.[13] Food in the hand is worth more than what's on offer. To tempt them, the food offered has to be a significantly more enticing option before they'll make the exchange. It's not that the apes think they will be cheated, but rather they find it difficult to give up possession of food. There is something so enticing about food – a bird in the hand is literally worth more than two in a bush. However, primates rarely exhibit similar attachment to other possessions such as tools, even when they are necessary to retrieve food. Once used, artefacts are discarded.

Humans, on the other hand, actively accumulate possessions. The whole of human history is a treasure trove of manufactured possessions, the oldest of which we now put on display in our museums. We admire the possessions of others. Personally, I love to marvel at these historic items to make a connection with our distant relatives, as a way of identifying our similarities as much as our differences. The Upper Palaeolithic era was a golden era for prehistoric production as there was an explosion in the archaeological record of sophisticated artefacts, especially in the southwest of France beginning around 40,000 years ago. Prior to this period, the earliest example of non-tool manufacture was jewellery in the form of eagle talons, dating to around 130,000 years ago, that were worn around the neck of a cousin of modern humans, the Neanderthals.[14] It is true that some animals can create beautiful material things, such as the sand sculptures of the male Japanese pufferfish or the elaborate bowers of the Australian bowerbird, but these temporary displays are solely for the purpose of attracting mates. Like animal tools, once their purpose is served, they are abandoned.

In contrast, early humans were painting caves and making figurines that must have had some symbolic meaning and, most importantly, were meant to last. They were creating possessions that were to be passed on in this life and the next. Both early humans and Neanderthals buried their dead with artefacts. Some of these items took many hundreds of hours of manufacturing effort, so they had value in terms of the sheer amount of labour invested. They were not discarded but, rather, must have formed part of rituals. We can only speculate about the reasons for this burial practice, but it seems reasonable to infer that these items either belonged to or were given to the deceased in a belief in an afterlife.[15]

Arguably, as humans accumulated possessions of worth, these were traded for food, territory, services and sex. Tempting the opposite sex with nuptial gifts, however, is not unique to humans; animals also use bribes. Many species of male insects, including flies, spiders and crickets, provide food parcels to potential female mates. Male chimpanzees offer meat to potential partners to increase the likelihood of mating, even though this may take some length of time with repeated offerings.[16] However, humans were the first materialistic animals that valued possessions in their own right. These possessions were symbolic, aesthetic, valued as extensions of our identity, carried around, protected, revered and, ultimately, passed on to others. Such transfers could only take place by understanding ownership rules. Abiding by the rules of ownership ultimately enabled stable societies to emerge, societies built upon the foundations of property accumulation and transfer of wealth.

RELATIVE VALUES

After the last ice age, human activity shifted from migrating hunter-gatherer subsistence to settled communities that began to cultivate crops and domesticate wild animals. As we transitioned into agricultural societies, humans began to produce surpluses of resources that could be stored or stolen. This is when ownership became crucially important. We can speculate that property laws emerged in civilizations as ways to organize and control their members. Transient societies became established ones, with ordered structures that passed from one generation to the next, providing continuity and stability.

Ownership was a powerful accelerant in this process. Social hierarchies were fuelled by the desire to accumulate wealth, through commerce and military campaigns. These hierarchies became the ruling elite with political power to control citizens. Economic wealth created a mechanism for prosperity that freed individuals from the daily chores of survival. Artisans and intellectuals thrived, supported by a system where they did not have to manually labour to maintain subsistence. Ownership provided a legitimate and sustained justification for the order that citizens grew up in.

Today most parents want their children to succeed, and this usually encompasses a good education, career and marriage. These are the ingredients not only for a happy life, but also for long lineages. As parents, we devote resources to improve the lives of our children, which sounds like a sacrifice but, in biological terms, is simply a strategy of the genes to get themselves replicated from one generation to the next. This 'selfish gene' perspective, familiar to many through the popular science writing of Richard Dawkins, still grates with most parents who believe they are acting selflessly.

Even in death, we could pass on our advantages. In most human societies that have ever existed, some form of inheritance takes place, though there are wide cultural variations. A survey of 16,000 people in fifteen countries conducted by HSBC Bank in 2013 revealed that, overall, 69% of respondents planned to leave a will, with the highest rates in India (86%) and Mexico (84%), whereas only 56% of US respondents and 57% of Canadian parents expected to give inheritances to their children.[17] There are a number of reasons for this variation, including better social-security systems in the developed countries, but another primary factor is the cultural differences in family-oriented attitudes, with those in industrialized nations expressing more individual-oriented, short-term goals compared to the collectivist societies of other nations.

Attitudes towards inheritance are also changing as economic circumstances shift. A report by the Prudential insurance company in 2011 revealed that around half of UK adults expected to leave an inheritance to their children, but the percentage had halved again to around a quarter in 2016.[18] 'Spending the kids' inheritance' or 'SKIing' describes this generation of baby boomers who do not plan to leave the bulk of their money to their children, demonstrating that biology may not always win out when it comes to predicting human behaviour.

A more charitable reason for the decline of inheritance in the UK is that parents are already supporting their family members with hand-outs. Increasingly, the 'bank of mum and dad' is the only way that millennials can ever hope to own property. Significant financial gifts and loans from parents and relatives play an important role in helping younger family members to take important steps in adult life, including paying off debts, getting married and buying their first home. A report by the UK mortgage company Legal and General revealed that parents had loaned their children £6.7 billion in 2017, a 30 per cent increase from the previous year, making the bank of mum and dad equivalent to one of the top ten mortgage lenders.[19] Today, the ability to get on the housing ladder is more to do with whether your parents own a home than it was a generation ago. This means that the situation can only get worse in the future, as the gap between the 'haves' and the 'have-nots' widens. Whether within our lifetime or after we die, most of us pass on our wealth to our children in one way or another.

Remarkably, biology also plays a role in this benevolence. It seems obvious to most parents to leave our wealth to our kids, but an analysis of inheritance trends reveals some surprising patterns. When we pass on our inheritance, bequests are greater for genetically related kin and spouses, compared to unrelated beneficiaries. The more genetically related, the more the bequest. That's to be expected. However, not all children benefit equally, depending on whether they are male or female and whether the family is wealthy or not.

In the early 1970s, psychologist Robert Trivers and mathematician Dan Willard proposed an ingenious model to predict patterns of inheritance that vary with environmental circumstances. According to the Trivers–Willard hypothesis, there is a bias to favour male offspring when times are good but female children when times are hard.[20] Wealthier families leave more money to sons than daughters, whereas the opposite pattern is found in poorer families. The reason being that in hard times, without the benefit of a welfare state, wealthy males are more likely to have more children that survive compared to males who are less well off. Wealthy males can attract more potential mates and invest in their offspring. Males can also produce many more offspring than females, so wealthier parents should bias their investment towards sons rather than daughters in order to produce the maximum number of grandchildren. However, poor daughters are more likely to have children than poor sons, so they represent a better investment for poorer families.

These various predictions were tested in an analysis of 1,000 Canadian wills selected at random. First, it was revealed that 92 per cent of the beneficiaries were relatives, while only 8 per cent were non-relatives.[21] Spouses were the most likely beneficiaries, which makes a lot of sense as they are partners who in the majority of cases have a vested interest in the survival of any children that have resulted out of that partnership. The average amounts that were bequeathed mirrored the pattern of genetic relatedness, with around half of wealth given to relatives who were one-half related, around 10 per cent to relatives who were one-quarter related and only 1 per cent to relatives who were one-eighth related.

Children received more than a parent's siblings, and the relative proportion given to sons and daughters depended on the size of the inheritance. Just as Trivers and Willard predicted, sons received twice as much as daughters for the wealthiest estates whereas this pattern was reversed in the poorest estates. When there were both brothers and sisters, fair distribution was the most common pattern, with no difference in 82 per cent of cases. However, there was a bias towards daughters in 7 per cent of cases and towards sons in 11 per cent, which does not look too different until you consider the size of the estate. In line with the Trivers–Willard hypothesis, those with a son bias were wealthier than those with no bias, and those with no bias were wealthier than those with a bias towards daughters. This pattern of parental favouritism is echoed in the value of gifts bought for children. A 2018 study of online purchases revealed that wealthier Chinese parents spent more on sons than daughters, whereas the opposite pattern was observed among less well-off parents. Parents in the middle economic bracket showed no preference for sons or daugthers.[22]

While spouses are by far the most likely beneficiaries of wills, it does depend upon who dies first. In a study of Californian wills dating back to 1890, men who died before their wives left the majority of their estate to their spouse.[23] However, when wives died before their husbands they were more likely to cut their husband out of the will and give their wealth directly to the children. Again, there is a good biological reason for this. When a husband reaches an age where he is about to die, most wives are beyond reproductive age and unlikely to have further children. For the husband, it makes sense to make provision for the mother of his children. However, if a wife is about to die, her husband can go on to have another family with another woman, which is why dying mothers tend to leave their estate to their children rather than giving it to the husband and any potential wicked stepmother.

It's not only the parents who make provision for the children. Other relatives have something to be gained when it comes to looking after offspring. For example, mothers can be 100 per cent sure that their children carry their genes, but fathers may not be the biological parent. Even today, according to the US National Opinion Research Center's 2010 General Social Survey,[24] the number of wives having extramarital affairs is around 15 per cent. In our ancient past, there would have been more uncertainty over paternity. Indeed, in some South American tribes the practice of 'partible paternity', where children are considered to have multiple fathers, existed because it was believed that conception depended on the accumulated semen of multiple males.[25] One thing that is considered certain in all societies is that the child comes from the mother who gives birth. Therefore, the grandmother on the mother's side can also be pretty sure that her genes are present in the grandchildren (unless they were switched at birth), whereas the grandfather on the mother's side cannot be certain; he, too, may not be the father of his own daughter. The paternal grandparents have no such guarantees, as their son may be a cuckold and their grandchildren not genetically related to them in any way.

These varying degrees of biological relatedness and potential for deception manifest in the generosity of relatives. On average, maternal grandmothers invest more in grandchildren than do other grandparents, and grandparents invest more in their daughters' children than in their sons' children.[26] For example, a recent survey of US parents with a child under five years of age asked about grandparental generosity and help with raising the children. As many of the grandparents in this study had remarried, it was possible to compare biological and step-grandparents. On average, biological grandmothers gave their grandchildren $680 annually, compared to just a measly $56 from the step-grandmother.[27] Maternal aunts and uncles also invest more in their nieces and nephews than paternal brothers and sisters.[28] Even though paternity uncertainty is relatively low in modern society, these strategies of providing different levels of support represent an evolutionary legacy from a time before parents were certain who was the father.

ARE YOU GOING TO STAND BY AND DO NOTHING?

'The only thing necessary for the triumph of evil is for good men to do nothing.'

Edmund Burke

In 1754, the French philosopher Jean-Jacques Rousseau noted that: 'The first man, who, after enclosing a piece of ground, took it into his head to say, "This is mine," and found people simple enough to believe him, was the true founder of civil society.'[29] This capacity to abide by rules freed individuals to expand their activities with the understanding that their ownership would be acknowledged and not challenged. Thus, a moral code ('Thou shalt not steal') was borne out of a primitive pragmatic solution. When you no longer have to keep your stuff in immediate possession under your watchful eye, you are freed up to spend your time accumulating more wealth. You can invade other territories and come back in the knowledge that your home will still be there.

Territorial behaviour is common in the animal world, with many species marking, patrolling and defending 'property'. A variety of animals build nests and burrows that they defend. Hermit crabs fight over discarded seashells. Probably the most dramatic example of home construction is the beaver dam. In the winter, to protect themselves from predators and provide ready access to fish under the frozen ice of rivers and lakes, beavers build elaborate homes out of trees they fell by gnawing through the trunks. These are floated into position to create a structure with an underwater entrance set at just the right depth to prevent it freezing up. This sanctuary provides safety for their family. Beavers would not have evolved this behaviour if rivals had open access to this resource. If these habitats or territories are not defended, or they are abandoned, then there is very little to prevent others from taking possession. They are homes so long as they are possessed.[30]

Unlike possession, however, ownership is sophisticated because it requires the cognitive machinery to calculate whether a resource can be claimed and, if so, an understanding that ownership is retained even when the owner is not present. Like leaving your coat on a seat when you go off to get an ice-cream at the cinema. It depends on imagining the consequences of actions and planning for future contingencies. It requires anticipating retribution and punishment if you take what is not yours.

Enforcing ownership necessitates action with the associated potential costs. Before the advent of laws and policing, it would have meant fighting for what is yours. Protecting your possessions from theft is straightforward second-party retaliation that is going to benefit you directly. However, stable growth and civilization could not thrive with constant internal conflict. For ownership to work, there had to be mechanisms that defended the property of the weakest as well as of those who were temporarily absent. There had to be a policing system whereby potential thieves were discouraged from taking possession – namely, third-party punishment, where an individual comes to the defence of someone else's property. Unlike second-party punishment, third-party punishers do not stand to gain directly, yet potentially suffer a cost to the benefit of others. This is going to be particularly necessary in large-scale communities where not everyone is known to each other and individuals rarely, if ever, encounter each other directly.

Many species engage in second-party defence of their property, but there is little evidence of third-party interventions among non-humans.[31] Dominant chimpanzees and macaques have been observed to wade into fights among others, but this is more to do with maintaining the status quo of the group than assisting others in property disputes. When the opportunity for third-party punishment over the theft of food has been deliberately set up, chimpanzees do not help others but rather only defend or retaliate against theft of their own food.

In contrast, from an early age, human children will intervene to protect someone else's property. Initially, two-year-olds only get upset if someone tries to take away their possessions and are less likely to kick up a fuss if it is someone else's property that is being violated. But at three years old, children will complain if a naughty teddy bear attempts to take away someone else's property.[32] Such third-party enforcement is critically important to ownership as its power depends on individuals abiding by the rules even when the owner is not present. Turning a blind eye undermines the whole value of ownership. Societies and co-operation among groups would collapse without third-party punishment, which is why it is one of the defining features of ownership not observed among non-humans.

Why do children start to demonstrate an understanding of third-party punishment around their third birthday? One answer is a developing sense of others and their stuff. Crucially, this may be linked to what psychologists call a 'theory of mind', an intuitive capacity to mentally place one's self in someone else's shoes so as to understand their thoughts and behaviours. Theory of mind is one of the most studied research topics in human and non-human cognition because such mental capacity is so valuable in social interactions and for predicting what others will do. If you can read the mind of another, then you can anticipate their next move, or you can manipulate them by feeding them false information. There is evidence for rudimentary theory of mind in other species, but it is most sophisticated and common in humans from about three to four years of age.[33] Prior to that, infants and toddlers do seem to register that others have minds, but they are not adept at reading them in the same way as older children. The strengthening of theory of mind around three years of age enables children to start considering others' beliefs and attitudes concerning the things they own and the emotional consequences of loss, which is why they are willing to punish others who transgress. It makes it much easier to enforce social norms and the rules of ownership when one can appreciate others' feelings.

Theft is a violation of ownership that is understood early in child development, but concepts of theft vary among adults. Members of hunter-gatherer societies have few personal possessions, which makes sense as they are constantly on the move and need to travel lightly.

They do not consider it theft to help themselves to others' possessions if they are not in use. They are therefore less likely to administer third-party punishment.[34] It is not that they don't understand ownership but rather that most possessions are owned by the group, and so if one member of the tribe is not using something then another is entitled to take temporary possession. This is known as 'demand-sharing': if you've got it and I need it, then give it to me. Even when they ask permission to use something, it is not because they acknowledge personal ownership but rather to establish that it is not in use. Don't be surprised if you leave your shoes outside the tent when visiting a hunter-gatherer tribe to see someone walking around with them on the next day. After all, you were not using them.

Demand-sharing evolved as a strategy among hunter-gatherers who were constantly on the move. We know this from mathematical models that can simulate the efficiency of different strategies when it comes to how we used to live. Analysis reveals that demand-sharing families that continuously moved between camps in response to their energy income were better adapted to survive in the unpredictable environments typical of hunter-gatherers, while non-sharing families and sedentary families perished.[35]

There are very few traditional hunter-gatherer societies left today. Most humans live in the same place surrounded by many others where the risk of theft by strangers is a constant threat. The whole point of ownership is appreciating that resources cannot be freely taken when the owner is not about. As part of this social contract, we expect others to protect and respect our property rights. But consider the following scenario and answer honestly. What would you do if you saw a young man in his twenties, looking furtive, trying to cut a security chain on a bike with a pair of bolt-cutters? When someone passes, the man stops and pretends that he is doing something else. I expect you would make a quick risk-benefit analysis: Maybe it is his bike? But why stop when being observed? Maybe he is a dangerous criminal? Somebody should stop him, but I am not sure I want to get involved.

When people witness an apparent theft, they often fail to confront individuals who are stealing. To illustrate this point, filmmaker Casey Neistat made a video of himself acting as if he was stealing a bike in various locations around New York in 2012 that has been watched by over 3 million YouTubers.[36] It looked exactly like a theft and yet no one stopped him until he tried the stunt in the busy Union Square in New York with a power tool, at which point the police turned up. This reluctance by members of the public to get involved is an example of the so-called 'bystander effect', the phenomenon whereby adults do not offer help or assistance if others are present. The more people, the stronger the bystander effect, as if responsibility is diluted.

If ownership depends on third-party policing, how can we square the bystander effect with the need for intervention? Humans do not always protect the property of others. Consider household burglar alarms, a deterrent based on the assumption that a neighbour, security guard or police officer will be summoned quickly. In truth, this rarely happens. In the UK and US, almost all alarms that are triggered are false. In the UK, it is standard policy for the police not to respond to an unmonitored alarm unless a crime taking place is independently corroborated. Interviews with habitual thieves reveal that they generally do not consider alarms a major deterrent, in comparison to other security measures, as they know the police rarely turn up.[37]

If three-year-old children intervene when they witness stealing, then why the bystander effect in adults? It turns out that the bystander effect is not due to apathy but rather a combination of ambiguity and fear. Many situations are ambiguous and, rather than dashing in, most of us prefer to tread lightly to establish what is going on. If someone is so brazen as to try to cut the chains off a padlocked bike, then we reason it must be his or hers in the first place. Adults, like children, infer that people interacting with objects are usually the owners, which is statistically more likely in a lawful society. Alternatively, if the person is someone who is not afraid of others, then that means they might be violent. In which case, is it really worth the risk of personal harm for the sake of someone else's bike? Would they do the same for me? It's simply not worth it.

The bystander effect does not always win, however. Adults are more likely to intervene when they witness a property violation if they are alone. In this situation, there is no one else to rely on. Such evaluations also depend on where the crime takes place. City urbanites are much less willing to intervene compared to those living in rural towns. It could be that in rural areas there is more willingness to challenge or less ambiguity about the situation. When we live in smaller communities, we tend to not only know our neighbours but identify others as strangers. People who live in smaller groups also feel more obligation and responsibility to look after their neighbours' interests, including protecting and defending their neighbours' property. The bystander effect disappears when the group witnessing something suspicious all know each other, which again makes perfect sense. Such a group reduces ambiguity, enables communication and, together, there is a shared common interest to protect against property crimes.[38]

TRAGEDY OF THE COMMONS

It is for the collective benefit of all of us that we take responsibility and police our resources. This need is increasingly more pressing as our species changes the planet we inhabit. Since the birth of modern civilization around 12,000 years ago, the human global population has rocketed from some 5 million to more than 7 billion people today. Not only were there fewer people before civilization got started but they lived in small migratory groups that were dependent on the vagaries of the environment. Civilization changed that. With our technological advances in health and wealth, our population has risen exponentially, reaching a size that now threatens our planet. Not only are there fewer natural resources now to exploit, but our industrial activities have changed the environment in ways that affect the climate, which, ultimately, will affect all life on Earth.

This precarious state of affairs was predicted in a 1968 paper by the late ecologist Garrett Hardin, published in the prestigious journal *Science*, on the dangers of over-population and entitled 'The Tragedy of the Commons'.[39] In it, Hardin drew attention to the problem of human behaviour as the major contributing factor. In short, people are motivated to reproduce, compete and act out of self-interest for themselves and their families. Hardin pointed out that the consequences of selfish behaviour were not necessarily intentional. Rather, it was in our human nature and, as such, he argued, there is no clear technological solution to changing human motivation.

Hardin considered the problem from the perspective of classical economics. In *The Wealth of Nations* (1776), the father of modern economics, Adam Smith, put forward the notion of an 'invisible hand' that operates to improve society. He wrote that an individual who 'intends only his own gain' is, as it were, 'led by an invisible hand to promote . . . the public interest'. In other words, by acting out of self-interest, individuals produce cumulative changes in society for the better. Probably the clearest example of this is the relationship between markets and innovation. If some product is in short supply and there is high demand for it, innovations will arise to increase the availability of the desired good through technological and economic advances. This is what entrepreneurs are constantly looking out for – opportunities to provide solutions that will make them money.

This belief that individuals are the drivers of economic growth remains core to political perspectives that emphasize the autonomy of the individual as the most important factor to advance civilization. This logic may work reasonably well for economics (though we shall see in later chapters that it has problems), but when it comes to what's best for society, Smith's invisible hand is decidedly a bad one.

Writing in 1833, the mathematician and economist William Forster Lloyd presented a formula that explained why Smith was wrong.[40] He gave the example of individuals allowed to freely graze their herds on communal pastures, or commons as they were known in England. Through their desire to prosper, spurred on by the competitive instinct, individuals would be motivated to increase the size of their herd, which would eventually lead to calamity. To the individual herdsman, the value of adding one more animal to his herd would be +1, but the cost of increased overgrazing would be divided among everyone using the commons. From the individual herdsman's perspective, adding an extra animal makes perfect economic sense, but the problem is that everyone operates with the same logic. Eventually, everybody increases the size of their herds, until the land is overgrazed and the grasses die off, leading to the collapse of the commons.

Hardin took this example in his influential paper, calling it a tragedy because there was an inevitability that was clearly evident, but not solvable. The problem is that everybody on the planet is caught up in a real-life tragedy of the commons played out by individual nations that believe they have the lawful rights of ownership. Over the past generation, we have increasingly begun to understand Earth as a delicately balanced ecosystem, and that the right of destruction of resources by owners (*jus abutendi*, again) conflicts with the rights of us all to occupy a habitable planet. One country may have the right to cut down trees to make way for farming, but the consequences of destroying rainforest are catastrophic for the rest of us.

Since the beginning of human civilization, the planet has lost half of the trees that it previously supported.[41] Fossil-fuel burning, the acidification of the oceans and all the other markers of human activity indicate that we are producing problems that will affect the future of life on Earth. Climate change is a direct consequence of human activity, but the necessary actions required to address the problem conflict directly with an individual country's ownership rights to exploit its resources as it wishes. This is why international co-operation and treaties are the only way to combat the ecological disaster that threatens us, and why unilateral protectionism – as epitomized by the slogan 'America first' – is so short-sighted, dangerous and, ultimately, self-defeating.

The economist John Gowdy argues that our current dilemma was not inevitable, since for 90 per cent of human history we lived as hunter-gatherers and did not compete in an arms race of ownership.[42] Ownership is a burden for nomadic peoples. Hunter-gatherers spent considerable amounts of time eating, drinking, playing and socializing. Ironically, they are, by definition, materially poor, but they regularly enjoy the sorts of leisure activities that only the very rich, who do not have to work, can afford today. Most hunter-gatherers actually have far more leisure time than modern people in the industrialized world. Hunter-gatherers typically work an average of three to five hours per day and often take a day or two off each week.[43] Moreover, much of that work includes hunting, fishing, and picking fruits and berries, the very same activities that are considered recreational in the West. Jason Godesky – a primitivist with ambitions of forming a functional hunter-gatherer tribe in the future – believes that even the hardest possible life for a hunter-gatherer compares favourably to the most leisured life one can expect in the world's most wealthy industrialized societies.[44]

While this utopian vision is somewhat sentimental and romantic, one cannot help but conclude that the pursuit of material wealth has led to our own current environmental predicament. But John Gowdy is not as pessimistic about the future as was Garrett Hardin, and he recommends a number of changes we need to make to counter the tragedy of the commons. Some of these are familiar, such as environmental sustainability, reduction of wealth inequality, social-security support and greater international co-operation.

Missing from that list, however, is an understanding of how we learn about ownership and shape it in the first place. It may arise from biological imperatives, but the concept of ownership is one that is constructed in the human mind and shaped during child development. If psychological ownership is really one of the root causes of our current situation of over-consumption and relentless materialism, then we must find ways of changing people's perceptions. But before you can change perceptions, you need to know where these come from. This is the question we turn to next.

3
Origins of Ownership

WHO OWNS A BANKSY?

In 2010, the old Packard Automobile plant in Detroit, Michigan was being redeveloped when a picture of a child holding a bucket of paint and a brush and the message 'I remember when all this was trees' was discovered painted on a concrete wall that was scheduled for demolition. It turned out to be the work of the renowned British graffiti-artist Banksy, immediately recognizable by his iconic stencil images, his witty sense of humour, his daring, unobserved, guerrilla-style execution (often in the middle of the night), and most famous for his total anonymity. The general public does not know who Banksy is or what he looks like, and he never claims ownership of his art. Banksy simply acknowledges that he creates the images via his official website, pest-controloffice.com – again, typical Banksy humour. If he doesn't claim ownership of his labour, who owns a Banksy?

Very few of us, in fact, because they are so valuable. When it became known that a Banksy had been discovered at the old Packard plant, the local Detroit-based 555 Arts gallery removed the 7-by-8-foot, 1,500-pound cinder block of concrete with the intention of saving it from the bulldozers because the workmen would not have known what they were destroying.[1] However, when the landowners discovered this rescue, they claimed the wall was worth over $100,000 and took the art gallery to court on the grounds of theft. Overnight, a worthless wall scheduled for demolition was valuable. The court had to decide who was the legitimate owner of the graffiti. The artist who painted it on the wall? The company that owned the land? The workmen who found the painting? Or the art gallery that put effort into removing and preserving the artwork? Eventually the Detroit Banksy case was settled with the 555 gallery paying $2,500 to the land-owners for outright ownership. It was a good deal. Five years later, in 2015, the Banksy graffiti wall sold for $137,500 to a couple from California, much to the consternation of Detroit residents who thought that the work should have remained in Michigan as they believed Banksy had gifted it to their city.

Banksy seems to relish provoking situations that prod and poke at the concept of ownership. He challenges us to address not only what art is but who owns it. Each one of the claims for ownership described above can be called into question. All buildings are owned, either privately or publicly, and so the walls he adorns are not his to alter. Graffiti is considered defacement and generally devalues the property. In most Western societies, it is considered a form of crim-inal damage, punishable by fines and imprisonment. In the UK, the estimated cost of cleaning up graffiti in 2017 was £1 billion.[2] Is a Banksy destruction or construction? In his home city of Bristol, the local officials have protected Banksy murals, giving them the status of public art. There are tours of his street art and, in 2009, the Banksy exhibition at Bristol City Museum generated £15 million for the city from visitors coming to admire his work.[3] Others see it a different way. In April 2007, one of Banksy's most famous pieces, on a wall near Old Street tube station in London, depicting the actors John Travolta and Samuel L. Jackson's *Pulp Fiction* characters, pointing bananas instead of guns, was painted over by London Transport workmen despite having an estimated value of more than £300,000.[4] Asked to comment on the mural's destruction, a Transport for Lon-don spokesman replied, 'Our graffiti removal teams are staffed by professional cleaners not professional art critics.'

Ironically, Banksy's most creative work to date was an act of destruc-tion. It took place at Sotheby's London auction house on 5 October 2018 during the sale of one of his iconic images of a girl letting go of her heart-shaped balloon. As soon as the auctioneer's hammer came down on the sale, an alarm sounded from within the frame as the picture started to self-shred in front of the shocked crowd. In his video post on Instagram, Banksy revealed how he had built a shredder into the picture frame years earlier just in case it was ever sold at auction. He also posted a photograph of the telephone bidders assembled in the showroom looking on aghast at the spectacle, with the witty tag, 'Going, going, gone ...' It was his most creative work because, as Banksy added, 'The urge to destroy is also a creative urge – Picasso.' Normally a half-shredded work of art would be rendered worthless by such destruction, but not a Banksy. The winning bidder decided to keep the remnants of the picture and frame as they were worth even more given the publicity that the stunt attracted. Banksy appears to be the King Midas of the art world, with everything he touches turning to gold.

Every time he produces a public work of art, Banksy reveals the tensions in the way that we establish ownership. The artist provides the intellectual property with his brilliant ideas and actual labour, but then abandons the product of his efforts, leaving others to fight over the ownership. Each Banksy creation is a reminder of Bentham's dictum that ownership is a mere concept, a product of the mind.

Conceptual art was launched into the public mind by the French artist Marcel Duchamp, who displayed a common porcelain urinal, entitled *Fountain*, which he submitted to the first annual exhibition of the Society of Independent Artists in New York in 1917. The Society's board of directors, however, bound by its own rules to accept all members' submissions, took exception to *Fountain* on the grounds that it was indecent and not a work of art. The whole point of the Society of Independent Artists was to tear down the stuffiness and elitism of the art world that had dominated until then. The exhibition was supposed to have no juries, no judgements, no prizes and all the works were to be displayed in simple alphabetical order according to the artists' surnames. Yet the board objected to one of the works of art on grounds of decency.

Disgusted, Duchamp reclaimed the urinal, which had been stuck behind a partition at the exhibition, and took a photograph of it to the leading New York gallery owner and photographer of the day, Alfred Stieglitz. He had a different reaction, writing of the work: 'The "Urinal" photograph is really quite a wonder – Everyone who has seen it thinks it beautiful – And it's true – it is. It has an oriental look about it – a cross between a Buddha and a Veiled Woman.'

All that survives of *Fountain* is the 1917 photograph, as the urinal was dumped soon after. After all, it was only meant to be a statement. Duchamp had deliberately provoked his fellow Society members because he wanted to challenge the concept of art. Some say the artist was

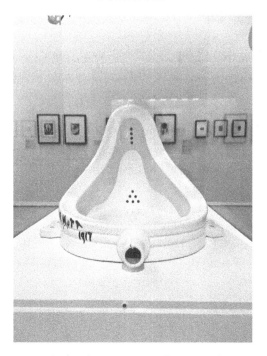

One of Duchamp's replicas of *Fountain* in the Pompidou Centre, Paris
(Image: author)

inviting the audience to urinate on the concept of art, but, when he was
interviewed in 1964, Duchamp said he was, 'drawing people's attention
to the fact that art is a mirage'.[5] Like ownership, art is elusive.

In a 2004 poll conducted by the sponsors of the Turner prize,
Fountain was considered the single most important artwork of the
twentieth century by leading figures in the art world.[6] The original
Fountain may be gone but there are replicas in prestigious art galler-
ies around the world, including the Museum of Modern Art in New
York, the Tate Modern gallery in London and the Pompidou Centre,
Paris. Conceptual art is now a genre of its own, with works exchanging hands for considerable sums of money. In 2002, one of the replica
urinals that came from Duchamp's studio was sold at auction for
over $1 million – a large price to pay for a piece of art that exists only
in the mind.

The reason that art is relevant to ownership is that both are conceptual. Our world is full of concepts constructed by the human mind,

but how? As a developmental psychologist, I have spent my career researching the development of concepts in children, in everything from their understanding of the physical world to belief in a supernatural one. In every realm, concepts appear to develop from basic, fundamental principles that we are born with and that become more sophisticated through experience. Likewise, ownership is a concept that develops in children from the primitive principle of possession – something that humans share with the rest of the animal kingdom.

Before there was ownership, there was possession. Possession is simply the control of physical access to some resource such as holding it, carrying it or even sitting upon it. As noted in the last chapter, many animals acquire and defend possessions. In child development, before there is the concept of ownership there is also possession. The psychologist Lita Furby has analysed the development of possessive behaviour and has come up with two principles of possession that operate around the world.[7] Based on interviews with children aged from five years to adults in their fifties, all of them agree that possession gives you control over something. Secondly, they all agree that possessions can form part of your identity. This is the psychological ownership that we described in the first chapter that comes from seeing a personal connection with your property – an extension of your self.

Initially newborn infants have little control over objects, nor do they have a developed sense of self. And yet they have an intrinsic curiosity to interact with the world. The psychologist Robert White theorized that all animals, including humans, are motivated to produce effects in their environment, and that feeling of efficacy is a universally sought-after source of pleasure.[8] When you watch your pets at play, it is quite clear that they get much satisfaction out of controlling various objects that they paw or bat repeatedly. These objects are in their possession because they are under their control. This desire for control is the motivating factor in Swiss child psychologist Jean Piaget's theory of intellectual development where he described infants discovering the nature of the world around them by interacting with objects and learning about their properties. This is one of the reasons why young babies repeatedly hammer the table with their utensils or drinking cups, and why they love to push things off their high-tables to make parents pick them up – over and over again. Piaget recognized these behaviours as a way that the infant begins to explore the nature of the world around them, exert control over it and discover what is in their possession.

Control also depends on contingency. Infants are particularly attracted to experiences that are contingent, or timed to their own actions. Turn-taking is one of the characteristics of many parent–infant interactions. This is why peekaboo is such a universally popular game played with babies in variations across the world, because it involves contingency.[9] Through these fundamental drives for control and contingency, we establish possession of things, and also of our personal thoughts and actions. The American psychologist Martin Seligman proposed that 'those "objects" become self that exhibit near-perfect correlation between motor command and the visual and kinesthetic feedback; while those "objects" that do not, become the world.'[10]

As adults, when we lose control of these contingencies, we experience a disconnect. We lose the sense of ownership of our thoughts and actions and experience depersonalization, a fractionation of our personality because the integrity and control of our self is compromised. In such psychotic states, we say that we are the ones who are *possessed*, as if another person or spirit has taken control of our minds and bodies. When there is a mismatch between the voluntary control of thoughts and actions, as occurs in a number of psychiatric conditions such as schizophrenia, patients experience delusions of external control and possession from elsewhere.[11] In a sense, who we are both in mind and physical body comes down to what we exclusively control and therefore own.

CARROTS AND STICKS

If the urge to possess is borne out of a primitive drive to control the physical world around us, then parents generally allow infants access to most things that are not going to harm them. Infants start out as the apples of their parents' eyes, the centre of family attention. The next time you visit someone with a toddler, take note how often they interrupt the conversation by bringing objects to show the parent. This is a common way to command attention and control the situation, which is why much of the social interaction with parents during these early years involves physical objects.[12]

Infants are curious animals who want to push the boundaries of exploration. With increased mobility, they suddenly have access to most of the objects in their environments. However, these encounters could often result in damage or destruction, which is why adults and older siblings try to curb the child's curiosity. This is when infants start to learn about restricted access and what is and what is not under their control. Objects which are under someone else's control thwart feelings of possession when the child tries to explore them. This gives rise to an appreciation of things being out of bounds, whereas those objects that infants are at liberty to control belong to them.

When they do interact with peers, the youngest toddlers are also more likely to do so with an object rather than through speech. They know which toys to take that will upset their sibling most.[13] Outside the family home, when the toddler enters the nursery, they embark on a campaign to take control over all the objects that they can possess. Some of the earliest observational studies revealed that three-quarters of quarrels between eighteen- to thirty-month-olds in a nursery were disputes over possession of toys.[14] When there are only two toddlers present, then these disputes rise to around 90 per cent. Obviously, the 'first possession rule' from the animal kingdom is not fully operational at that age. By the time they reach three years old, these arguments drop to around half of all disputes.

Initially children prefer the toys that others like the most. It is not uncommon for toddlers to drop a toy in their possession and go after an identical one simply because it is in the possession of another. Long before they are aware of status symbols, toddlers appreciate the value of acquiring stuff that others want. Initially toddlers are fairly self-centred when they play with objects, but this soon shifts to increased joint play with their peers which involves toys.[15] As the child psychologist Edward Mueller described, ownership of toys is the 'carrots and sticks' of social development, fostering social inter-action both by invitation and by demand.[16]

Possession also becomes a means to establish where you are in the nursery pecking order. Taking control of objects is far more frequent than hitting, and arguably a more salient characteristic of dominance than violence, which is transient and likely to lead to retaliation or punishment.[17] When it comes to ownership, what is remarkable is that toddlers may bring their home environment experiences into the nursery. One study showed that toddlers who take objects relatively frequently from their peers have mothers who take things relatively frequently from them; conversely, those toddlers who offer objects more frequently to their peers have parents who offer things more frequently to them.[18]

Territorial disputes and aggressive possession tend to decline over the pre-school period and be replaced by negotiation. This is where language plays an important role in settling ownership disputes. Children who are language-delayed continue to rely on brute force to claim ownership.[19] No wonder, then, that these children are the ones who are rejected by their peers. Boys, who are comparatively more aggressive and slower to communicate compared to girls, are also the ones most likely to resort to violence when it comes to ownership disputes. They are also less likely to share.[20] Child psychologists have long argued over whether male aggression is a natural inclination or cultural stereotype, but the universal language delay in males is biologically rooted.[21] Could it be that the inability to negotiate over possession has its origins in this aggression, or is the inability to negotiate possession the origin of this aggression?

One intriguing shifting pattern observed over this period of early childhood is that dominance hierarchies tend to be the first to emerge, with friendship structures following and altruistic structures developing later still. Children learn to wield ownership as a means to establish themselves socially, first by force, then by co-operation and finally by reputation. 'Mine' may be a very small word that children first learn to use, but it remains one of the most powerful in a world dominated by ownership.

IS THAT YOURS?

Many of the property dilemmas we face involve absent owners. Imagine you are on a long, tedious train journey without a companion to talk to or a smartphone to alleviate the boredom. You spot an interesting magazine you would like to read on an empty seat. Determining whether you can pick it up or not comes down to working out who it belongs to. Is it the woman who is sitting in the seat next to the magazine? Is it the man who was sitting there a moment ago but who got off at the last stop? Or does it belong to the train company, which often distributes free promotional materials for passengers to read? Maybe somebody put the magazine there to reserve the seat while they go off to the buffet carriage. Is the magazine owned or not? Your theory of mind engages as you try to solve this puzzle. Or you may not care and simply pick it up, but most of us are sensitive to ownership and conditioned not to offend by taking without permission. At the very least, we would ask the woman first before picking it up. After all, she is closest to it and may have a priority claim over it.

For trivial items, such as magazines, we probably don't agonize over ownership, but with most valuable possessions we do: land, in particular, and where we can and cannot go. Security guards, gates and fences protect many restricted areas, but others are less clear where trespassing can have lethal consequences. In the US, innocent trespassers have been shot and killed by homeowners. Sometimes the trespassers are intoxicated, sometimes they're lost, or sometimes they're foreign visitors and don't appreciate the homeowner's right to use deadly force to defend their property.[22]

Contrary to widely held assumptions, the use of lethal force for home defence is *not* legal in the US, but in many states it is perfectly acceptable to shoot and kill a trespasser if one fears for one's safety. Based originally on English law that came over with the colonists, the 'Castle Doctrine' is the right to use force to defend property and can be traced to the seventeenth-century lawyer Sir Edward Coke, who wrote that 'a man's house is his castle'.

Trespassing can be unintentional. There are even cases of Pokémon Go players who, while following the GPS on their smartphones to capture virtual cartoon creatures, have been fired upon for wandering on to private property.[23] Every year some hapless individual is shot, supposedly in self-defence, but in reality it's because they did not have permission to be on the property. But how do you know when you are trespassing? In some cultures, the concept of trespassing does not even exist. You have to know the conventions and learn to read the signs, even when they are not visible.

Humans use signals to demarcate territory because they are a proxy for a person. Names, addresses, signs and flags all indicate ownership. However, sometimes there are no markers to indicate ownership. If you visit one of the many US National Parks, such as Yellowstone in Wyoming, and happen to see an interesting stone lying on the ground, you might want to take it home. However, despite its being a natural object, created in the bowels of the Earth millions of years ago, and that no one but you is aware of, you are, nevertheless, prohibited from taking it.[24] Many parks now have signs telling visitors that natural things cannot be removed. You cannot take ownership of flowers and rocks from many National Parks because in a sense everyone owns them – they are owned by the State. The trouble is, how would you know? One stone looks much the same as any other. Ownership controls each and every one of us and we have to abide by it or face the consequences, but the rules are not always evident. How do we acquire something so intangible as ownership?

For the developing child, there are two plausible routes to establishing ownership: visual association and verbal instruction. Simple visual association leads infants to assume a degree of connectedness between people and things that they observe on a regular basis. They see Mummy speaking on her smartphone every day so they come to assume that this object is part of who she is. Identifying specific people with specific objects is a skill that they have probably had since they were twelve months old at least.[25] However, establishing ownership relationships also requires some deliberate interaction with the object that is fairly exclusive. Otherwise, infants would be making associations with just about every type of household object paired with a person they see on a daily basis. It would become an overwhelming amount to keep in their tiny minds – refrigerators, cups and cutlery, televisions and so on that do not really reflect exclusive ownership per se. Rather, having something in your possession and interacting with it seems to trigger ownership assumptions.[26]

Once the visual association is established, children spontaneously verbally label the object with the person they associate with it. Scholars of early language development have noted how common it is for infants to point at objects associated with someone, such as a smartphone, and say 'Mummy', as if to illustrate that there is an early appreciation that objects are an extension of individual identity. This label can then be reinforced and elaborated to identify the name of the object: 'Yes, that's right – that's Mummy's phone.' However, at no point would a typical child point at her mother and say, 'Phone'. This shows that before their second birthday, infants understand the relationship between people and possessions as one of owner and the stuff they own.

Toddlers don't just use language to discover who owns property; they use it to claim possession. When we hear, 'This is John's', because it is a possessive phrase, then we know that it belongs to him. Young toddlers appreciate this, but then can over-apply the command as if establishing ownership simply requires saying, 'Mine!' Studies of peer interactions between eighteen-month-olds reveal that the possessive pronoun 'mine' was most frequent when grabbing toys from another child.[27] Children with siblings also use possessive pronouns earlier and more frequently in their speech than those without older siblings, indicating that children use 'mine' to verbally stake their claim when there is potential competition.[28]

By the time they reach their second birthday, children can also refer to possessions when the owner is not present. If they are shown a familiar possession from a family member, they can answer the question, 'Who does this belong to?' with 'Daddy' or 'Mummy'.[29] If you think about it, this seemingly simple ability of identifying someone's possessions when they are not around is actually a considerable achievement. It demonstrates that the concept of ownership exists in the minds of pre-schoolers as thoughts of absent individuals and the stuff they own. The ability to represent the relationship between people and their property, when they are not present together, is a level of conceptual understanding that stretches the mind further still.

Learning by association and labelling is all very well, but how do you establish ownership when dealing with new people and unfamiliar items on a first-time basis, which make up most cases in real life? How do you work out whose magazine it is on the train? When it comes to understanding the world, children look for patterns to establish general principles. The child psychologist Ori Friedman has spent the past ten years studying how children work out who owns what. Like little Sherlock Holmeses, he argues that children are intuitive sleuths, using deduction to recreate the history of an item so as to determine its likely owner. To do this, they apply a set of rules. They consider what can and cannot be owned.

WHAT CAN BE OWNED?

Imagine walking in the park and spotting three items on the ground: a pinecone, an old bottle cap and a diamond ring. Which of these items are owned? It seems fairly obvious to most adults. One is natural and the other two are manufactured. Of the two manufactured items, one is likely to have been discarded whereas the other is likely to be lost. From at least three years of age, children understand that pinecones are natural objects and not as likely to be owned as diamond rings, which are man-made. But consider a leaf you see on someone's desk. Is this owned? You are going to reach different conclusions about ownership if their office window is open and it is a windy day with trees outside, compared to finding the same leaf on an office desk on the thirtieth floor of a skyscraper.[30] In the first case, there was probably no intention to acquire the leaf but simply the effects of the wind. As for the leaf in a skyscraper, someone must have intentionally put the leaf there and so it probably has some significance to someone.

Intended effort is one signal of the production of property. Like many doting parents, I have expressed gratitude for the leaves, sticks, stones and other natural things collected by my children. Our kitchen used to be festooned with our infant daughters' works of art that to outside observers must have looked more like scraps with squiggles. Not so. A lot of effort and intention had gone into these creations. As my colleague Melissa Allen has argued, when it comes to art, it is the intention, not the craftsmanship, that determines what it is. It is the intention of the creator that defines art – something that children understand from the age of two.[31]

Establishing intentions, goals and effort are all factors in our ownership decisions when we are asked to adjudicate in property disputes. Just as the courts argue over ownership of a Banksy, is it any surprise that children and cultures reason differently about ownership? In our research, we have shown that pre-schoolers, like adults, initially believe whoever put in the effort to create or acquire something is the rightful owner.[32] However, they don't care about who owns the original materials that are used in the process. Three- to four-year-olds think that taking someone else's modelling clay to make a new object is fair and gives them ownership rights, whereas adults are more likely to ask who owns the clay. We have found that the bias towards creative effort over material first possession is true in other cultures too, except that Japanese adults are much more likely than British adults to be concerned about where the material came from.[33] This suggests that, in comparison, Japanese adults are much more sensitive over taking possession of another's material irrespective of the creative act. British adults also take into consideration whether labour significantly alters the value of the newly created object. If an artist like Banksy puts in the effort to transform a worthless block of concrete into a work of art then they are considered the rightful owner, compared to the artisan who takes valuable gold and makes a piece of jewellery.[34] It is the relative increase in wealth through effort and labour that is considered to be the most important factor.

The amount of effort and the skill in creating something influences our decision about who owns an object. But how to judge that skill? A Jackson Pollock painting might look like an explosion in a paint factory to some, but for others his creative genius makes the canvas worth millions of dollars. Some paintings are considered graffiti, whereas others are masterpieces. Then there are works that to the untrained eye simply look like blank canvases but sell for exorbitant amounts of cash. In 2014, a white-on-white painting by the American artist Robert Ryman sold for $15 million.[35] When it comes to conceptual art, it is the intention of the artist that determines whether something qualifies as property worth owning.

WHO CAN OWN WHAT?

In 2010, Bret Carr filed a lawsuit in Florida challenging the will of his late mother who left around $11 million in assets and funds to look after her pet dogs.[36] Some people leave their wealth not only to animals but also to art collections, buildings and lands that they want to preserve and protect. Clearly, people can leave their wealth to schemes set up to look after anything.

It does seem odd that animals and artefacts could be thought of as owners of inherited wealth. Even young children understand that it is usually people who own things. In one set of studies, children aged between six and ten were asked a series of questions about who could be owners, including humans, animals and artefacts.[37] They were asked questions such as 'Can a little baby own a blanket? Can a dog own a ball? Can a couch own a pillow?' Although there were a few exceptions, on the whole even the youngest children thought that only humans could be owners. If the animal in question was a pet, however, then children would apply ownership rights. When my daughters first started to keep pets, they reasoned that the various bells and climbing frames in the cage belonged to their pets. They reasoned that possessions were an extension of identity. It would seem that when we establish unique identity, we use ownership as part of that concept. But, again, there are exceptions. Children initially believe that humans have to be conscious to own something.[38] Someone who is asleep is not considered capable of owning.

These exceptions provide clues as to how children may be establishing ownership. Adults consider ownership as an extension of the individual irrespective of the state he or she is in – whether they are tied up, paralysed, asleep or in a coma. Even the dead can own property until it has been established who are the rightful heirs to their estate. It seems then that children must consider ownership as the capacity to act upon a thing, a legacy of what motivates the drive for possession in infants in the first place – the ability to control. Remember, young children think that whoever is interacting with an object is the legitimate possessor – a bit like demand-sharing observed among hunter-gatherers. They still do not understand that once ownership is established it remains a right of access unless it is transferred by the owner. This raises the untested prediction that if the youngest children understand theft is wrong, is it the case they consider that ownership eventually transfers if the thief continues to possess the stolen property?

You may consider this an obvious no, except that in both US and

English law, a legal process known as 'adverse possession' entitles a transfer of ownership of property by occupation if the original owner does not contest the interloper who has taken possession for a period, usually at least ten to twelve years. Given enough time, squatters can legally claim ownership. Ownership is not for ever and unless you exercise your use of property, then others can take it away from you.

If establishing ownership requires a bit of sleuthing, then one of the strongest clues is who is likely to own a particular possession. Stereotypes emerge early and, increasingly, we are beginning to understand just how strong and influential they can be. At as early as three years of age, children are obsessed with identifying gender. Psychologists Carol Martin and Diane Ruble have likened toddlers to 'gender detectives', since they seek out gender information with which to construct their notions of what it is to be a boy or a girl.[39] Not only do they start out as gender detectives but they become 'gender police', where they insist, for example, that only girls can own dolls or only boys can own toy soldiers as these objects are stereotypical of each gender. Of course, there are always exceptions and some parents try to find gender-neutral toys, but in general, there is good evidence that children themselves exhibit early preferences. These may have a biological basis as young female primates, both human and non-human, have a stronger preference for dolls compared to males when offered a choice of toys. There are even reports that young female chimpanzees use sticks as rudimentary dolls and care for them in an attempt to emulate their mothers.[40]

As the child develops more elaborate models of identity, including gender, race and age, they include within those concepts the appropriate possessions as typical of that group defined by the cultural context.[41] Like Sherlock Holmes, children apply deductive reasoning in establishing ownership. In one study, three- to four-year-olds were shown two characters, a boy and a girl, who were each depicted playing with a beach ball separately.[42] When asked who owned the ball, the children deferred to the first possession bias to assume the first child seen playing with the ball was the owner. However, in a second set of studies, rather than a beach ball the objects being played with included a toy truck, a jewellery box, football equipment and a doll. Presented with this additional information, children attributed ownership based on the gender stereotype of possession irrespective of who was seen to be playing with the object first. The possessions were reflections of the likely owner.

TEDDY BEARS AND BLANKETS

As children learn to solve who owns what, they increasingly view possessions as part of identity. One possession that young children will not share and will defend vigorously is their attachment object – usually a soft toy or blanket that they have had since they were infants. Children tend to be inconsolable when such items are lost. These are sometimes called 'security blankets' as they provide a sense of reassurance and often form part of a routine to settle the child. I've been researching attachment objects for over twenty years. It is such a peculiar, but common, behaviour that it must arise from a fundamental need in many of us to hold on to someone or something that is familiar. It is one of the strongest examples of psychological ownership, and one of the earliest. Where does it come from?

The psychoanalyst Donald Winnicott called these security blankets 'transitional objects', since they fill in as the child makes the psychological break with their mother.[43] He thought that infants form such a strong bond with the mother that when she is not available the child fills the void with an object to transfer their emotional connection from the mother. Various estimates place the number of Western children who form emotional attachments to soft toys and blankets to be around 60 per cent.[44] Interestingly, childhood attachment objects are not typically seen in the Far East, where studies have reported much lower levels of use.[45] One explanation comes down to traditional sleeping patterns.[46] In the West, middle-class families typically put infants into separate sleeping places from around the first year, whereas in traditional East Asian families children will continue to sleep with the mother well into middle childhood. To our Western eyes, this practice seems odd, but it is simply a cultural norm. In addition, many East Asian families, especially in the densely populated cities of Japan, sleep in small apartments where having your own bedroom is unusual. So not only does this parenting practice influence emotional attachment, because children traditionally are kept close to the mother, it also reduces the need to seek comfort from possessions.

When children are separated from their mothers to sleep, they have to establish a routine and these possessions become critical triggers. My elder daughter, Martha, started to attend a nursery in Boston at around the age of twelve months, when her mother had to go back to work, and we were instructed to provide a blanket for nap time, an established routine where all the children had to learn to settle down at the same time. We provided a garish, multicoloured, polyester fleece blanket, and very soon 'Blankie' became a regular part of Martha's life – and still is today. Clearly, a pattern of association between comfort and an object was soon established. In our case, by the time she was two, Martha was inseparable from the blanket, which caused many moments of anguish whenever Blankie went missing.

Nor can attachment objects be easily replaced. In one study, we convinced three- to four-year-olds that we had built a machine that could duplicate anything, like a photocopier for objects or a 3D printer.[47] We did this with a simple conjuring trick using two scientific-looking boxes with lights and dials. Objects were placed in one box, which was then 'activated' by pushing a button. After some more noises and lights, the second box was opened to reveal a second, identical object. Children were convinced that this machine could copy any physical object to make another exactly the same. Of course, we had two identical-looking objects and there was a hidden experimenter putting the duplicate into the second box. We did this because we wanted to see if the child would agree to have their personal possession copied and, if so, which one they preferred to keep. The pattern was clear. If it was simply a toy they owned, they were indifferent to the copying and preferred the brand-new toy. It was cool after all. However, if it was their attachment object they wanted the original back. As if it was an original piece of art, they didn't want a copy even if it was indistinguishable.

Maybe you never had an attachment toy. My younger daughter, Esmé, did not, even though she was raised in the same household as Martha. Why not? This is the type of question that parents often ask about their children. Why are they so different? This is where studies of identical and non-identical twins are so valuable in trying to tease

apart the contributions of biology and environment to individual differences. One recent twin study found that attachment toy ownership
is half to do with genes and half to do with the environment –
especially for those children who spent longer times away from their
mothers.[48] My graduate student Ashley Lee, who is studying attachment object behaviour in adults, just happens to be an identical twin.
She never had an attachment object whereas her sister, Rachel, still
has hers. According to their mother, when she was a baby Rachel had
to spend several months in hospital after getting an infection, where
she was separated from the rest of the family. This is when she first
became attached to her object.

This relationship with an inanimate object may start as a simple
routine but it can soon change to something very different indeed.
Many children act as if their attachment objects are alive, giving them
names and worrying about whether they are happy or lonely. They
spontaneously interact with them as if they have minds of their own. In
psychological terms, they anthropomorphize them, or treat them as if
they were human. Along with my colleague Thalia Gjersoe, we tested
to see whether children believed that these possessions had mental
lives.[49] We did this by showing them a picture of an animal or another
child's toy and told them that, when placed in a box, the animal got
lonely but the toy simply got dusty. We then asked the child what would
happen to their attachment object if we left it in the box. Children
responded that, while other toys might get dusty, their attachment
objects were more like the animals, with sad thoughts and feelings.

You might imagine that children grow out of this behaviour, but many
do not. Ashley investigates students who still have their attachment
objects. My daughter Martha is now twenty-four and still has Blankie!
Would they be willing to damage them? We couldn't ask adults to damage their possessions so we used a bit of voodoo instead. We asked them
to cut up pictures of their childhood toys while we measured their gal-
vanic skin responses, which is basically an indication of how much sweat
they produce. It's one of the measures of stress used in lie detectors. Even
though they knew that there was no potential harm that could come to
their beloved possessions, the act of cutting up a picture was so sym-
bolically distressing that their anxiety measures went wild.[50] They
were emotionally connected to their attachment objects.

Each year, I recruit subjects from our student population at the University of Bristol to take part in our studies. When I ask them about attachment objects, I always see a mixture of perplexed faces and giggles from those who are sheepish about this peculiar aspect of their personal lives. We normally find that around two-thirds of students remember having had special toys in childhood, and around half of them still have them at university. Clearly these are sentimental possessions that people are reluctant to discard because of their emotional value.

Up and down the country, adults are finding their partners' filthy blankets and ragged dolls stuffed under pillows or in drawers. It's a guilty secret that many are too ashamed to admit. Others are much more open. I have spoken to many adults who are quite happy to talk about the emotional relationship they have with their childhood attachment possessions. Sometimes their confessions can be quite embarrassing. I once talked about this research at a dinner party when a female guest, presumably more forthcoming after some wine, admitted that she always had to turn her teddy bear to face the bedroom wall when she brought boyfriends back. She was simply too embarrassed by what her teddy might see.

Sentimental ownership is common for humans but not normally observed in wild animals. They can be made to become emotionally attached to inanimate objects but only if you take them out of their natural environments. In the 1960s, Harry Harlow performed his infamous studies of raising infant macaque monkeys isolated from their mothers, providing them with 'surrogate' wire mothers that were either covered in soft terry towelling fabric to simulate fur or bare wire cages with a feeder attached.[51] He was trying to establish whether infant monkeys would become emotionally attached to the mother who was a source of food or the mother who provided comfort. The research showed that the monkeys clung to the furry mother and, when distressed, they would seek reassurance from this surrogate, which suggests that primate attachment is mostly motivated for emotional security and not by the drive for food. Normally, a mother is readily available in the wild so there is no need for primates to make the choice.

Animals kept in captivity, however, have been shown to become spontaneously attached to possessions. As many dog owners discover, pets can form emotional attachments to toys just like human infants,

Dogs form emotional attachments to inanimate possessions (Image: courtesy Jo Benhamu)

especially when separated from their mothers. But, again, this is not a behaviour observed in their ancestor, the wolf. Dogs have emerged from a long process of domestication by humans, which is known to induce juvenilization in animals – an increase in the period and extent of dependency – so attachment to possessions may have been a by-product of this process. Human children, on the other hand, are almost totally dependent on others. And we grow up depending on others. We also spend our lives accumulating possessions in the belief that owner-ship is the root of happiness. Psychological ownership is a consequence of social evolution where we form emotional attachments to significant things – both people and possessions.

BEYOND SIMPLE POSSESSION

We have established what makes humans unique when it comes to our relationship with possessions. Many animals fight over possessions, but humans evolved the concept of ownership as a way to establish control in our absence and to signal who we are. Like art, concepts are generated in the mind, but ownership, because it is a socially agreed convention, requires learning the rules. While the rules of ownership may be opaque, the need to possess is appreciated from an early age. Infants protest when someone tries to take their stuff away, but this is just a simple reaction to being dispossessed. Ownership is more to do with personal identity and not breaking the rules.

At first, ownership focuses on physical objects, though parents may be considered property in that infants expect exclusive rights of access. Owning land and ideas, on the other hand, are somewhat more sophisticated and appear much later in development. Even adults contest these. It would seem then that children first identify significant others such as family members, and then elaborate their mental photograph album of people with the possessions they own. The idea that we extrapolate from bodies and minds to possessions is consistent with one of the main themes of this book – that ownership represents an extension of our self-concept. If this is true, then our sense of self will differ depending on the social contexts we grow up in. What we can call ours depends on the mutually recognized conventions of ownership that we share with others. These rules are not cast in stone but change over time and between cultures.

When there is a property dispute, establishing ownership comes down to making a choice as to who has the strongest claim. But the strength of a claim depends on what a society values the most. In Western societies, with our emphasis on the individual, the bias is for those who can exercise the most control, either through first possession or exclusive access. In other, more interdependent societies, these would not be considered the most important factors as need and communal value play greater roles, as evidenced by the hunter-gatherer tradition of demand-sharing. Wherever they grow up, children must learn the appropriate norms for their community or face the danger of being ostracized – something that must be avoided at all cost.

Our identities are socially constructed and that includes our attitudes towards ownership. In the distant past, our social groups may have been fairly restricted, but, as we are increasingly living together in greater and greater densities on a planet of limited resources and restricted size, that self-identity will be forced to realign with the needs of the many if we are to avoid the ultimate tragedy of the commons. To do that requires us to teach our children a set of ownership values that deny unbridled self-interest. One of the most important values to adopt is sharing with others, something that conflicts with our competitive instinct but is essential for co-operative living. Like ownership, sharing undergoes considerable development and cultural variation, which we examine next.

4

It's Only Fair

'Do not worry about poverty, but rather about the unequal
distribution of wealth.'

Confucius

When it comes to wealth and poverty, life is unfair. Throughout his
presidency, Barack Obama called economic inequality 'the defining
problem of our time' as the gap between the world's rich and poor
reached staggering proportions. In 2015, a Credit Suisse Bank report
revealed that the top 1 per cent of the world's population owned 50
per cent of the world's wealth, whereas 70 per cent owned less than 3
per cent.[1] In America the poverty gap has been increasing steadily
over the years. In 2012, a typical company CEO earned over 350
times the salary of a typical worker, whereas it was just 20 times their
salary only two generations earlier.[2]

With statistics like these, you might think that a second American
revolution is long overdue, but the truth is most Americans prefer
inequality. In one study of over 5,000 Americans who represented all
strata of the wealth divide, adults were shown three anonymous pie
charts that reflected the real wealth distributions of the US and Sweden as well as a fictitious communist country where all wealth was
evenly distributed.[3] Each pie chart was divided into five quintiles that
showed how much each 20 per cent of the population owned in terms
of the nation's wealth. Participants were then asked to imagine moving

to one of the countries and being randomly assigned into one of the quintiles. Which country would they prefer to live in? Very few chose the fictitious communist country. But they did not want to move back home either, because they did not recognize the gross imbalances of the US pie chart as representing the country's actual wealth distributions. Rather, nine out of ten Americans said they would prefer to live in Sweden, based on the Swedish pie chart that showed a much more even distribution of wealth compared to the inequality of the US. This preference for some degree of inequality is not just restricted to Americans. In a 2018 online study of another 5,000 adults, when presented with the opportunity to play Robin Hood, the majority of both Americans and Germans preferred not to take from the rich in order to redistribute wealth to the poor.[4] Clearly, we expect and prefer inequality in life.

We do not start out accepting inequality. Simple experiments suggest not only an early sensitivity to inequality but an aversion to it. Infants as young as fifteen months are surprised when crackers are not shared evenly between two recipients.[5] Toddlers know to share equally between third parties, even though they still keep most for themselves.[6] When there is an odd number of treats to be dispersed between two recipients, six- to eight-year-olds would rather dispose of the odd treat in order to maintain an equal share.[7] Children also prefer individuals who have been shown to share equally compared to those who show favouritism.[8]

The psychologist Christina Starmans points out that there is no contradiction between the research studies that demonstrate children's aversion to inequality and the evidence that adults prefer to live in unequal societies. It is not the unequal distribution of wealth that upsets people, but rather whether that distribution is considered fair.[9] This is because fairness and equality are not the same thing. Studies claiming to show a natural disposition towards fairness have typically set up a situation where recipients are equally eligible to receive rewards. If you divide resources among individuals who have worked for them, it is unfair if you give everyone the same amount even though some worked hard while others lazed about. When differences of effort are taken into consideration, the lab studies start to look more like real life. Children who are told that one child has worked harder to clean up, reward them with more because they consider it fairer.[10] They believe in rewarding merit.

Perceived fairness also explains attitudes towards wealth distribution. The reason most residents of capitalist countries are content with the unequal state of economic distribution is that they believe that people who work harder than those who don't should be rewarded more. Meritocracy is central to the capitalist ideology that if you work hard, you will succeed and benefit from the fruits of your labour. If citizens are unhappy about the current state of affairs then it is not because of inequality per se, but rather because they think the distribution is unfair. From the richest to the poorest, everyone wants to see less inequality, but not a totally equal society (apart from communists, of course, but no communist society has yet to achieve this full equality).

One problem for this perspective on fairness is that, just like when estimating other people's salaries, we are not very good at predicting the actual distribution of resources. The same participants from the study above, who revealed a preference for Sweden versus the US, were asked what they thought would be an ideal fair distribution, and to estimate the real distribution of wealth in the US.[11] Respondents thought life would be fair if the top 20 per cent owned around a third of a nation's wealth and the bottom 20 per cent owned around one-tenth of the wealth. When it came to estimating the actual US distribution of wealth, they were correct in guessing that the top 20 per cent in the US own most of the nation's wealth compared to the poorest, but they grossly underestimated the extent of that inequality. In fact, the top 20 per cent own around 84 per cent and the bottom 20 per cent own only 0.1 per cent of the nation's wealth. Clearly the perception of equality and fairness is much greater than it really is. One of the reasons for this misperception is the common belief in the 'American dream'.

The American dream is one based on meritocracy – that people are justly rewarded for their efforts. If so, it naturally follows that anyone can be successful if they work hard enough. This leads to the assumption of social mobility, where anyone can reach the top and should be rewarded for their efforts. People prefer unequal societies because without the motivation to succeed no one would strive to better their lives and the lives of their children.[12] Why bother if you do not reap the benefits of all your hard work? The fairness principle explains the general tolerance of inequality in the US, and less support for the redistribution of educational resources or wealth by taxing the richest more heavily in comparison to countries such as Sweden.[13] We all want to live in fairer societies, just so long as we are the ones at the top. The UK may not have the equivalent British dream, but there is still income inequality. We have better social-support systems than the US, especially with welfare and the National Health Service, but again the top 10 per cent benefit from around 45 per cent of the total UK wealth whereas the bottom 50 per cent have only around 8 per cent of the national wealth.

The meritocratic ideal partly explains the rise of the political right during the modern era and the appeal of Donald Trump. Although many commentators considered his election to the presidency as an economic protest vote from the poorest in society, economic inequality is not the only factor operating across the political spectrum where populism has arisen, as we saw in the first chapter. Indeed, there are few politicians as privileged and wealthy as Donald Trump, and yet many economically disadvantaged voters voted for him because they viewed him as a product of the American dream – a self-made man. His opponent, Hillary Clinton, on the other hand, represented the establishment, her husband being a former US president. Even though Clinton's Democratic Party has traditionally promoted more egalitarian policies to distribute wealth that should have favoured the least well-off in society, many of the poorest resented this continuity of privilege from one political dynast to the next. They felt that their economic predicament was due to the elite classes controlling the system that kept them subjugated. They wanted to take back ownership and control of their lives.

History will tell if the shift to the right produces a better world, but one thing is clear: people do not always behave in their best self-interests – as the current political upheavals demonstrate – but, rather, make decisions based on principles. This is particularly relevant in the case of ownership. If ownership is the exclusive control over resources that enable individuals to thrive, then there is a strong moral component as to what society considers acceptable ownership inequalities. We can accept inequalities when individuals have deservedly earned their wealth, but ownership is inherently unfair because life is not a level playing-field.

Each of us benefits to a greater or lesser extent depending on who our ancestors and relatives are. And it is not just through financial inheritance but genetic dispositions too. If someone works hard then maybe they are physically more capable than others to begin with. Some of our top athletes are paid exorbitant salaries, but is it fair if they were born that way? If someone is naturally more numerate, do they deserve a higher salary than someone who is not? Then there is financial luck and windfalls as much as bad luck and disasters – events that are out of our control but change our lives. How do we respond to the inequalities that make or break our fortunes as a result of life's random events? As individuals, we must decide what is fair and just, but how?

Ownership creates inequality and, by the advantage of inherited privilege, it perpetuates unfairness in society. But it also empowers individuals to share their resources with those who have less, and so the imbalances created by ownership can be corrected by the moral compass that guides our generosity towards others. Contrary to the competitive instinct, humans can be remarkably kind to strangers; but if life is simply a competition, why? To get a better understanding of this, we turn to the field of behavioural economics to discover how our generosity is determined by a developing sense of morality and fair play.

THE DICTATOR GAME

Nicholas is a dictator. He is not the leader of a fascist regime, nor does he deliver strident nationalistic speeches like Hitler or Mussolini. After all, Nicholas is only seven years old. But he is the one calling the shots and has the power to decide what he can keep for himself – in this case, some shiny animal stickers.

Nicholas has just taken part in a study where he talked about his friends while my graduate student Sandra Weltzien drew a picture based on his description. After the interview, she thanked him for his time and said that, as a treat, he could choose six stickers from a bag of goodies to take home. After he'd selected the six best ones, Sandra told Nicholas that he could keep them all, or, if he wanted, he could share some of them with the next child who was coming into the lab by leaving some in a blank envelope. It was entirely up to him. He really liked the stickers and wanted to keep them all. What should he do?

After Nicholas left with his mother, Sandra opened the envelope and tipped out three shiny stickers on to the table. Why did Nicholas give away half his stickers? After all, no one would have known if he'd taken all of them, and it wasn't as if he knew the child who would receive them. By the time they reach seven or eight years old, most children share when asked to even though they do not know the recipient. Is it because they have learned that they must share, or do they think that it is the right thing to do? Why do we share or help others? Is it out of the goodness of our hearts or are there other motives for kindness?

In 2017, Americans donated $250 billion to charity, while Britons donated £10 billion.[14] When it comes to charitable donations, there is no expectation to receive something in return. Why do people share and give away their resources if not for pure altruism? Such kindness is a concern that has preoccupied our greatest thinkers since Socrates, the father of moral philosophy. It constantly arises across the humanities, sciences and theology, but selfless generosity has not occupied a central role in economic theories because it is illogical from a purely rational viewpoint. Kindness is difficult to reconcile with classical economic models that are largely influenced by thinkers such as John Stuart Mill and Adam Smith.

In *The Wealth of Nations*, Smith wrote: 'It is not from the benevolence of the butcher, the brewer, or the baker that we expect our dinner, but from their regard to their own interest.' In other words, humans operate rationally to maximize what they can get by contributing as little of their resources as possible. They are motivated by commerce to buy low and sell high, and, so long as the market exists to adjust to the needs of buyers and sellers, Adam Smith's invisible hand of economic influence that we discussed earlier will guide citizens towards prosperity. This idealized consumer who always operates rationally has been called 'Homo Economicus', an individual who has evolved solely to maximize their own interest.[15]

It is ironic then, that the major problem with Homo Economicus is ownership. This is because we make ownership decisions that reveal that most of us fail to maximize our own interests – and can act against our best economic interests when it comes to valuing things. Individuals are prone to over-value certain items, such as personal possessions or objects associated with significant others, which we address in later chapters. More problematic for Homo Economicus, however, is charity and generosity. Humans regularly give away resources to others even when there are no opportunities for payback. We share when we see others in need. Just like Nicholas and his gift of stickers to the unknown child, we are often kind to strangers, which runs counter to the business principles of Homo Economicus.

If our economic drive is self-maximization and our biological imperative is to make copies of our genes at the inevitable cost to others, then why is there altruism at all, if life is just a competition? Why is the world full of generous people and kind acts? Why do charities exist? What motivates people to be kind? To address these questions, we need to look to biology for answers.

I'LL SCRATCH YOUR BACK

As we have already seen, biology can explain patterns of generosity to others, especially those who are kin. Kin selection predicts we are more likely to help our relatives because they carry varying proportions of our individual genes, but it cannot be the only mechanism. The problem for kin selection is that we often engage in pro-social acts that are not accounted for by genetic relatedness. For example, many of us donate blood even though we will never know the recipients. What is the advantage of helping a total stranger with whom you do not share genes?

One answer is pooled benefit. Co-operation is one of the major characteristics and strengths of social species. Working together, our ancestors learned to hunt animals as massive as mammoths that no lone hunter could easily bring down on their own. Other social animals have also learned the benefits of mutual effort. Wolves and other pack predators co-ordinate to capture prey larger than any one individual member. Our nearest cousin, the chimpanzee, is a group hunter when it comes to tracking and capturing red colobus monkeys for meat. Frisky colobus monkeys are swift and difficult to catch unless cornered by multiple chimps working together. Sometimes prey is so small and numerous that a group effort is more efficient. One of the most unusual and spectacular examples of this collaborative effort is 'bubble net' fishing by humpback whales. They swim in circles around shoals of fish to confuse and corral them by blowing out bubbles of air through their blow holes, before each whale takes their turn to swim up the centre of the column to gulp down the amassed prey.

All these examples of hunting require co-ordinated activity in order to achieve a common goal. However, animals also share food even when their bounty does not require co-ordinated hunting. Take the South American vampire bat. Vampire bats must feed off the blood of other animals at least every forty-eight hours or they will starve, but not every bat will have a successful hunting trip on each outing. When this occurs, other bats will regurgitate blood to help their neighbour even when they are not related as required by kin selection.

This form of altruism seems charitable, but it is really a strategy to bank favours. Bats keep track of those who helped them in the past and give them preferential treatment if they need food in turn. Studies of bats kept in zoos reveal that individual bats who are deliberately segregated and starved by experimenters will benefit from neighbours if they have donated blood previously to others, whereas bats with a reputation for being selfish tend to be ostracized when they themselves require food.[16] This 'reciprocal altruism' is an evolved strategy to get individuals through lean times.

In our human history, reciprocal altruism would have been a necessary mechanism for survival. The evolutionary psychologist Michael Tomasello thinks the origins of human morality evolved from our capacity to share the spoils from our collaborative efforts.[17] This co-operation arose from interdependence, where we depended on each other. Sometime in our evolution, early humans discovered the truth of the proverb 'many hands make light work'. We were interdependent because it was more beneficial for us to work together. We learned that it was in our interest to forego some personal goal for the potential of greater rewards through collaboration.

Reciprocal altruism depends on keeping track of those who return favours and those who cheat. Otherwise, freeloaders would come to dominate the group. This is especially true with ownership where we need to keep in mind who owns what and which individuals owe a favour in return. This is also motivated by emotions of anger and outrage, as we seem to be especially sensitive to someone who breaks the rules. Keeping track of others requires a social brain that is characteristically found in species that not only co-operate and live together in small groups but also spend a long period of time rearing their young. Long childhoods provide ample opportunity to learn about helpers and cheats. Consider the vampire bat again. It is a particularly social animal, rearing its young on average for nine months, in contrast to other species of bat that are usually independent by one-month-old. This extended childhood is also true of other species that form enduring social bonds, providing learning opportunities to discriminate between other members of the group as well as how to behave reciprocally. This may be why social animals spend long periods engaged in grooming each other; this is also true of the vampire bat, which grooms fourteen times longer than other bat species.[18] This grooming is not promiscuous but rather selectively directed to those who have shown past reciprocity. The same is true of humans and other primates. Chimpanzees will groom longer and more often a partner who has previously groomed them.[19] Grooming is the original reciprocal act of 'I'll scratch your back, if you scratch mine!'

HONEST HYPOCRITES

If young children recognize and expect fairness in others, then it seems hypocritical that they appreciate the fairness principle, expect it from others, but do not demonstrate it in their own behaviour. They recognize fairness from infancy, but still have to be told to share until around six or seven years old, when it starts to become routine. In many ways, however, younger children are being more honest than older children and grown-ups. Adults typically consider themselves to be fair, but most of us are hypocrites when the potential rewards are high and we think our unfair choices will be undetected. In one study, adults were presented with two tasks: one that had potential reward and one that did not. The majority (between 70 and 80 per cent) assigned the lucrative job to themselves when their decision was anonymous.[20] The same is true for avoiding pain or punishment. Even when adults are instructed that the fairest way to allocate jobs is to flip a coin, only about half elect to do so, with the remainder showing the same self-bias to choose the best job or to avoid tasks with associated electric shocks. What's more remarkable is that 90 per cent of individuals who agreed to flip a coin still chose the best job anyway. They want to appear to be fair but cheat when they think they will be undetected.

There are a number of ways our selfish behaviour can be moderated, especially when attention is drawn to us. For example, simply looking in a mirror forces adults literally to self-reflect, which studies have shown reduces cheating on a test.[21] This effect of mirrored self-focus on morality is consistent with classic studies demonstrating that children tend to help themselves less on Halloween night when the bowl of treats is placed in front of a mirror.[22] When we think we are being watched, we tend to behave ourselves. If the fear of exposure regulates our transgressions, then religions with an all-seeing God may operate to foster moral behaviour precisely because followers think that they are constantly observed.[23] Most of the world's religions promote pro-sociality in their teachings and practices. There is a common assumption that religions foster kindness and generosity, as epitomized by the parable of the Good Samaritan in Christianity.

One problem with this moral view of religion is that, despite the stereotypes, there is very little evidence that religious people are more generous than non-religious people.[24] It is true that many religions engage in activities that help the less fortunate, but that kind of organized altruism does not necessarily operate in worshippers' daily lives. Also, there is no difference in the generosity of religious and non-religious players in the Dictator Game unless religious players are reminded of God in subtle ways. For example, if they are asked to unscramble sentences that contain the words 'spirit', 'divine', 'God', 'sacred', or 'prophet', then they act generously.[25] Even environmental cues work. Moroccan traders in the Marrakesh markets are much more willing to donate money to a charity when the Muslim call to prayer can be heard in the background.[26] But this generosity is not restricted to the religious: everyone is more generous when they are reminded of secular ideals of equality through subtle priming with the words 'civic', 'jury', 'court', 'police' and 'contract'.[27] What these studies tell us is that we carry around a legacy of our early childish self-interest, but can be nudged to be more pro-social by subtle cues.

Even if people are kind and generous in one context, it does not necessarily translate to every situation. This hypocrisy is known as 'moral self-licensing', where individuals who behave in a moral way in one situation can later display behaviours that are inconsistent in another.[28] Past good deeds can liberate individuals to engage in behaviours that are immoral, unethical, or otherwise problematic; behaviours that they would otherwise avoid for fear of feeling or appearing immoral. Someone who volunteers to help at their church fundraiser to help the poor may later decide not to donate to another charity. When asked to write either about their positive or negative moral traits, those that describe themselves as more generous donate less to a charity, whereas those who reflect on how bad they are, donate more.[29]

There is also a social cachet in being seen to be generous, especially when it comes to donations. For every philanthropist there is some building, prize, award, grant, wing or ward named after them. There are some anonymous donors but, in general, most benefactors (and their families) take pride in these public acknowledgements – unless, of course, others deem the source of benefaction to be the product of ill-gotten gains. Consider the controversy over Edward Colston, a seventeenth-century Bristol merchant and philanthropist who made a fortune from slavery. Across Bristol there are churches, schools, halls and institutions named after him. But not for much longer, as many Bristolians regard such commemorations as hypocritical and have lobbied successfully to have these institutions renamed to cut ties with Colston and disown his legacy.

Assuming your sources of wealth and intentions are honest, sharing stuff empowers you to form and strengthen social bonds. It signals that you are kind, generous, empathetic and an all-round good person. Nobody likes a miser or a hoarder. Whether from religious teachings or the wisdom of elders, we are warned about greed, avarice, envy and all manner of negative emotions associated with the pursuit of material wealth. Up and down the country, many parents are constantly reminding their children to share because it will make them more popular and acceptable to the rest of society. Failure to do so can result in retribution and ostracism.

GETTING EVEN

The flipside of fairness of course is that when others try to take advantage we seem readily prepared to administer punishment. Not only are we wary of those who do not share, but we are prepared to pay for the opportunity to punish them. Imagine the following scenario. Would you willingly accept $10 for doing nothing if there were no strings attached? Why would you ever say no? Now imagine a different scenario, where I offer $100 to another person who would be allowed to keep some of it but only if they shared some with you. Whether or not they keep any money depends on your decision because you ultimately control the outcome – hence the name of this scenario, the 'Ultimatum Game'. Now if they offered you $10 and kept $90 for themselves, would you accept the terms?

Your answer depends on who you think the other person is, and which part of the world you are from. An ambitious study set out to examine the Ultimatum Game in fifteen small-scale societies.[30] Responses were mixed because participants, presented with the strange Westerner offering money in a game, try to relate it to similar situations in their own cultures. In the gift-giving societies of Melanesia, on average they offer more than half the money in the Ultimatum Game. But even that generous amount might be rejected because in these societies, accepting gifts, even unsolicited ones, implies a strong obligation to reciprocate at some future time. In other words, 'What's the catch?' At the other extreme, the African hunter-gatherer Hazda tribe of Tanzania typically offer small amounts, and also suffer high rejection rates in the Ultimatum Game. These people live in insular societies with little co-operation, sharing or exchange with outsiders or strangers.

In Western cultures, most adults playing this game offer nearly half the money, and very few receivers will accept an offer less than $20. Even though this is a one-off opportunity, we would still reject the $10 offer – why? In both scenarios, you would get exactly the same amount of money for doing nothing, and yet half the people questioned think that in the second scenario it is unfair to be offered anything below 20 per cent of the total. Brain-imaging studies reveal that this is largely an emotional response, as these low offers are associated with areas activated by negative experiences such as disgust.[31] We feel vengeful in that we would prefer to punish the other person at our own expense rather than accept something for nothing.

The Ultimatum Game is clearly a hypothetical scenario, but it does reveal something profound about human nature. It challenges the notion of selfless giving as well as that of Homo Economicus, because rejecting offers is neither kind nor is it self-maximizing. An altruist should not care what is offered because rejection leads to no one benefitting, whereas Homo Economicus should accept whatever is offered because it is better than nothing.

The reason for rejecting offers is not economic, but rather psychological. When the Ultimatum Game is played against a computer, people take whatever amount is offered.[32] We only seem to be sensitive to offers from other humans, which is why it is a fascinating glimpse into the psychology of fairness. Moreover, in another version of the game, where the proposer gets to keep any money knowing the receiver cannot veto their offer, they still tend to offer something. This indicates that our behaviour is guided by fairness, a principle that we apply to other humans but not machines and rarely to animals. Our closest cousin the chimpanzee, playing a version of the Ultimatum Game, is happy to accept any offer.[33]

Reciprocity is a predisposition to share with others, and to punish those who violate the norms of fairness. Remember the tragedy of the commons as an explanation for why individuals who act selfishly threaten the future for all? Could retaliation and fear of punishment be the way to solve the tragedy of the commons, by threatening individuals who help themselves to some shared resource more than others? Martin Nowak, a Harvard mathematical biologist, thinks that retribution is neither common, nor the best way to resolve the tragedy of the commons. When we believe that others are cheating in real life, we may simply withdraw and refuse to co-operate. Rather than punishment, Nowak has found that the best way to solve the tragedy of the commons is by a combination of communication, reward and ownership.

The problem of the tragedy of the commons is that we rarely have the opportunity to punish individuals ourselves. In fact, identifying those who cheat on a common resource is not that easy. We may dislike cheats and feel anger, but who are they? Do you know who cheats on their taxes? It is not something that people readily admit. For these reasons, Nowak argues that people are motivated by shared interest, and the best way to encourage that is to reward them for contributing and to give them a sense of ownership. Yes, punish the cheats through the strong arm of the law, but reward individuals who co-operate through the power of reputation. Becoming known as a team player generates a positive motivation in most of us, which, in turn, means that a) we will be more liked by others, and b) we are less likely to transgress. In his book *SuperCooperators*,[34] Nowak advocates that paying car workers bonuses for greater productivity is much more effective than fining them for falling behind. An even more powerful motivator for contributing to a joint effort is mutual ownership. We are more likely to share when we believe that we have worked together to achieve a common goal.

We hinted at the opportunity for retaliation when we considered the rise of political populism in Chapter 1. We may not often get the opportunity to punish specific others, but we can express our indignation at the voting booth.[35] In 2016, the Yale psychologist Molly Crockett wrote in the *Guardian* that human behaviour in these economic games could help to explain why the least well-off in UK society voted for Brexit, even though they were warned that they would suffer the greatest negative consequences. At the time of the referendum, there was so much disinformation and uncertainty circulating that the electorate were never really in a position to make an informed decision about what would be the best outcome, but even if they had many would still have preferred to vote for a change that they thought would hurt those in power. They had nothing to lose but, rather, had an opportunity to express their anger at a system that they felt had kept them down. Other leave voters felt they were losing control of the country and were resentful at what they perceived as a loss of sovereignty and traditional values. Both groups wanted to express their anger.

This need for self-expression is predicted by behaviour on the Ultimatum Game. Those individuals who are most likely to reject offers also endorse statements such as 'I do not want someone to interfere with my business' and 'I do not like having someone else's opinion imposed on me', clearly echoing the same sorts of sentiments expressed by the Brexiteers.[36] What is remarkable is that the need to express

anger is so strong that individuals will still reject offers in a version of
the game known as the 'Impunity Game', where the proposer is not
penalized for a rejected offer but gets to keep their payoff.[37] In other
words, if I am offered $10 knowing that the other person will still get
$90 irrespective of my decision, I'd rather reject the offer anyway,
even if that choice is private, in order to keep my integrity.

The implications from this research for the political sphere is that
all this pent-up resentment could have been avoided if the Brexiteers
had been listened to, rather than dismissed as ignorant or embittered.
Again, the Ultimatum Game reveals that if recipients are able to communicate their anger to proposers, then low offers are more likely to
be accepted.[38] Even if their frustration and anger does not reach the
proposer, but is simply broadcast to others, then responders are more
willing to accept derisory offers so long as everyone knows that they
are not a pushover.[39] Giving people the opportunity to complain is
sufficient, even if it is ineffectual, because it restores an illusion of
control and ownership of opinions. Communication is critical when
it comes to resolving differences, not retaliation.

Molly Crockett ends her article with a stark warning that one should
not rely on economics when it comes to predicting human behaviour,
and that the same perceived sense of injustice is fuelling the rise of
populism across Europe and in the US: 'Those who wish to engage
with these voters would be well-advised to recognise the human need
to feel that someone – anyone – is listening.' If only the Democrats had
listened to her; her article was published in July 2016, four months
before the US election that heralded the arrival of Trump.

LET'S PULL TOGETHER

Young children are sensitive to inequality, expect it from others but
not of themselves and are reluctant to share. There is, however, one set
of circumstances which seems to trigger spontaneous sharing in children: those situations where they have to work collaboratively in order
to gain a mutual benefit. Michael Tomasello and his colleagues in
Leipzig set about testing his idea about the importance of co-operation
in the evolution of human pro-sociality.[40] Pairs of three-year-olds had

to work together to pull on two ropes simultaneously in order to dislodge four marbles. The apparatus was rigged so that it delivered three marbles to one child but only one to the other. In this situation, the 'lucky' child gave one of his three marbles to the 'unlucky' child. However, when there was no need for a collaborative effort, such as a windfall, they did not share.

In the face of a selfish bias, nothing brings people together more than a tragedy where they have to work together. In 2017 the UK suffered a spate of terrorist attacks in London and Manchester. Each of these atrocities revealed the dark side of human nature in the callousness of individuals to inflict suffering on innocent others, but also the willingness of the majority to come to the assistance of those in need. The general public responded to these attacks with a wave of support for the survivors and the families of the victims. The blood-donor centres in Manchester received over 1,000 calls per hour following the bombing of the Ariana Grande concert.[41] People responded to the plight of others and wanted to help in whatever way they could.

This humanitarian reaction is something that we develop first as children. In 2008, a team of researchers were studying sharing in six- and nine-year-olds from the Sichuan province of China using the Dictator Game when an earthquake, registering a massive 8 points on the Richter scale, struck, killing over 87,000 people.[42] Here was an unexpected chance to measure children's altruistic behaviour in a real setting where people were suffering. Prior to the earthquake, Chinese children were just like others around the world. Nine-year-olds were more generous than six-year-olds, as measured by the Dictator Game. One month after the disaster, almost all the children studied had been left homeless and in dire straits. Now, the Dictator Game revealed a change in altruistic behaviour. Six-year-olds in the affected region became even more selfish, sharing less than before the earthquake, whereas nine-year-olds did the opposite: they shared even more. Three years after the Sichuan disaster, patterns of sharing on the Dictator Game had reverted to those typical of six- and nine-year-olds across the world, suggesting that generosity is sensitive to adversity and may be a coping mechanism. By the time we reach middle childhood, we have thrown off our earlier self-interest and come to the aid of others when they need help.

Wealth empowers individuals. The privileges provided by owner-ship accumulate, leading to an ever-increasing advantage as the wealthiest have access to opportunities not available to the least well-off. These include better education, health, housing, stable home environments and all the other factors that contribute to success. Most wealthy people pass those advantages on to their children (with some notable exceptions), but many also share their wealth either indirectly, through government intervention, or directly through acts of charity.

In understanding the economics of human behaviour and, in particu-lar, charitable donations, a pure model of altruism has failed and been replaced by impure altruism, where donors give to help others but also because they gain some comfort from the act of giving; that is, they experience a 'warm glow' from the joy of giving.[43] Standard mathemat-ical models of gift-giving fail to take into account that human nature is motivated by pride, empathy, guilt, shame and all manner of emotional states that are at the root of why people want to help others.

In every realm of human activity, we strive for those positive experi-ences associated with helping and avoid those associated with guilt and shame. In one clever study, adults were told that they would earn $10 for their participation and at the end they could also make a donation to their favourite charity.[44] There was one important rule. Potential donors were told that their selected charity would receive no more and no less than $10, with the difference being made up by the experi-menter running the study. In other words, if you donated $4, the experimenter would contribute an additional $6 to make the total up to $10. If you decided to donate nothing, the charity would still get $10 given to them by the experimenter. It did not matter what the partici-pants did, as the charity would still get a $10 donation in total. Just over half the adults (57 per cent) still decided to make an average don-ation of $2, even though they did not have to. The only reason that they could have done this was because they thought it was the right thing to do, as their behaviour had no additional benefit for the charity.

We encourage our children to share because that is the right thing to do, but they also develop their own sense of responsibility. During their second year, infants start to become aware of when they have done wrong and experience negative emotions related to their trans-gressions. It is not clear whether this is a consequence of being told off or being punished, but most children become increasingly concerned about doing wrong. They develop a guilty conscience.

Guilt is a negative emotion that motivates our behaviour. When we give to the poor, are we really being kind? To what extent is a motive to feel better – or less worse – truly altruistic rather than self-interest? When Abraham Lincoln explained, 'When I do good, I feel good. When I do bad, I feel bad. That's my religion', he was stating the common-sense view of morality, which is why we fail to understand others who seem to be cruel. We ask 'How could you?' or 'Have you no shame?' We may take the moral high ground, but, then, are we any better? Over our childhood, the rules and expectations of society are encoded into our emotional systems, creating everything from the warm glow of giving to the ruminations of guilt in our minds that torment us.

By internalizing the opinions of others, we become intrinsically motivated. We do things because it *feels* right, which is why we are suspicious of others who have ulterior motives or who are extrinsically motivated. This is why paying people for their kindness backfires. Take blood donation again. We do this without expectation of reward. In his book *The Gift Relationship*, comparing blood services in the US and the UK, the sociologist Richard Titmuss concluded that paying blood donors (as happens in the US) was not only dangerous, because it incentivized the wrong individuals and created dubious practices and safety concerns, but that if the practice was introduced in the UK it would remove people's intrinsic motivation to express altruism, and erode the communal efforts that are the bedrock of the National Health Service.[45] To test his claims, Swedish researchers carried out a study where adults were asked to donate blood voluntarily, or received the equivalent of $7 in payment, or could donate this payment to a charity. In line with Titmuss's prediction, blood donations dropped significantly when donors were offered payment, but not if the money could be donated to a charity.[46] This phenomenon, known as 'crowding out', sullies the good intentions derived from helping others because it removes the intrinsic value we get, which is why rewarding people financially for acts that are supposed to be morally motivated is considered sordid. When blood donors and non-blood donors were tested with the charitable Dictator Game described above, in which additional financial donations made no difference to the final amount received by the charity, blood donors still gave more relative to non-blood donors for the sheer warm glow they experienced.[47]

Where do these good and bad feelings come from? Not from us, but from everyone else. Our pride comes from basking in the imagined praise of the group. Our indignation and rage explode when we feel we have been cheated by others. This is why socialization is so powerful, so ubiquitous everywhere you look. To feel good, we care about what others think. As we develop from young children dependent on the approval of our parents, we turn into adolescents obsessed with the opinions of our peers and, from then on, we lead adult lives seeking the validation of others and spreading the very same values that shaped our lives. Those values include how we acquire stuff and what we do with it when we have it.

ADIOS HOMO ECONOMICUS

There is little evidence that Homo Economicus was ever a plausible account for human behaviour as there are many occasions where we do not maximize our self-interest. Although considered one of the first proponents of Homo Economicus, Adam Smith was also well aware that humans often acted out of kindness, when he wrote on the origins of morality:

> How selfish soever man may be supposed, there are evidently some principles in his nature, which interest him in the fortune of others, and render their happiness necessary to him, though he derives nothing from it except the pleasure of seeing it. Of this kind is pity or compassion, the emotion which we feel for the misery of others, when we either see it, or are made to conceive it in a very lively manner ... The greatest ruffian, the most hardened violator of the laws of society, is not altogether without it.[48]

In other words, all of us can recognize the suffering of the less fortunate, and there is something about human nature which makes us want to help. Of course, we can become immune to the suffering of others through familiarity or fatigue, but when we are stirred to act that compassion is often a reflection of our own good fortune. When we see another individual suffering, we put ourselves in their shoes and imagine how bad it would be if we were them. This view, expressed hundreds of years ago, is supported by today's neuroscience, which shows that our brains emulate and mirror the plight of others such that we can literally feel some component of their suffering which registers in regions associated with pain.[49] Under this light, attempts to alleviate another's suffering that we witness through acts of charity help to reduce our own discomfort. In this sense, charity is not selfless altruism but rather self-interest.

The competitive instinct should make humans all the more selfish in times of need when resources are low because the consequences of failure are more catastrophic, and yet adversity seems to bring out the best in people. If we work together on a common problem, then we naturally distribute our resources in difficult times. Facing up to a common threat as a group seems to be the solution, rather than as deindividuated bystanders who are more likely to act out of self-interest. Maybe this is why armed conflict seems to generate so many acts of altruism. War is never to be condoned on any grounds, but one can understand why events that threaten the group generate a sense of collective responsibility. Unfortunately, we do not seem to have reached a point yet where the greatest threat to humanity – climate change – is perceived to be imminent enough for all nations to begin working together. It is entirely understandable why developing nations think it is only fair that they get a larger share of the pie because there are rich industrialized nations who have benefitted from the exploitation of natural resources for centuries. It is only fair that each society has the opportunity for each of its members to live in peace and comfort. The trouble is that enough is never enough. In the next chapter we turn to the central question of *Possessed*: why do we want more than we need?

5

Possessions, Wealth and Happiness

CLIMBING THE LADDER OF SUCCESS

'The rich man glories in his riches, because he feels that they naturally draw upon him the attention of the world . . . The poor man, on the contrary, is ashamed of his poverty. He feels that it either places him out of the sight of mankind, or, that if they take any notice of him, they have, however, scarce any fellow-feeling with the misery and distress which he suffers.'

Adam Smith[1]

In 2010, when Bhisham Singh Yadav, a New Delhi wheat farmer, spent over $8,000 to fly his son just two miles to his wedding by helicopter, it generated so much attention that the story made the pages of the *New York Times*, 7,300 miles away.[2] Bhisham, one of India's so-called nouveau riche farmers, who had been born into poverty, was now benefitting from the country's economic boom and appeared to be spending money recklessly. He had just sold three acres of his farm for $109,000 and wanted to put on a lavish wedding for his son. Even without such windfalls, poor families around the world spend disproportionately large amounts of their income on luxuries when they could be buying necessities. The poorer these families are, the greater the percentage of their meagre incomes they spend on things they do not need.[3] Why?

Bhisham was being extravagant. He was not so rich that he could easily afford to spend a tenth of his windfall on a helicopter ride just to impress his wedding guests. He is not alone, however, as many use wealth to send ostentatious signals of importance – even those who should not need to succumb to vanity. When Jennifer Gates first met Donald Trump at a horse show gala he organized in Florida, she was surprised when suddenly he departed, only to return twenty minutes later by helicopter. Her father, Bill Gates, the founder of Microsoft, concluded that Trump must have been driven away from the event so that he could make a grand return entrance.[4] Whether you're an Indian farmer or an American billionaire, as Adam Smith noted, it is just as important to be seen to be wealthy as it is to be wealthy. We like to show off, and one way we do that is through our wealth.

We have always had stuff, but we seem to have an unquenchable thirst for more. This is clear from the exponential rise in household consumerism. In his book on the excesses of ownership, *Stuffocation*,[5] James Wallman informs us that the critical flashover point – the time it takes for a domestic fire to reach a temperature that causes house contents to spontaneously combust – used to be around twenty-eight minutes thirty years ago, but has shortened to just three or four minutes today because of the amount of household possessions we now typically accumulate. Yet the passion for accumulating household goods has a long tradition. Just take a look at this picture of a nineteenth-century Victorian parlour room in a country estate close to where I live in Somerset, England.

Victorian parlour room of Tyntesfield House, North Somerset (Image: author)

How many different items can you identify? There are carpets, tables, chairs, stools, couches, cabinets, desks, tablecloths, cushions, coverings, mirrors, photographs, paintings, drawings, books, bookcases, candles, candleholders, fireplaces, fireguards, lamps, switches, a hand-bell, a letter opener, plates, bowls, vases, plant holders, jars, statuettes, ornaments, boxes of various sizes and all manner of knick-knacks. I have studied this image and counted over a hundred different items in this one room alone. Each time I look again, I spot something new. Some are exotic items from the far away continents of Asia and the Americas. The room is resplendent with mahogany, ivory and silks that are not native to the British Isles. It is a snapshot of the British Empire at the height of its power and ownership of foreign lands.

Although this parlour room was in the home of wealthy people, such cluttered rooms were considered the aspirational norm for many middle-class families across the country at the time. This level of wealth contrasted sharply with the abject poverty and the workhouses that Dickens wrote about so vividly in his various tales of social injustice such as *Oliver Twist*, *Little Dorrit* and *A Christmas Carol*. The photograph is also a testament to the industrial revolution. Many of the items were mass-produced in domestic factories. During the nineteenth century, no other country could compete with Great Britain in terms of industrial output. The industrial revolution that had begun with the invention of steam engines and mechanization in the eighteenth century marked the beginning of modernization in the Western world. Before the industrial revolution, most British people lived in the country. They may not have been landowners, but they were relatively self-sufficient, leading simple lives. However, as smallholders grazing their herds on the commons, this meant they were also vulnerable to the vagaries of the seasons, so life was hard and unpredictable. With the promise of regular wages, the country population flooded into the cities to become workers in the new factories. As the cities grew, so did the desire to own.

THE ESTEEM MACHINE

Historians have traditionally connected the rise of consumerism to the industrial revolution and the birth of cheap, mass production. Yet people have always wanted to own more stuff, and especially things that were new and difficult to get hold of from foreign lands. In his exhaustive account of consumerism over the last five hundred years, *Empire of Things*,[6] the historian Frank Trentmann argues that consumerism pre-dates the industrial revolution. Concerns over consumption, a term that had previously meant the using up of resources, had been around since antiquity. The Greek philosopher Plato, who wrote of the immaterial world, warned of the dangers for society in pursuing material goals, and these concerns over ownership have been echoed across the centuries by most religions and various political thinkers, including Hobbes, Rousseau and Marx. Their fears were directed at not only the immoral folly of relentless ownership and social inequality, but also the economic consequences of spending money on foreign imports.

According to Trentmann, it was not the industrial revolution but rather increased trading that fuelled the rise in consumerism over the last half millennium. The opening of new trade routes and the growth of imperialism provided opportunities for consumers to buy more stuff. As trade expanded, most states enacted 'sumptuary laws' to prohibit the purchase of goods from abroad. The rationale was that any wealth spent on foreign goods was not being spent on domestic produce – a concern that still resonates today, with many countries introducing global trade restrictions as a form of protectionism. However, there were also social reasons for sumptuary laws. Imported goods were typically more expensive and so became status symbols of the elite. Sumptuary laws were enacted to prevent commoners being mistaken as gentry. In England at one point, commoners were forbidden from wearing silk, eating red meat or having more than a certain number of guests at their weddings. By the time the industrial revolution arrived in the eighteenth century, almost all sumptuary laws had disappeared. What the industrial revolution did was simply feed an insatiable appetite for ownership that was already well-established. There was no need to persuade the general public to want more things in life even if they did not need them: it seems to be a basic desire.

Wealthy people had always been capable of purchasing, but the industrial revolution created a new class of consumers who also wanted to own as much as possible. Prior to the eighteenth century, products were largely made by hand and were costly in terms of the number of labour hours that went into making them. For example, before automation in the textile industry, an individual working with a spinning wheel could only produce one spindle of thread at a time. When the Spinning Jenny was invented in England in 1764, and then later powered by a waterwheel, it could spin a hundred reels at a time. Mechanization and the invention of steam engines to drive the machinery not only sped up the process but also reduced the number of worker hours required.

Production costs plummeted and output escalated. In her historical analysis of the rise of consumerism,[7] the Australian engineer Sharon Beder points out that while the US population increased three-fold between 1860 and 1920, manufacturing output increased twelve- to fourteen-fold, which created a substantial problem of over-production. Across the industrialized West, the same picture emerged. Falling production costs meant that fewer labour hours were required, but rather than shortening the working week, business leaders decided to raise wages in order to increase the buying power of households to sustain the demand for goods.

During the boom years of 1910–29 in the US, salaries increased by 40 per cent. Workers were spending more on products and money was pouring into stocks and shares, which created an unsustainable prosperity bubble based on market speculation. This would eventually burst in the Wall Street Crash of 1929, triggering the Great Depression and the subsequent world recession that would last for another ten years. After the Second World War and the years of austerity, consumption continued to rise as workers sought higher salaries rather than shorter working hours. The standard of living became defined by what people could buy.

Increasing numbers of women entered the workforce as provision for childcare increased during the so-called 'Golden Age' of prosperity during the 1950s and 60s, when ownership triumphed over job satisfaction as workers opted for higher salaries to spend on more consumables.[8] Previously, workers had been encouraged by what they could make; now they were incentivized by what they could own. In the 1970s and 80s, Western politics fuelled this desire to own more. Leaders such Margaret Thatcher and Ronald Reagan encouraged ordinary citizens to take control of their lives rather than rely on others. In 1914, only one in ten homes were privately owned in the

UK. One hundred years later, two-thirds of homes were owned.[9] Private ownership replaced public housing and public services as societies shifted towards increased personal independence.

In the West, we witnessed the rise of the 'Greed is good' 'yuppies' of the 1980s, as personified by the character of Gordon Gekko in Oliver Stone's iconic depiction of corporate corruption in the film *Wall Street* (1987). The political policies of the day actively encouraged consumption and, just like in the lead-up to the Great Depression, history repeated itself with widespread speculation and the subsequent financial crisis of 2008. The US subprime mortgage crisis that began a year earlier was a direct consequence of an inflated housing bubble; ordinary people got swept up in the rising tide of house prices and the financiers were all too happy to profit from the commissions they were earning from lending money. Rather than renting, people wanted to own their homes because ownership, they were told, was a mark of success. People borrowed more so that they could buy more, but when the banks called in the loans, the financial system crashed. Each boom–bust economic cycle has been fuelled by our human obsession to own more and more stuff that we don't really need.

THE PEACOCK'S TALE

The rapid rise of consumerism enabled by industrialization was not without its critics. In 1899, the economist Thorstein Veblen observed that silver spoons and corsets were markers of elite social position. His critique of the excesses of consumerism introduced the term 'conspicuous consumption' to describe the willingness of people to buy more expensive goods over cheaper, yet functionally equivalent goods. As he wrote, 'The motive is emulation – the stimulus of an invidious comparison which prompts us to outdo those with whom we are in the habit of classing ourselves.'[10] In other words, consumers spend money on luxuries to show how much more affluent they are in comparison to others around them. Why do people do this? The reason is rooted in evolutionary biology.

As we saw in Chapter 2, all animals compete to survive. That competition also includes success at reproduction so that our genes are transferred to our offspring. Genes build the bodies and brains that control our actions that produce the next generation containing the very same genes. So, in addition to staying alive, we compete to reproduce. One way to succeed in reproduction is to fight off competitors, but that brings with it the risk of injury or death. An alternative strategy is to advertise how good we are to the other sex so that they choose us to mate with rather than our rivals.

Many animals evolved attributes that signal their suitability as potential mates. These signals include appendages such as colourful plumage and elaborate horns, or ostentatious behaviours such as bellowing calls or the intricate, delicate courtship constructions made by the pufferfish and bowerbird. These physical attributes and time-consuming behaviours come at a cost but must be worth it because natural selection would have disposed of such costly adaptations unless there was some benefit.

Costly signalling theory explains why these apparently wasteful attributes are reliable markers of other desirable qualities. Poster child for costly signalling is the male peacock, who has an elaborately coloured fantail that evolved to signal to peahens that its owner possesses the finest genes. The tail is such a ludicrous, ostentatious appendage that in 1860 Charles Darwin wrote, 'The sight of a feather in a peacock's tail makes me sick.' The reason for Darwin's nausea was that the peacock tail is not optimized for survival. It weighs too much, requires a lot of energy to grow and maintain, and, like a large Victorian crinoline dress, is cumbersome and not streamlined for efficient movement. With all these disadvantages, how could the peacock's tail ever have evolved?

Heavy displays of plumage are a conspicuous disadvantage in terms of the dangers and inconveniences they entail, but they signal genetic prowess. For example, the more eyespots on the peacock's tail, the better its immune system.[11] Peacocks that are ill may lose feathers and have poor plumage, which reflects in their less glorious tails.[12] Larger tails are correlated with other genes that confer better survival adaptation in spite of the disadvantage bestowed by expensive displays.

Signalling also reduces the need for physical confrontation with potential rivals. In the same way that the first possession rule evolved as a means of avoiding conflict over territory, many males in the animal kingdom use signals to warn competitors just how fit they are. Posturing, roaring, charging, splashing waves or beating chests are all forms of behaviour intended to display the potential harm an opponent might suffer so as to deter others from actual physical contact.

Humans also respond to signals. We have physical features that potential mates find sexually attractive, such as symmetrical bodies and good skin. Some of us are better endowed with these features than others, which is why we call them beautiful – though, of course, there is considerable cultural variation and individual preference when it comes to what we find attractive. If you are not particularly gorgeous, then possessions can signal your success and potential suitability as a mate. If you were not born beautiful then ownership enables you to compensate by emulating the peacock's tail. Designer clothes, an expensive watch, even a helicopter can increase approval by signalling success.

This biological explanation of conspicuous consumption as a way to impress potential mates is supported by a recent study of the effects of administering the sex hormone testosterone to men, who were then asked to rate different watches that varied in their status value.[13] Across the animal kingdom, testosterone is associated with a range of male reproductive and social behaviours – especially those linked to status, such as competition. Adult males were asked to rate three identical watches that were described as either being of high quality, powerful excellence or status enhancing. Men who had previously been administered with an inert gel rated all three watches as equally desirable, whereas those who received a gel containing testosterone preferred the watch described as status enhancing. We attract mates and intimidate competitors through our possessions, which is why such conspicuous consumption is a form of social peacocking.

DRESS TO IMPRESS

The global luxury market is worth an estimated $1.2 trillion, with personal goods representing $285 billion of that amount.[14] Branding is the visible identity of a product and a vital component of luxury goods. Having a simple logo on your chest can be surprisingly powerful. In one study, people who wore luxury brands (Tommy Hilfiger or Lacoste) were more likely to be considered for a job, were better at raising money from others, and were generally more effective at getting people to comply with their requests than people who wore clothes from the local thrift or charity store.[15]

Manufacturers vigorously defend brand identity by prosecuting rip-offs and fake merchandise. Customers equally value authenticity. Thalia Gjersoe and I tested this in a study of over eight hundred US and Indian adults, where we told participants to imagine a duplicating machine that could make exact copies of items such that they were indistinguishable from the originals.[16] We then asked them to put a price on each. Adults from both cultures valued copies less than the originals, but the effect was more pronounced in the West. The same is true for luxury goods. People expect originals when they buy luxury and feel cheated if the item is not authentic even if it is effectively indistinguishable from the real thing.

To be an effective signal, luxury should also not be affordable to everyone. This is what makes luxury goods exclusive and embodies their appeal for those who buy them. They are signalling a string of privileges and opportunities that make them elite. We tally up all these signals when it comes to judging the pedigree of others. If you attend a good school – signalled by your college scarf – then chances are that you either come from a wealthy background (tick) or possess exceptional skills (tick). You will be exposed to other successful individuals that share these attributes and so increase your chances that you benefit from the same mechanisms through networking (tick and tick). Employers will value the same selection process and so hedge their bets, thus perpetuating a system geared to favour the successful (more ticks). To do otherwise would be fairer, but also riskier.

If you never had those opportunities or privileges, then you can invest in expensive purchases to deceptively signal that you are successful even though you did not go to the best schools. Or you could try faking it until you make it with knock-off copies, because the chances are that perceived success will generate opportunities for future success. Even those who should not need to fake their success still seem susceptible to signalling deception. According to the actor Charlie Sheen, Donald Trump gifted the actor a set of his own platinum and diamond cufflinks that he was wearing at an event dinner as a present for Sheen's forthcoming wedding.[17] Only months later did the actor discover that they were cheap counterfeits. Whether they were fakes or not, this spontaneous gifting was still a gesture which was intended to signal power. Sheen told this story on national television as evidence of the weak character of the future president, but aren't we all guilty of succumbing to the allure of status symbols?

We are so easily impressed and make judgements based on superficial evidence, but sometimes luxury provides a psychological boost to confidence that improves our well-being. Wearing designer clothes can make us feel better about ourselves, which then becomes self-reinforcing. When we put on our luxury apparel we feel special and behave accordingly. Luxury goods light up the pleasure centres in our brain. If you think you are drinking expensive wine, not only does it taste better but the brain's valuation system associated with the experience of pleasure shows greater activation, compared to drinking exactly the same wine when you believe it to be cheap.[18] What's important here is the belief – not the actual luxury. Francesca Gino, a professor at Harvard Business School, found that people who wore what they believed to be fake Chloé designer sunglasses (but were in fact genuine) felt like frauds and were more likely to cheat on tests.[19] You may be able to fake until you make it, but deep down, if we do, many of us feel like imposters.

Luxury ownership signals wealth, but – ironically – it is often the very wealthy who prefer to look cheap. Countersignalling is when you go out of your way to show that you do not need to go out of your way. It has become almost a point of honour in Silicon Valley not to wear expensive clothes or suits, but rather jeans and trainers, which signals that you are more interested in tech than status. This style has been undoubtedly influenced by Facebook's Mark Zuckerberg with his ubiquitous hoodie and casual wear. Gino has shown that countersignalling by wearing atypical clothing leads to higher regard in the right context. In one study, she asked Milan shop assistants working in high-end designer stores to rate two shoppers, one in gym clothes and the other in a dress and fur.[20] The assistants were far more likely than the general public to think the gym-clothes wearing shopper would spend more and be in a position to buy the most expensive items in the boutique. They had learned from experience how the rich often countersignal.

Countersignalling only works if one deliberately violates the norms as a sign of defiance and confidence. Studies have shown that professors who wear T-shirts and sport beards at prestigious universities are better respected by students than well-dressed, clean-shaven instructors, but the reverse is true if the university is not prestigious.[21] Gino calls this countersignalling the 'red sneaker' effect, after she wore red trainers with her business suit to a seminar where the executives assumed she charged higher fees and had a larger client list. When the A-list actress Cybill Shepherd wore orange Reebok trainers to the 1985 Oscars she claimed it was for comfort, but she was also demonstrating the red sneaker effect. A lesser actress with lower status would have suffered in silence wearing high heels rather than signalling she thought she was so important that she could get away with wearing whatever she wanted to the prestigious gala.

One problem for manufacturers of luxury goods is that they want to sell as much of their products as possible, but if everyone has them they are no longer perceived as high-status and cult-worthy. During the early 2000s, the luxury British clothing company Burberry suffered a significant drop in UK sales when its trademark camel-check design became popular among 'chavs' – a pejorative term for a low-income social group obsessed with brand names, cheap jewellery and football. This chav association tarnished the brand value of Burberry, forcing the company to raise its prices in an effort to move upmarket.[22]

Another problem for luxury signalling is that it can be easily faked or temporarily acquired. You can rent luxury clothes and cars by the day to send out the right message. The conspicuous signalling value of a brand rises with price only up to a point, beyond which the truly wealthy would rather not be seen to be owning it. In an ironic twist on Veblen's concept, a new phenomenon known as 'inconspicuous consumption' has emerged at the high end of the market to distinguish those who would prefer to pay more for quality goods that are less obvious. These elite products have switched to subtle branding, as in the case of Louis Vuitton, which removed the iconic 'LV' logo from its upmarket bags. The super-successful and rich do not need to compete with the masses and, as we shall see shortly, are more cautious about evoking public envy. That does not stop them enjoying the cachet of subtle signals that only the true elites can afford and decode, which is why more high-end brands do not have flashy logos, compared to more mainstream luxury brands that rely on mass sales.[23]

We signal not only our financial status, but also the virtues and personality traits we would like to portray to others. Charitable acts raise an interesting question about the motivation to help others. Cynics believe that acts of kindness and sacrifice are not necessarily benevolent but rather self-serving, used to indicate positive qualities by 'virtue signalling', or letting others know that we are good people. This phenomenon has been found in cultures across the world. Anthropologists Eric Smith and Rebecca Bliege Bird studied this type of generosity in the context of the Meriam turtle hunters of Northern Australia.[24] The Meriam people fish for turtles either by collecting them or hunting them. Anyone can collect turtles from the beaches during the nesting season, but only the best warriors can hunt them in the open sea. Hunters rarely keep any of the turtle meat, however, but instead give it away to neighbours or during feasts. This is not reciprocal altruism like the blood donation of the vampire bats, where there is an expectation to receive meat in return at a later date, but rather an act to signal virtue and status. As the hunting is so skilful, this increases the value of the signalling and if a hunter is thought to be strategic in their generosity, this is frowned upon. The generosity must be considered unconditional even though everyone knows it is a signal to be seen to be generous, which in turn generates favourable opinions of the individual.

RELATIVITY MACHINES

Conspicuous consumption and signalling are both just ways of competing with others. We buy luxury goods to signal our status, but this creates the problem of luxury fever, where we spend increasing amounts of money to get ahead of others.[25] This leads to a constant battle of one-upmanship because there is always someone wealthier than us. Even if there isn't, we are so poor at making judgements because, as we saw in Chapter 2, when it comes to salaries we feel under-appreciated and think that our contemporaries are doing better. This competition could be considered constructive if we increase our own productivity to earn more and outperform our rivals, but if there are others who are always better off, and we are putting all our efforts into a competition we cannot win, then the danger is not only ultimate disappointment, but a failure to find happiness and enjoyment in the things we already possess.

We are focusing on the wrong priorities. Rather than the relentless pursuit of material possessions and wealth, we should take the time to reflect upon what we have. Consider these two individuals, 'Tina' and 'Maggie'. Who are you most like? (You can always substitute 'Tom' for Tina and 'Michael' for Maggie if you are concerned about gender.)

> Tina values her time more than her money. She is willing to sacrifice her money to have more time. For example, Tina would rather work fewer hours and make less money, than work more hours and make more money.

> Maggie values her money more than her time. She is willing to sacrifice her time to have more money. For example, Maggie would rather work more hours and make more money, than work fewer hours and have more time.

In a study of over 4,500 adults, those who identified with Tina or Tom, saying that they valued time over money, reported that they were significantly happier than those who identified with Maggie or Michael.[26] This is strange because, given the choice, people often say in surveys that they would prefer more money than time. Certainly, this fits with the trend for increased consumerism we have witnessed over the last century. We think we want more money, but if you actually interview workers during their daily commute they say they would prefer to have more time.[27] Presumably, they resent the daily grind of commuting but justify it in terms of the financial rewards and belief in the greater happiness it will bring. We think more money will make us happier because we can buy more luxuries, but it is the luxury of time that we should be valuing.

Many of us set out in life to earn as much money as possible because we are convinced that this is the secret to happiness. Around 13,000 first-year students were interviewed in the 1970s and asked their reasons for attending college. The most common reason given was to make money, but those who rated themselves as more materialistic ended up being, on average, more dissatisfied with their lives twenty years later, with higher rates of mental illness. This was a correlational study, and those who ended up the wealthiest were not necessarily the most unhappy, but the expectation that financial success is the root to more happiness is common, but false.[28]

Why doesn't wealth make us happier? Why do we fail to appreciate what we already have and strive for more? To understand this, we need to shift gear for a moment from the complexity of happiness to how the brain makes decisions at the most simple level. We have to consider some basic principles of how we make judgements in life. One of those principles is relativity. Relativity is not only a fundamental physical law of time and space in the universe, as Einstein described, but it is also one of the most important organizing principles of life on Earth. Every creature operates using the principles of relative comparisons. Even the simplest building blocks of our brains are relativity machines.

The brain is a complicated processing system, breaking information down into patterns of electrical activity propagated across networks of brain cells that interpret the world and produce all the thoughts and behaviours we experience. Our brains enable our bodies to interact with the world in all its complexity through these networks of electrical activity. This information is processed by changes in the rate of firing of brain cells called neurons. If you listen to the electrical activity of an individual neuron transmitted through a speaker, it sounds a bit like a Geiger counter, ticking over with the occasional burst before rattling off like a machine gun when it receives incoming information that there is something new of interest to be considered.

In this way, information is processed and stored as patterns of distributed activity in the brain. These thresholds, however, can adapt over time and with repeated activity. If the same sets of signals keep coming in, the network eventually adapts its firing threshold. In other words, it learns. A neuronal network will then require a relatively greater level of activation for it to respond again. When we experience some event over and over, we get habituated or bored with it and so we have a natural preference for novelty, which generates renewed interest. It is because our brains get bored that we are motivated to seek all sorts of novel experiences, from simple sensations that stimulate neurons to the rich diversity of human activities – something as complicated as buying stuff. No matter what the experience is, we are always on the lookout for something new.

Novelty is one of the motivating factors that keeps consumers seeking new products. We want the latest cool thing because we are bored with what we have and we want something different.[29] It is no coincidence that advertisers are at pains to highlight that products are either 'new' or 'improved' so that you can expect something different. The attention systems in our brain are stimulated by the prospect of some new reward, which creates our wanting and desire. But just like most experiences, our pleasure habituates. Once you acquire whatever it was you wanted, you start looking around for the next best thing in a constant cycle of what's known as 'hedonic adaptation'.

Even the most stimulating of experiences can become boring. With repeated intercourse, sexual interest declines in many species, especially among males. However, novelty induces what is called the 'Coolidge effect': the reinvigoration of interest and mating capabilities when a novel sexual partner is introduced. It's one of the reasons why pornography is so popular, because it provides a seemingly endless supply of novel images to satisfy sex drives. The name is attributed to a trip by President Coolidge and his wife to a government farm in the US where Mrs Coolidge observed a rooster mating frequently and was told by the attendant that the cockerel performed this dozens of times a day. Mrs Coolidge is alleged to have said, 'Tell that to the President when he comes by.' Later, upon being told of his wife's remarks, the President asked, 'Same hen every time?' The reply was, 'Oh, no, Mr President, a different hen every time.' President Coolidge laconically replied, 'Tell that to Mrs Coolidge.'

CHOOSING THE RIGHT POND

What is true at the neuronal level is true all the way up the network. Every aspect of complex behaviour will adapt. Whenever you experience some sensation such as sight, sound, taste or smell, that experience is always relative. In other words, all judgements are based on comparisons. You experience this every waking moment. Your life is one big exercise in making relative comparisons. Whether you are tired or alert, hungry or famished, bored or interested, happy or sad, it's all a matter of comparison. And what is true of the basic experiences is true of how we think of ourselves and what we value in life.

Relativity, as noted by the economist Robert H. Frank, is one of the fundamental principles in human economic behaviour. In his book *Choosing the Right Pond*,[30] he makes the point that our economic decisions are guided by status, which is really a relativity issue. It explains why people would prefer to live in a 3,000-sq. ft apartment if their neighbours live in 2,000-sq. ft apartments, rather than in a larger, 4,000-sq. ft apartment in a neighbourhood of 5,000-sq. ft apartments; and why people would prefer to earn just $50,000 if their colleagues earned $25,000 rather than earn $100,000 if colleagues earned $250,000.[31] We would prefer to have less so long as it is more than everyone else. We measure our success relative to others. One of the most surprising examples of this comes from an analysis of emotional reactions to winning Olympic medals.[32] To even reach the Olympic Games should be considered an extraordinary achievement, and yet analysis has revealed that Olympians can sometimes experience disappointment even when they win a silver medal. The reason that the silver medallists are not happy is because they are comparing themselves to the winners. In contrast, the bronze medallists compare themselves to all the other competitors who did not get a medal, so they perceive themselves better off and happier. Relativity is how we judge our sense of achievement. It is better to be a big fish in a small pond than a big fish in a bigger pond.

Just about everything we do can become a competition with others. From eating to running a race, the mere presence of others makes us up our game in a process known as social facilitation.[33] We may consider ourselves fast runners, but that ability really depends on how fast others can run. Like the joke about the two athletes running from the lion in the Serengeti, it is the relative comparison that is the most important measure, not the absolute value, when it comes to thinking about ourselves.

Car ownership is a classic example: many people seek status by the value of the car they drive. Expensive cars are generally more powerful, better made and equipped with all the latest gadgetry, but it is the cost of the car that impresses the most. Drivers are less likely to honk at the car in front at a green light if it is an expensive sportscar compared to an old banger.[34] Such luxury items are called 'positional goods' because of where they place you on the status ladder; their value is relative rather than absolute. They may be bought as a way of enhancing one's perceived status but luxury items change people's perceptions of the owner. This becomes critically important for those who live in social groups where the need to signal status cannot be satisfied with houses, titles and education, but by expensive personal possessions they can carry around with them.

Our susceptibility to status symbols comes from our deep need to be accepted, but it is also a way of protecting ourselves. We depend on each other, which creates a corresponding vulnerability to isolation that affects not only mental well-being but also our physical health. Remarkably, and this is something that has only recently been appreciated, social isolation increases your likelihood of an earlier death by about 30 per cent and presents a stronger morbidity risk factor than either obesity or moderate smoking.[35] If we want to be noticed then we need to signal. We need to be valued and appreciated by others, which is one of the reasons conspicuous consumption is such a powerful signal for most of us. We want to impress others because, in doing so, we are securing our position not only within the group, by being placed further up the social ladder, but also by avoiding the lowest rungs where those less fortunate in society run the risk of being ostracized.

Our sensitivity to evaluation with and by others is a fundamental component of our psychology. Humans are constantly comparing themselves, as articulated in the psychologist Leon Festinger's social comparison theory. As he pointed out in his seminal paper in 1954, there is no objective appraisal of oneself because most measures of human aptitude depend on who we compare ourselves with.[36] What is true of personal attributes is also true of ownership. We are always comparing what we have with that of others, but not just anybody. Very few of us think that we are well off in comparison to the Bill Gateses and Mark Zuckerbergs of the world, so we do not generally compare ourselves to them. Nor do we compare ourselves to the multitude of poor living in the slums and shanty towns. Rather, we judge ourselves relative to the neighbours and our colleagues at work as these are our most relevant comparisons. And given our distorted perspective, psychologically, we are constantly in the silver-medal position on the rostrum of life.

BLING CULTURE

Anyone who has watched hip hop videos cannot fail to notice how there is constant reference to flashy, ostentatious trappings of gold, expensive cars, beautiful people and champagne. These are commonly referred to as 'bling'. What is remarkable is that even those who cannot afford these luxury goods will still sacrifice in order to acquire desirable designer goods in an attempt to emulate those who have succeeded. In 2007, economists published a study looking at conspicuous consumption and race in the US, and found that African Americans and Latinos spent 25 per cent more of their disposable income on jewellery, cars, personal care and apparel compared to whites in the same economic bracket.[37] What might be the cause of this?

Take trainer shoes, a trademark of hip hop style, as a good example. The trainer began life as the 'sneaker' in the late nineteenth century as a multipurpose rubber-soled casual shoe designed for activities like playing croquet and beach walks, but the shoes reached the height of popularity in the 1980s when they became associated with famous basketball players. In 1985, Nike introduced the first of the 'Air Jordan' range, named after the legendary Chicago Bulls player Michael Jordan, which retail for just over $1,000 for the top model today. Another in the Nike range, the 'Air Mags', is currently the most expensive trainer and sells for nearly $9,000.

There have been multiple muggings and murders associated with Nike thefts. Why would anyone spend that sort of money, especially if they cannot afford it, on shoes that place their lives at risk? For a start, these shoes have recognized street credibility that makes them highly desirable as status symbols. Secondly, owning luxury goods produces a sense of well-being. Just like Bhisham, our Indian farmer, the poorest derive greater satisfaction from spending on luxury items than wealthier individuals. This is supported by a recent analysis of over 34,000 households in India, which revealed that conspicuous consumption was associated with higher levels of subjective well-being, and the effect was most pronounced in the poorest families.[38]

There is, however, a racial stereotype that needs to be explained when it comes to the bling culture. Why is it that African Americans and Hispanics in the US, more than whites at comparative income levels, are spending more of their income on non-essential goods? It depends on where they live and comes down to social comparison again. When economists looked at blacks living in more affluent parts of the US, they found there was proportionately less money spent on conspicuous consumption.[39] In other words, racial minorities were spending proportionately more on luxury goods because they were living in the poorest neighbourhoods. Why?

When your ethnic group is largely poor, there is pressure to distinguish yourself by conspicuous consumption because the situation is so much more competitive with many more rivals. However, that need to impress disappears if you live in more affluent areas where there is less direct competition from members of the same ethnic group. Blacks and Latinos did not feel the need to compete with their rich white neighbours because they were not the relevant comparison group. But does this pattern hold for other groups, especially those in other countries less affluent than the US where the impact of spending money on conspicuous consumption has greater consequences for disposable income on basic requirements such as health and medical services? Indeed, it does. South African society is characterized by huge differences within and between social groups. Applying the same analysis of relative expenditure within social groups in over 77,000 households between 1995 and 2005 revealed that coloureds and blacks spent between 30 and 50 per cent more on conspicuous consumption goods and services than comparable whites, with the magnitude of the effect more pronounced in the poorest households.[40] In these dire situations of poverty, signalling trumps the need to address basic living requirements.

This desire to flaunt possessions can create a vicious circle. Money spent on luxuries is not spent on the sorts of investment that might help to alleviate social inequality such as education. However, that argument underestimates the true extent of the racial inequality in the US. According to an Economic Policy Institute report of 2016, the black–white wage gap has been increasing steadily since 1979.[41] A college education does not reduce this gap, since black college-educated males experience the greatest disparity with their white counterparts. To make matters worse, any benefits of economic growth over the decades have gone to the top wage earners – predominantly white males – thereby increasing the disparity that already prevents minorities from prospering.

GREEN-EYED MONSTERS
AND TALL POPPIES

Coveting is one of the seven deadly sins, specifically identified as to be avoided in the Bible's Ten Commandments: 'You shall not covet your neighbour's house. You shall not covet your neighbour's wife, nor his male or female servant, his ox or donkey, nor anything that belongs to your neighbour.' Both the Talmud and the Koran also specifically warn about the dangers of wanting what others have. In ancient times, prior to mass production and where everyone knew each other, there were fewer goods to go around and so coveting inevitably led to competition and the desire to acquire at the loss to another.

We covet items, but envy people. However, envy can create the negative emotion of resentment and rumination about another's perceived advantages. The negativity can be so consuming that people would even prefer to burn their own money in order to reduce the earnings of someone they envy.[42] It leads to that peculiar pleasurable experience felt at another's misfortune that the Germans call *schadenfreude*. Clearly envy is irrational, contradicts standard economic behaviour and leads to malicious behaviours and thoughts. It creates a distinct register in the emotional circuitry of the human brain active when we are thinking about others.[43] We envy because of the relativity principle described above. We envy those that are closest to us and especially if their good fortune is something that could have easily fallen upon us.

But sometimes comparing ourselves to others can spur us on in an aspirational sense. Aristotle first drew a distinction between two forms of envy: malicious envy, where we begrudge the success of others, and benign envy where we admire and wish to emulate the successes of others. This distinction exists in other languages that have separate words to express the difference between positive and negative envy. Whereas English and Italian have only one word for envy, Polish and Dutch have two. In Dutch, there is *afgunst* (malicious envy) and *benijden* (benign envy). In both cases of envy, there is a perceived imbalance between what we have compared to others. However, malicious envy is related to *schadenfreude*, while benign envy is not.[44] Moreover, the motivations that imbalance creates lead to different coping strategies. In malicious envy, we prefer to take away the successes of others to redress the imbalance – to pull down. Whereas with benign envy, we prefer to acquire what others have in order to be on an equal footing – to pull up.[45] Clearly malicious envy leads to a zero-sum game where no one benefits. In contrast, benign envy can lead to a competitive race that improves the situation for all, as when we up our game. Whereas in the past we were warned about coveting our neighbour's possessions, as well as about showing off too much, today we seek the benign envy of others. We want others to admire us, but not to begrudge us.

Benign envy is the goal of advertisers who want to motivate consumers to acquire items that inspire them to be like others. Celebrity endorsement is used to stimulate benign envy as we try to emulate those whom we admire. In one study of smartphone purchasers, students were asked to imagine working with a group of fellow students where one member was demonstrating the latest features of the Apple iPhone they had just acquired.[46] Participants were told to imagine desiring this phone, as well as being provided with information about the individual who owned it. In one group, the person was described as undeserving, so as to induce a sense of malicious envy, whereas another group were told that the owner was a deserving individual, so as to induce benign envy. A third group were told nothing about the iPhone owner but asked to reflect on the desirability of the phone. Those who experienced benign envy were willing to pay an average of $100 more for the purchase of a similar iPhone, compared to those experiencing malicious envy. However, those experiencing malicious envy were prepared to pay *even more* for a different phone, the BlackBerry, just to distance themselves from the iPhone owner whom they regarded as undeserving. This finding partly explains the brand tribalism that exists between Apple and non-Apple users and speaks more to the ownership of group identity than objective product evaluation.[47]

We may be jealous of those brandishing products as tangible measures of their success, but salaries are probably the most contentious issue when it comes to social comparisons. In 2017, the ratio between the average salary for a chief executive working in one of the top UK companies and one of their workers was 130:1. In other words, an ordinary worker earned less than 1 per cent of the top executive's salary.[48] In the US, the discrepancy is even greater. Data from 2014 reveals that the average ratio of CEO salary to worker was 354:1.[49] Some of the annual salaries of executives represent a lifetime of wealth for the average worker. According to *USA Today*, the average CEO salary in 2016 was $11 million per year.[50] Is it any wonder that there is such a public appetite to see these fat cats get their comeuppance through some personal misfortune or scandal? The term 'fat cat' was coined by journalist Frank Kent of the *Baltimore Sun* in the 1920s to describe rich political donors who yearned for public honours as recognition. Scandals sell newspapers, not only because they are titillating but because they are a welcome opportunity to feel better about our own lives when someone on a higher rung of the social ladder has a fall from grace. This is why newspapers continue to publish such stories, to trigger feelings of just deserts in their readers.[51]

Seeking to level those who have risen to an elevated position is called the 'tall poppy syndrome'. The name comes from the story in Livy about the last king of Rome, Tarquin the Proud, who, when asked about how to maintain power, took a stick and cut off the heads of the tallest poppies in his garden: a metaphor for executing the most eminent citizens. Nowadays, it's the press, especially in the UK, who conspire to cut people down to size if they get too popular.

The tall poppy syndrome is also well-established down under. Australians are renowned for their self-deprecating humour and this comes from a reluctance to brag too loudly about achievement to avoid jealousy. Australians even refer to successful people as 'tall poppies', and cutting them down to size is known as 'tall-poppying'. When she appeared on a US chat show with Seth Meyers in 2017, the rising Australian TV actress Ruby Rose rebuked the host when he described her as 'famous', saying: 'I'll get in so much trouble if you say that . . . They don't like hearing that back home . . . You're going to get me slaughtered.'[52] Fear of malicious envy is why many successful individuals engage self-deprecating strategies to ward off potential criticism. Or they may display generosity towards others they think will become envious. Traditionally, when a Polynesian fisherman caught fish and others did not, he would give away all his catch. If he did not, the others would talk negatively about him back in the village.

Bragging about wealth may be a signal of success but it runs the risk of generating malicious envy. So, you might predict that when inequality is visible, the wealthy would feel guiltier and be motivated to do something about it, like the Polynesian fishermen. In fact, the opposite is true. When wealthy people discover just how much better off they are than their neighbours, they are much less likely to reduce the imbalance. This counterintuitive effect was first observed by Nicholas Christakis, a Yale psychologist who created two virtual worlds of online citizens who lived in two different sets of 'countries'.[53] One set of citizens was randomly assigned to rich and poor roles within three societies with different levels of inequality as measured by the Gini coefficient. A Gini score of 0 per cent is perfectly egalitarian, with everyone on an equal footing. A score of 100 per cent would be a severely unequal society. Some of the world's poorest countries (the Central African Republic, for example) have some of the world's highest Gini coefficients (61 per cent), while some of the wealthiest (e.g. Denmark) have some of the lowest (29 per cent). Interestingly, Denmark operates a tall poppying code of conduct known as the 'Law of Jante' that emphasizes the virtues of being average and not thinking that you are better than others. (They also have the concept of *hygge*, which captures the enjoyment and contentment of simple things shared with other people – which partly explains why the Nordic countries top the league of the happiest nations. A few years back, *hygge* became a craze in other countries, with numerous bestselling books on the topic as well as a spike in sales of socks and candles. People were seeking the promise of happiness through *hygge*.) Another term, *lagom*, which translates from the Swedish to mean 'just the right amount', captures the Scandinavian countries' preference to shun excessive consumption or ostentatious acts.

In Christakis's virtual world, one society was set to a Gini coefficient of 0 per cent, another was set to 20 per cent (which is close to Scandinavian countries) and the third was set to 40 per cent (which corresponds to the US). One set of societies could 'see' the wealth of its neighbours, whereas the other set was blind to the wealth of its competitors. Christakis and his team then got the citizens to play repeated rounds of a co-operation game similar to the tragedy of the commons we described earlier, where 'citizens' could either opt in to contribute to the common wealth of the group, or defect and take advantage. The major factor that determined play was not the level of inequality but rather whether players could see each other's wealth. When wealth wasn't visible, the rich and poor converged towards more egalitarianism at around 16 per cent on the Gini scale. That's a pretty co-operative society typical of Scandinavian countries, which may reflect an inherent bias, which is why, as we discovered earlier, Americans would prefer to live in Sweden when offered a choice of hypothetical wealth distributions. However, when wealth was visible people became as much as 50 per cent less co-operative, less friendly and less rich – regardless of the initial level of inequality. Moreover, when wealth was visible, the rich exploited their poor neighbours. Of course, unlike for the Polynesian fishermen, this was a virtual world so there were no real consequences of defection or exploitation. However, it would appear that, when it comes to economic inequality, ignorance is bliss. These experimental findings suggest that signalling wealth can backfire. Rather than generating admiration through benign envy, excessive visible wealth may generate malicious envy, stoking the fires of rebellion.

THE WEALTH OF NATIONS

After the Second World War several economies, most notably the US, experienced a marked increase in wealth, and yet, as observed by the economist Richard Easterlin, they did not seem to experience an increase in reported levels of happiness.[54] As wealth rose, levels of happiness remained constant. This 'Easterlin paradox', first identified in the 1970s, has since been studied extensively in nations across the world, with mixed results. Both the UK and the US fit the general picture that increased income does not make you happier. Indeed, many indicators of mental well-being seem to show the reverse. Writing in the *Financial Times* in 2006, British economist Andrew Oswald criticized the Chancellor of the Exchequer, Gordon Brown, for pursuing a strategy of economic growth precisely because of the Easterlin paradox.[55] Both the US and UK were experiencing increased wealth but also increased rates of depression, work-related stress and suicides. At the time, such was the concern that economic policies were generating unhappiness, that a group of respected academics produced a manifesto – 'Guidelines for national indicators of subjective well-being and ill-being' – identifying the importance of mental health as a priority over economic growth.[56]

The Easterlin paradox is still a contentious issue as the experts argue over the data. Both sides of the debate have evidence to support their positions. Each country differs on so many dimensions that a simple relationship between economics and psychological well-being is problematic. People are complex, and discovering the association between wealth and happiness is fraught with difficulties. Indeed, defining happiness is complicated. In 2010, the psychologist Daniel Kahneman and his economist colleague Angus Deaton published an analysis of subjective well-being and income in a sample of 450,000 US adults.[57] They asked about happiness in terms of positive affect, not feeling blue and the number of stress-free days they had recently had. They also asked the respondents to rate their lives in terms of success on a scale of 0–10, with 0 being the 'worst possible life for you' and 10 the 'best possible life for you'.

There were two basic findings. Life got better in terms of happiness with more money, up until around $75,000 of annual income; after that, happiness flattened out so that extra income made no difference. However, the second important finding was that individuals continued to feel that they are more successful on the ladder of life as their income increased. Clearly the link between wealth and happiness is only true up to a certain point, after which money does not have much effect. Poor people are not as content as richer people but, as Kahneman and Deaton conclude, high income buys life satisfaction but not happiness. In other words, we rate our lives as much better with more money, but we are not necessarily happier. Yet, most of us are still compelled to strive for greater financial success. We believe that being a success is measured by how far up the ladder we have climbed even if it doesn't always make us happier.

If money can't buy happiness, then maybe it's because it is being spent on the wrong things. There is now a substantial body of research that indicates people gain greater satisfaction from spending money on experiences rather than possessions – the difference between 'being' versus 'having'. Psychologist Tom Gilovich has shown that the benefits that people derive from experiential consumption such as holidays, concerts and meals out tend to last longer than the consumption of material possessions such as luxury items of clothing, jewellery and electronic gadgets.[58] That satisfaction holds from both the anticipation of the experience as well as upon reflection.

One simple reason goes back to habituation again. The things we acquire often sit around accumulating dust, whereas memories are constantly reinterpreted and gilded in our minds. We are more willing to talk about our experiences than our recent material purchases, and where we see faults in our purchases we are much more inclined to reflect upon the positive side of experiences. We walk around with rose-tinted glasses when it comes to reminiscing about our trips rather than remembering how arduous or awful they really were. In one study of parents' recollections of visits to Disneyland – 'the happiest place on earth' – the average experience was less than magical with long queues, cranky kids and hot weather. However, after time, the trip was considered much more fun and an opportunity for family bonding.[59] As we noted earlier, the good old days are a product of bad memories.

The reason we are so easily fooled is that memories are not cast in stone but reconstructed with every retelling. The psychologist Elizabeth Loftus has shown that our memories are readily modified over time and with every recollection to the extent that, eventually, we cannot tell reality from fantasy.[60] This is because memories are stored in dynamic neural networks that code for multiple experiences and adjust their content over time and new events. And if we are retelling events to impress others, then they are subject to the 'Pollyanna principle'.[61] The name comes from the eponymous 1913 book by Eleanor Porter, who created a girl who could only see the best in every situation in her 'Glad Game'. Today we would call it a positivity bias when it comes to evaluating memories. With this malleability, memories can easily take on positive embellishments in a bid to out-experience someone else's anecdote. How often have you overheard dinner conversations where there is a competitive one-upmanship to outdo another's experiences? 'Oh, you must see Machu Picchu. It will blow your mind! It was the best trip we ever had.'

Where once exclusivity was the cachet for luxury items, so it also holds true for experiences. In retelling experiences, they become part of our identity and increase our social capital, the resources people accumulate through their relationships. Compared to material consumption, which tends to be a solitary affair, experiences by their nature tend to be social events involving other people. Through the social media platforms of Facebook and Instagram we can display just how amazing our experiences are. We may think that such information is simply sharing experiences, but in posting the best possible images we are in fact social peacocking again and generating envy in others. Whether that envy is benign or malicious really comes down to whether our friends and followers think we deserve the experiences.

In seeking happiness, it would be an over-generalization to say that we should simply spend more on experiences, because consumers are only really happy if they buy experiences that fit with their personality type. An extravert is going to enjoy spending money on parties and restaurants more than an introvert who finds such experiences challenging.[62] This is why an analysis of 76,000 bank transactions reveals that introverts are happier buying books rather than visiting bars.[63] We need to look at our personal values to make the right choices of what we want.

Seeking experiences sounds like a carefree, non-materialistic existence in the pursuit of hedonism without the hassle of mortgages and commitment. In reality, these experience seekers are often affluent individuals who have the wealth to enjoy bohemian lifestyles, outsourcing material requirements as needed. It is not a model for life that will work for all. A recent large-scale analysis of purchasing happiness shows that while the rich do enjoy experiential purchases more than materialistic ones, the opposite is true for those who are less well off.[64] This is because those with access to abundant resources can afford to indulge themselves with self-improvement.

Moreover, the notion that experiential consumerism is more environmentally friendly than material consumerism requires closer scrutiny. For example, travel is on the increase. For the past five years, the UK has experienced a year-on-year increase in travel of between 5 and 10 per cent to and from the British Isles by visitors and residents.[65] Airbnb, the house-renting online platform, has increased travel – with the associated carbon footprint that entails – rather than reducing it. The fact that growing numbers of Western millennials cannot afford mortgages and move more often has been given as a reason for increased expenditure on experiences. According to *Forbes* magazine, 78 per cent of millennials, compared to 59 per cent of baby boomers, would rather pay for an experience than material goods.[66] If you are laden down with stuff, moving is a hassle. Yet the shift to experiences does not necessarily mean a reduction in consumption. Just think about how wasteful and inefficient hotels are, in terms of providing cleaning, fresh linen, disposable toiletries, food, air conditioning and all the other luxuries that we have come to expect in our travels but not in our homes. To indulge travellers, 2 million bars of soap are thrown away every day in US hotels and 50 per cent of waste in the hospitality industry is food waste, at an annual cost of $218 billion.[67]

Global tourism is a $1.2 trillion industry, and it's growing every year. Previous estimates of the tourism industry's carbon footprint put it at between 2.5 and 3 per cent of total global carbon dioxide emissions. However, a recent study of tourism in 160 countries found that, between 2009 and 2013, tourism's global carbon footprint had increased four times more than previously estimated, accounting for about 8 per cent of global greenhouse gas emissions.[68] Transport, shopping and food were the most significant contributors and the majority of this footprint was made by the wealthiest countries. As the authors conclude, the rapid increase in tourism demand is effectively outstripping our goals of decarbonization of tourism-related activities.

We need to find better ways to occupy our time and spend our limited resources. While we may think that we will be more satisfied with our lives if we own more stuff, research into life satisfaction and happiness reveals that, once we have achieved a moderate income, we are no happier with more possessions. Whether it is through our purchases of things or experiences, we are still seeking something to show that we are different. We are still trying to signal our status and project who we are.

6

We Are What We Own

Nusrat Durrani looks like a rock star. When I met him in 2017, he was a senior executive at MTV, but even if you did not know that, you probably would have guessed he came from the media world just by looking at him. He wears designer clothes, most often black or leather, over his slight frame, has an abundance of jet-black long hair and wears tinted glasses – an Indian Joey Ramone. Even among the colourful gathering of fashionistas, futurists, venture capitalists and entrepreneurs at the Kinnernet gathering in Venice where we met, you could tell that Nusrat was super cool. Except that, when we met, he was far from cool.

Nusrat had just arrived from Rome where, the evening before, he had been robbed in a restaurant by opportunistic thieves who had taken his bag of personal items. With around 40 per cent unemployment in Rome, petty crime and theft from tourists has become a main source of income for the poor. It was an inconvenience but Nusrat is a relatively wealthy man. He has the luxury of time and resources to travel the world. These possessions could be easily replaced. At first, he was relaxed about the incident and seemed calm and collected. But over the next few days of the meeting, he became increasingly agitated about it. Like many unwelcomed intrusions in life, theft generates initial bewilderment followed by a growing sense of rage.

Nusrat's reaction is common. We are often surprised by how much theft upsets us, no matter how well off we are or how cool and calm we would wish to remain. This is because possessions are an extension of our selves. When they are taken without permission, it is equivalent to a violation of our person. Household burglary is particularly distressing as it includes an invasion of our territory where we usually feel most safe. Almost two-thirds of those burgled in the UK are extremely upset, experiencing a variety of symptoms including nausea, anxiety, crying, shaking and ruminating well after the event. Insurance companies report that it takes around eight months to feel safe again, and one in eight never recover emotionally.[1] It is not just the financial loss that distresses us; rather, it is more an intense sense of infringement. Someone has come into our world uninvited and undermined our control.

Loss can also be upsetting when we are forced to give up possessions that we would rather keep. It is this reluctance to let go which is one of the more revealing aspects about humans and their relationship with possessions. Consider the storage unit industry that took off in the late 1960s, after the decades of post-war consumerism. Every year more of us are putting our stuff in storage rather than getting rid of it. Currently, there are more self-storage facilities in the US than there are branches of McDonald's, even though 65 per cent of storage users also have garages.[2] Many garages no longer contain cars but rather the overspill of possessions that we can no longer keep in the house. Why are we reluctant to relinquish our things, and why do we keep lock-ups full of personal possessions that are of little value? Why do we have this peculiar emotional dependency on our possessions?

The reason is that we are what we own. In 1890, the father of North American psychology, William James, wrote how the self was defined by what we can claim ownership over:

> In its widest possible sense, however, a man's Self is the sum total of all that he CAN call his, not only his body and his psychic powers, but his clothes and his house, his wife and children, his ancestors and friends, his reputation and works, his lands, and yacht and bank-account. All these things give him the same emotions. If they wax and prosper, he feels triumphant; if they dwindle and die away, he feels cast down, – not necessarily in the same degree for each thing, but in much the same way for all.[3]

James is describing what psychologists call 'self-construal', the way we think about who we are as well as the emotional consequences of loss, which reveals the special relationship we have with our possessions. It is not particularly surprising that we consider our bodies and minds as part of our self. After all, who else can claim them? However, many material things on the list are not unique to us and could be owned by another. Houses, lands and yachts are properties that we acquire. It is striking then that losing them can affect us so personally.

Many thinkers have considered the intrinsic link we have to our material possessions. Plato famously had little regard for the material world and thought we should aspire to higher, immaterial notions. He argued that collective ownership was necessary to promote pursuit of the common interest, and to avoid the social divisiveness of private property that leads to inequality and theft. His student Aristotle, always one to argue with his mentor, was a little more grounded, and emphasized the importance of studying the material world. He thought private ownership promoted prudence and responsibility but noted how we tend to envy and be jealous of others because of ownership. Two thousand years later, the French philosopher Jean-Paul Sartre maintained that the only reason we want to own is to enhance our sense of self, and the only way we can know who we are is to observe what we have – almost as if we need to externalize our self through our possessions. Our acquisitions are tangible markers of our success. Like the study of wealth in the US, we may not get much happier after reaching an income of $75,000 a year, but we are more self-assured that we are successful if we can see our possessions. Not only do we signal our self to others through our possessions, our possessions signal back to us who we are.

Sartre, in his book *Being and Nothingness*, realized the extent to which humans are defined by what they own: 'the totality of my possessions reflects the totality of my being ... I am what I have ... What is mine is myself.'[4] He proposed a number of ways in which this arises. First, by exerting exclusive control over something, one is claiming it for the self – something that we saw evidenced early in infants. Secondly, and in line with the views of John Locke, creating something from scratch means you own it. Finally, Sartre thought that possessions evoke passions.

One way that people express their passion for possession is through accumulating stuff. In 1769, another French philosopher, Denis Diderot, wrote about how possessions can shape behaviour. Diderot bought a new luxury dressing-gown that he thought would make him happy, but he was surprised how miserable this purchase made him and how this item changed his life. Rather than enriching his life, the luxury gown stood in stark contrast to the shabbier items he already possessed. Soon, he found himself buying new items to match the quality of the dressing-gown. But Diderot was not a rich man so this escalation in spending made him even more unhappy. In comparison to his old dressing-gown, in which he had felt comfortable cleaning the house, his luxury purchase meant that he no longer wore his gown to do household chores. As he wrote, 'I was absolute master of my old dressing-gown, but I have become a slave to my new one.' The 'Diderot effect', a term coined by the anthropologist Grant McCracken, describes the influence that individual items can have on subsequent purchases.[5] For example, if you buy one luxury item, you are tempted to aspire to more such items even though you may not need them. Many retailers capitalize on the Diderot effect by advertising to us items that complement our initial purchase. This is also part of the appeal of Apple products. The purchase of the iPhone was for many, according to McCracken, a 'departure good' which exerted a new pressure to acquire other Apple products because they reflect identity. Even though a different purchase may be good value, if it sends the wrong signal about identity then the purchaser will be less likely to buy it.

Probably the most excessive form of emotional attachment to objects is found among collectors. Collectors are emotionally invested in their collections. It is not simply the monetary value associated with their things but rather the effort and pursuit that collectors expend when amassing their desirable possessions. Sometimes, the prospect of losing them can be unbearable. In 2012, the German authorities discovered that Cornelius Gurlitt, a recluse living in Munich, had amassed a huge collection of art masterpieces estimated to be worth around $1 billion. The art had been stolen from Jewish owners by the Nazis and sold to Cornelius's father for a fraction of their true value during the war. Cornelius had come to regard the hoard as his personal responsibility to protect. He described the experience of watching the police confiscate his prized collection as hitting him harder than the loss of his parents or his sister, who had died of cancer that same year.

Cornelius told the authorities that protecting the collection was his duty to the extent that he had become 'intense, obsessed, isolated, and increasingly out of touch with reality'.[6]

One of the earliest studies to test James's claims regarding self-construal was conducted by the Yale psychoanalyst Ernst Prelinger in 1959.[7] He asked adults to categorize 160 items on a scale from non-self to self and found that minds and bodies were considered more relevant to the sense of self than personal possessions. However, possessions were considered more relevant to the self than other people (though, as we shall shortly discover, this is a very Western perspective). When children were asked to rank the same items, they followed much the same pattern as adults except that, with age, there was an increasing emphasis on the importance of possessions that reflect our relationships with others, which makes perfect sense as we grow up into cohabiting adults.[8]

The Canadian marketing guru Russell Belk has also written about the relationship between the self and what we own in a series of influential papers championing the concept known as 'the extended self'.[9] Building on the work of James and Sartre, Belk proposed four developmental stages in the emergence of the extended self. First, the infant distinguishes self from the environment. Second, the child distinguishes self from others. Third, possessions help adolescents and adults manage their identities, and finally, possessions help the old achieve a sense of continuity and preparation for death. As we age, we shift in our valuation more to those possessions that remind us of our relationships over the years such as mementoes, heirlooms and photographs – the sorts of things that people often say they would save from a burning house. Sometimes this is literally true. The legendary blues musician B. B. King was famous for his guitar he called 'Lucille', which went with him everywhere. He named it after the time when he was playing a gig in Arkansas in 1949, and a fight broke out between two men and a heater was kicked over that set the hall on fire, forcing everyone to evacuate. Once outside, King realized he had left his $30 guitar onstage, so he re-entered the burning building to retrieve it. The next day he learned that the two men were fighting over a woman called Lucille, so King gave his guitar – and every subsequent guitar he owned – the same name to remind him never to run into a burning building again for a guitar, or to fight over a woman.

COMMODITY FETISHISM

Possessions are an extension of our self, but the development of new technologies means that our physical connections with many material possessions will disappear as they are replaced by digital formats. Physical photographs and hand-written letters are a rarity in these days of Instagram and email. Interestingly, vinyl records and bound books were predicted to disappear a few years ago, but both are making a comeback as people appreciate their physicality. In 2017, vinyl record sales in the UK hit a twenty-five-year high as listeners returned to 'tangible music'.[10] The same trend is evidenced in the decline of ebook sales in favour of the physical article.

One reason for this reversal is that it is difficult to become emotionally attached to non-physical things. The desire to have and to hold tangible things is a form of fetishism. The word 'fetish' (derived from the Portuguese word *feitiço*, meaning 'charm' or 'sorcery') was used by European travellers to Africa who noted the practice of worshipping objects believed to have supernatural powers. Fetishism has since come to refer to the emotional gratification that people gain from inanimate objects: sexual fetishism of various types of clothing being one of the most extreme forms.

Any object has the potential to generate fetishism. In the opening chapter of his critique of capitalism, *Das Kapital*, Karl Marx wrote about commodity fetishism as the psychological relationship that people have with products.[11] He was describing the value we ascribe to things that is based on what people are willing to pay for them. This value transfers to the object as an intrinsic property even when it has no functional value. Hence, for most of human history, gold and silver were not intrinsically valuable (they have since been found very useful in electronics), but rather became valuable because of their rarity and usefulness as a convenient form of currency. As soon as the market considers some commodity to be valuable, consumers develop emotional reactions to it.

Valuable things can generate fetish thoughts. Who does not feel that special tingle at the touch of gold? Possibly a goldsmith who works the metal every day but, for the rest of us, gold has long been a magical metal found throughout folklore and fairy tales and associated with touch – remember King Midas? Fetishism makes sense if you think there is something to be gained from holding and touching things – a tangible connection. In the field of magical thinking, this is known as positive contagion, where there is a belief that some positive attribute will transfer from the item – which is why people want to touch objects of desire.[12] I was once shown around the Fellows' common room at Trinity College, Cambridge where a solid gold Nobel prize medal was displayed unguarded atop the fireplace. Everybody wanted to hold it. Even today, banknotes are not intrinsically valuable but, again, there is something special about holding a wad of cash.

In fact, positive contagion has real-world consequences. When adults were asked to putt using a club that they were told belonged to the US golfing pro Ben Curtis, who had won the 2003 Open Championship, their performance was much better compared to those who were told nothing about the putter.[13] Not only did they putt more accurately but they also judged the golf hole to be bigger, which gave them more confidence to be on target. This psychological boost is the explanation for supposed lucky charms. Students who bring their own lucky charms into a test situation perform much better on memory tests and solving anagrams compared to those students who have their charms taken away during testing.[14] In all of these examples, physical contact with a desirable object generates positive psychology.

Simply handling money changes the way we think and behave, but not always for the better. The behavioural economist Kathleen Vohs, who studies the psychology of money, has shown that holding cash makes both children and adults less pro-social, less interconnected and more selfish.[15] Like Gollum, the pitiful, grotesque character with his precious ring in Tolkien's *The Hobbit* and *Lord of the Rings* trilogy, some owners become psychologically obsessed with their possessions. From misers to drug lords, from Fagin in *Oliver Twist* to Walter White in *Breaking Bad*, the depiction of individuals gloating over their hoards is usually one of selfish greed.

When it comes to the way we regard our personal possessions as part of our self-construal, Russell Belk also thinks that we enter the realm of magical thinking:

> The possessions that we see as most a part of ourselves also show close relationship to the objects that we see as most magical, include perfume, jewelry, clothing, foods, transitional objects, homes, vehicles, pets, religious icons, drugs, gifts, heirlooms, antiques, photographs, souvenirs and collections.[16]

Recently, however, Belk has updated his extended self concept to include our increasing reliance on and inter-relatedness with the digital world and the rapid changes that have taken place over the last twenty years.[17] People are using the new technologies of social media to change their self-construal online to one that they would prefer to promote to others. One of the major concerns about social networking is that people create and broadcast inaccurate profiles of who they are, preferring to emphasize, elaborate or fabricate information that they believe will impress others. The reason it's a concern is that this online promotion creates unrealistic expectations of how happy and successful everyone else is, which contribute to feelings of inadequacy among vulnerable individuals.[18] We generate multiple versions of ourselves that reflect the differing contexts in which we interact with others; we all experience an illusion of selfhood, rather than a veridical, unchanging self that remains constant over time, from one situation to the next.[19]

Digital platforms enable us, and indeed encourage us, to share personal information promiscuously that previously would have been considered crass, boastful or even embarrassing. We are now much more inclined to social peacocking online, but there is also a threat to our self-construal from digital technologies. Our memories and experiences now exist in formats that do not fade naturally and can be easily retrieved and verified. Background checks of online profiles are now common practice among potential employers. Many naive students applying for positions in my laboratory are shocked when I tell them that we usually check their social media profiles in order to discover more about them that they may not have shared in their applications.

Digital memories can also undermine the growing preference for experiences over possessions when it comes to satisfaction. Remember, this preference depends on our constantly changing memory of events as being more pleasurable. It may be the case that the digital era eventually removes those rose-tinted spectacles when it comes to reminiscing, by reminding us exactly what happened and who we are.

More alarming is the prospect of the digital afterlife online. People continue to acknowledge birthdays of the deceased, and it has been estimated that the number of 'dead' profiles on Facebook will increase at a rate of roughly 1.7 million per year in the US alone.[20] Facebook has memorial accounts for the deceased, and legacy arrangements for others to manage your account upon your death. But death is a minor inconvenience when it comes to your digital self. Companies such as Eterni.me, an MIT start-up, can generate re-creation algorithms that mimic the preferences of a dead individual and write posts from beyond the grave, enabling the bereaved to stay in touch with the dead. Even if we don't want to pay for such services, just as my wife was reluctant to discard the items she'd inherited from her parents, grieving families will find it emotionally difficult to delete the online profile of deceased loved ones. Storing millions of digital remains online will accrue mounting archival costs and so there will have to be some financial model that keeps these files active. The digital afterlife industry may be weird, but such is the inevitability of death and the online self that Oxford ethicists have proposed guidelines to regulate the field.[21] Digital innovations will literally be able to extend the lifeless self well after we are gone.

WEIRD PEOPLE

The notion of the extended self, defined by what we own, turns out to be a characteristically Western phenomenon. One of the major criticisms of psychology is that it represents a field that has been based largely on research conducted upon white American college students over the past sixty years, motivated to participate in experiments for course credit. They have been called WEIRD – Western, Educated, Industrialized, Rich and Democratic. An analysis of studies published in six leading journals found that almost all the participants were WEIRD, and yet this demographic represents only around 12 per cent of the world's population.[22]

To that list of cultural differences we can add self-construal and concepts of ownership. In his book *The Geography of Thought*, psychologist Richard Nisbett argues that, political ideologies aside, cultures traditionally differ in self-construal – with a broad division between the West and the East.[23] The Western concept of the self is relatively individualistic compared to Eastern societies, where self-construal is considered more interdependent with others or collectivist. Western values emphasize the notion of the independent self: the 'self-made' person and so on. Personal possessions, individual achievements and a higher appreciation of one's differences from others are all part of the Western egocentric view.

In contrast, Eastern societies with long traditions of Buddhist and Taoist philosophies, which emphasize lack of self and the importance of the group, teach children from an early age to value the group over the self. Indeed, children from rural collectivist cultures tend to share more fairly and generously than children from industrialized Western countries.[24] A higher value is placed on belonging to family and community, and it is more common to live in larger households that extend beyond the immediate family. Eastern families are often more physically interconnected than those in the West. In some societies, multiple generations – grandparents, aunts, uncles, cousins – may live under the same roof.

These differences are even reflected in the way we describe ourselves. For example, people raised in collectivist societies often describe themselves in relation to others. My student Sandra Weltzien recently conducted a study of seven- and eight-year-old school children from the Indian city of Pune, where she asked them to tell her what made them special, only to find that they almost always described their achievements in relation to family members and friends. A typical comment was 'I am good at counting so that it makes my mother proud.' In contrast, UK children of the same age in Bristol were quite proficient in rattling off why they were so special without the mention of others.[25] In some cultures, this inter-relatedness to others extends back to ancestors. Elsdon Best, an ethnographer of the Maori peoples of New Zealand, noted that they would often refer to their tribe in the first person, for example when describing a battle that may have taken place a hundred years earlier they would say: 'I defeated the enemy there.'[26]

Are these broad stereotypes generally accurate, or just sweeping generalizations that we use to categorize foreigners? Remarkably, a variety of experimental evidence supports the distinction between East and West. Tasks that are characterized by either analytical processing (individualistic) or holistic group processing (collectivist) produce different performance profiles in individuals from across the cultural divide. Even the way we see the world depends on our cultural heritage. When shown complex underwater scenes with multiple fish and an array of reef structures and plants, Japanese and American students notice different things.[27] On recognition tasks, where they had to identify whether some feature was present in the original image, American students tended to only notice the large dominant fish, whereas Japanese participants noticed much more of the surrounding scenery. Japanese students were more likely to say that the picture was 'a pond', whereas Americans were three times more likely to say something focal like, 'It was a big fish, swimming to the left.' The Japanese were much more sensitive to context and relationships between features. This interpretation is supported by a simple demonstration. Take a look at the diagram below.

Imagine that I have presented you with the empty boxes on the right and have asked you to draw in the missing line. There are two ways you could do this. You could either draw a line of exactly the same length (absolute solution) or draw a line that is proportionally related to the frame (relative solution). When presented with this

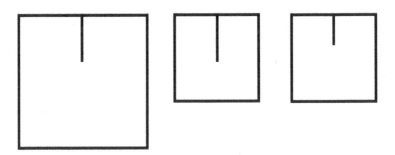

When presented with the box and line on the left, participants are requested to draw a line that is either identical (absolute) or proportional (relative) in length within a smaller empty box on the right. Participants from the West are more accurate judging absolute equal length, whereas those from the East are more accurate drawing the line proportionally to the box.

task, Japanese participants were much more accurate with the relative solution compared to the absolute responses, whereas American participants showed the opposite profile.[28] This indicates that there are cultural differences in the way we process the world: either through a piecemeal lens or more holistically reflecting the individualist versus collectivist self-construal.

What is more remarkable is that brain activation differs between individuals from independent and collectivist cultures when it comes to a number of tasks, including visual processing of complex scenes,[29] focusing attention,[30] mental calculation,[31] self-reflection[32] and reasoning about what someone else might be thinking.[33] All of this evidence suggests fundamental differences in our brains and yet these differences are not cast in stone or wired into our biology. Indeed, you can temporarily shift the way people think by using priming tasks, such as getting them to read stories that either emphasize individualist or collectivist storylines, or getting them to edit a manuscript circling the pronouns 'I' and 'me' or 'you' and 'them'.[34] Simply by refocusing attention on the self or others, you can shift self-construal. Indeed, after a couple of months, Americans living in Japan switch from the absolute to the relative bias, with a corresponding reversal in the opposite direction for Japanese students living in America.[35]

Simple manipulations can make you either more self-centred or less, and this shift in focus is mirrored by changes in brain regions activated by either self- or other-oriented thinking.[36] Our brains are constantly responding and adapting to the subtle cultural context around us. When you think about it, this biocultural brain is quite spooky. Most of us from the West assume that when we visit another culture we are bringing along our Western brain and observing through Western eyes. But the research on biocultural adaptation indicates that when you spend enough time within another culture your brain will adapt to see the world in the same way that others do. Indeed, over time, cultural self-construal has changed in the West – for example, the use of 'self' prefixes (such as 'self-regard' and 'self-made') did not appear in the English language until the rise of individualistic Puritanism in the seventeenth century.[37] The change in self-construal was partly a result of the shift in population away from close-knit village communities into the crowded, competing masses of the new industrialized cities.[38]

Historical events also play a role in these cultural differences. One common explanation for the independence and individualism that are fostered so strongly in the US is that it is a nation forged largely from immigrants seeking to make a better life for themselves. The American social hierarchy and values are based on meritocracy – as enshrined in the 1776 US Declaration of Independence, which states: 'We hold these truths to be self-evident, that all men are created equal, that they are endowed by their Creator with certain unalienable Rights, that among these are Life, Liberty and the pursuit of Happiness.' This political philosophy promotes the idea that everyone has the potential and the right to achieve success and stands in stark contrast to the prevailing class systems that many of the immigrants fled from. In Europe, you were either born into privilege or not, and there was nothing much you could do about it. In fact, social mobility was frowned upon as getting above your station in life. In the former colonies, however, the idea that one's fate was in one's own hands came to represent the American dream of becoming a self-made man (or woman).

Even within the US, however, there is differing self-construal from state to state, which reflects historical differences. Back in the 1920s, the historian Frederick Jackson Turner argued that the expansion and exploration into the west of the continent nurtured the 'frontier spirit', an independent self-sufficient ethos, as each pioneer battled the wilderness and each other for their own survival.[39] Research supports this romantic view. Collectivist tendencies are strongest in the Deep South, whereas individualist tendencies are strongest in the Mountain West and Great Plains.[40] Residents from the remote Midwest states score far more highly on measures of individualism compared to those on the densely packed coasts. It is probably no coincidence that someone like Donald Trump who represents the pinnacle of egocentric individualism was so popular in the former frontier states, compared to the more cosmopolitan states, during the US elections.

Probably the most compelling evidence to support this frontier hypothesis of self-construal comes from a study of Japanese residents of the northern island of Hokkaido.[41] Before the eighteenth century, Hokkaido was sparsely populated wilderness. Around that time, the central feudal government collapsed and many residents on the mainland settled in Hokkaido. Just like the pioneers of the US West, the first waves of settlers were motivated to start a new life. Even though mainland Japan has a long tradition of interdependence and collectivist values, the descendants of the original settlers of Hokkaido today score much more highly on measures of independence and self-focus and are more like Westerners than their fellow citizens on the mainland. It is not simply the geographical location that determines differing self-construal, but rather the historical origins of how a community came to be established.

Things are changing, however. A recent study of seventy-eight countries over the last fifty years has shown that levels of individualism have been rising globally with increased economic development.[42] (Even use of the pronouns 'me' and 'mine' has increased in collectivist cultures.[43]) However, the richer we get, the less we rely on other people – which is why increased economic independence is associated with increases in the divorce rate, living alone in a smaller home and not looking after your parents or grandparents.[44] It seems to be a hefty emotional price to pay for getting your way. If individualism is rising globally, then this has implications for the way in which humans use and value possessions as a material component of the self. Unless materialism can be decoupled from individualism, then we need to be aware that people will increasingly look to private ownership as a way of establishing status. If this happens, we need to avoid the corresponding problems arising from over-consumption.

SELFISH ME

Sometimes we give our stuff away as a measure of who we are. The reason self-construal is so relevant to ownership is not only that it reflects our attitudes towards our possessions, but also what we do with them. Ownership entitles you to share your resources with others. You can't share what you don't own, nor can you share that which belongs to others. If our possessions are part of our self-construal, then the cultural differences in individualist and collectivist processing style can explain the differences observed in sharing behaviour around the world. Someone who is self-focused is less likely to be generous to others compared to someone who thinks more about other people.

As every parent knows, children have to be constantly reminded to share with others, as we all start out fairly self-centred. Jean Piaget described the mental world of the young child as egocentric and demonstrated this in his perspective-taking games. In one classic study,[45] young children were seated directly opposite an adult. On the table in front of them was a papier mâché model of a mountain range with three differently coloured peaks of different sizes that were readily distinguishable. Some had conspicuous landmarks such as a building or cross on top. Children were then shown photographs of the mountain range taken from different angles and asked to select which picture matched what they could see. They were also asked to choose the picture that corresponded to what the adult could see. Below four years of age, children typically selected the photograph that corresponded to their own view, irrespective of where the adult was sitting. Piaget argued that this revealed they could not easily take another's perspective because they were so egocentric. This is one reason why it is unusual to see spontaneous sharing behaviour at this age. However, from an early age, children from the East are encouraged to be less egocentric and, as a consequence, share more than their Western counterparts, which reflects their collectivist upbringing.

What is remarkable is that our selfishness never really disappears. Both children and adults donate less to charity when they are not being watched, indicating that, privately, we still retain selfish motivation.[46] When they look to others, children in both urban America and rural India will reduce their sharing if stingy behaviour is modelled by an adult, but *only* Indian children increase their giving when generous behaviour is provided as a role model. One reason is that Eastern collectivist societies are more focused on reputation, whereas this is less of a concern for children from individualist societies.[47] But again, this can be easily manipulated. In her studies of Indian and British children, Sandra Weltzien showed that both groups become more selfish simply by being asked to talk about themselves just before they are asked to share. Again, the power of priming reveals that we can be shifted in our attitudes to what we own. Sharing is flexible and context specific but strongly influenced by others' expectations if we are reminded of them.

One of the reasons we are less likely to share our possessions is not so much that we do not think about other people, but rather we think too much about what we have. When we think about our self we are more task-focused, paying particular attention to things that are relevant to us. In a supermarket-sweep study,[48] participants were asked to sort a series of images of grocery and household items into a red or blue shopping basket, based on a colour cue on the item image. They were then asked to imagine that they had won all the items in one of the baskets, so all the items pictured in it belonged to them. After the sorting was over, participants were tested to see how many items they could remember. Both adults and children as young as four remember significantly more items they are told they have won compared to the items in the other basket.[49] This is known as the 'self-reference effect' whereby information encoded with reference to the self is more likely to be subsequently remembered than similar information encoded with reference to other people.[50]

The advantage for processing self-referential information registers in the brain as activity in the medial prefrontal cortex – where your temples are – but when associated with ownership also triggers corresponding activation in the lateral parietal cortex, an area further back just above your ears, which is usually active during object processing.[51] In other words, as objects are processed, they are given the additional ownership tag that registers in regions of the brain that are active when we think about ourselves. This explains why activation of this self-referential and object processing network is stronger in Western compared to Eastern subjects.[52] In contrast, when it comes to thinking about others, activation in Eastern subjects is stronger in brain regions that respond when reflecting about one's relationships with others.

If Eastern ways of perceiving the world are collectivist, does that mean they are less obsessed with social status and, if so, less likely to pursue status symbols? On the contrary, Asia is one of the strongest markets for luxury goods. How can competition to be seen to be successful through conspicuous consumption square with traditional collectivist values that emphasize group identity? How can an Indian farmer spend extravagantly on a helicopter ride, if Indian society is supposedly collectivist and other-focused?

Marketing expert Sharon Shavitt argues that in addition to the individualistic–collectivist dimension, there is also a critical vertical–horizontal dimension within cultures that explains the apparent contradiction.[53] Individualistic cultures with a vertical structure include countries such as the US, UK and France, where people distinguish themselves through competition, achievement and power. They are likely to endorse statements such as 'winning is everything' and 'it is important that I do my job better than others'. However, individualistic cultures with a horizontal structure include such countries as Sweden, Denmark, Norway and Australia, where people view themselves as self-reliant and equal in standing to others. They are more likely to agree with statements such as 'I'd rather depend on myself than others', and 'my personal identity, independent of others, is very important to me'. In contrast, collectivist cultures with a vertical social hierarchy include countries such as Japan, India and Korea, where people focus on complying with authority and enhancing the cohesion and status of their in-groups, even when that entails sacrificing their own personal goals. They are more likely to say, 'it is my duty to take care of my family, even when I have to sacrifice what I want', and 'it is important to me that I respect the decisions made by my group'. Finally, collectivist cultures with a horizontal structure, such as Brazil and other South American countries, are characterized by sociability and egalitarian arrangements of assumed equality. They are more likely to endorse statements such as 'to me, pleasure is spending time with others', and 'the well-being of my co-workers is important to me'.

When cultures have vertical structures, members are still going to aspire to social status through conspicuous consumption, irrespective of whether their self-construal is independent or collectivist. Cultures with horizontal structures will have more aversion to conspicuous consumption, bragging and showing off, and are more likely to promote modesty or engage in tall-poppying. These dimensions also explain why marketeers need to be sensitive to the cultural structures of countries. In Denmark, advertising appeals to individual identity and self-expression, whereas in the US, another individualistic society but with a vertical structure, advertisements are more likely to emphasize status and prestige.[54]

At birth, one human brain is much the same as another, but the emerging body of neuroscience research indicates that cultural self-construal manifests in different brain activation. These variations reflect historical, political and philosophical perspectives indicating that our brains are shaped by biocultural influences during development rather than through some evolutionary hard-wiring. If ownership is a major component of our self-construal, then it's how we raise our children that determines their attitudes towards possessions.

THE PROSPECT OF LOSS

When it comes to gaining and losing possession, the values we place on ownership should reflect rational economic choices. For centuries, economics was dominated by mathematical models of supply and demand proposed by the likes of Adam Smith and John Stuart Mill. However, as we noted earlier in our discussion of charitable donations, this mathematical approach to understanding market trading does not take into consideration human behaviour. People do not behave rationally when it comes to buying and selling – something that successful traders have known for thousands of years. Not only can a good trader recognize a potential buyer from the emotions they portray, but they can also manipulate the customer to purchase by playing to their emotions: 'Think how good you will look owning this!' The hard sell is invariably an assault on the emotional weaknesses of the potential customer. Nevertheless, many scholars, including Smith and others, produced models based on rational behaviour and maximizing profits to describe how economics works. All that would change when two Israeli psychologists, Daniel Kahneman and Amos Tversky, wandered the ancient streets of Jerusalem contemplating how humans actually make decisions.

We have already encountered Kahneman, but most of his Nobel prize-winning research was conducted in collaboration with his late friend and colleague Amos Tversky. They have been called 'psychology's Lennon and McCartney' because of their ground-breaking and creative work.[55] Both grandsons of rabbis, Kahneman and Tversky would employ the Talmudic tradition of structured debate over questions such as, 'Is it better to toss a coin to win $100 or take a sure bet of $46?' Over and over again, they would pose questions of choice, then rely on their intuitions as an insight into the human mind. They reasoned that if some decisions seemed self-evident to them, then they were likely to be the same for other people.

This methodological approach of examining your own mind, 'introspection', can be traced to the origins of psychology as a science, when early practitioners such as Ernst Weber and Gustav Fechner began the systematic study of subjective thresholds of perception. How bright did a light have to be before you could see it? How more intense did a tone have to be before it doubled in loudness? and so on. These pioneers of perception approached the problem like physicists looking for measurable experiences that could be mapped out in mathematical equations. They were *psycho*physicists measuring the non-material dimensions of the human mind.

Kahneman and Tversky used the same introspective approach to establish people's attitudes to risk, gambling and other financial transactions. Just like the discoveries of human perception made by the early German psychophysicists, Kahneman and Tversky discovered that people's attitudes to losses and gains were systematically biased. As an example of a bias, consider a pair of twins who do exactly the same job and have exactly the same attitudes and goals in life. Everything is identical about them. One day, their boss comes along and tells them they are due for a bonus: a pay rise of $10,000 or an extra twelve days' holiday. As they are both indifferent individuals, they toss a coin and decide who gets the pay increase and who gets the extra holiday time. Both are equally happy with the outcome. Now imagine that after a year, their boss comes back and says that it's time to switch over. How would each twin feel about the loss of $10,000 or the extra vacation time?

Even though each bonus was equivalent, Kahneman and Tversky pointed out that each twin would still be reluctant to switch. They called this 'loss aversion', and it is the reason that standard economic models fail under these circumstances.[56] If two resources are equivalent in value, then they should be readily interchangeable. However, once established or owned, people do not treat them as such. Biases in the human mind need to be taken into consideration when reasoning about economic decisions. What is it about human reasoning that seems so fickle?

In his bestselling book *Thinking, Fast and Slow*,[57] Kahneman argues that the human mind operates with two pathways to decision-making: System 1 operates fast and intuitively, often relying on emotional 'gut feelings', whereas System 2 is slow and ponderous, arriving at decisions much more slowly through rational logic and reasoning. We deploy both types of thinking, which often conflict when it comes to solutions. Standard economic models are based on the cold, hard logic and reason of System 2, but humans often succumb to their fast, intuitive biases of System 1, which is why our decisions can seem illogical when emotions are not taken into consideration. When you understand the difference between these two systems, the irrational aspects of ownership start to make more sense, as we will consider next.

BAD LOSERS

Imagine the following betting prospect. I will toss a normal coin and if it comes up heads, you will lose $10. How much would I have to offer you as a win before you took the bet? I expect you will want more than $10 otherwise there is no point in taking the bet. But how much would you require to be tempted?

On average, most people will not take the bet unless the potential win is at least $20. In fact, it doesn't matter whether it is $10 or $10,000; most people want at least twice as much in return in order to take such a bet. Why? When it comes to losing, the prospect of a loss looms larger in our minds than the prospect of a gain unless that gain is substantially more. System 1 is at fault once again. This loss aversion is perverse when you think of the bets many members of the general public make when they play the lottery. The odds of winning are so much smaller than 50:50 as in a coin toss, but then the cost of a ticket is completely swamped by the prospect of a megabucks win. In most people's minds, the unlikely chance to become a millionaire offsets the likely cost of the weekly lottery ticket. We are not very good at economic reasoning when it comes to taking risks, which is why national lotteries have been called an 'idiot tax'.

It's not idiocy, but rather System 1 operating. People love to dream about becoming rich, which is one of the reasons they gamble. And for many, a big win promises a better life that will make them happier. Clearly poverty is neither preferable nor desirable, but wealth does not always deliver the anticipated happiness we think it will bring. In a classic study of wealth and happiness back in 1978, researchers interviewed twenty-two lottery winners who had won prizes ranging from $50,000 to $1 million.[58] The relatively random nature of lottery wins provides an opportunity to assess the value that significant amounts of money contribute towards enhancing well-being without factoring in work and effort. Winners were asked to rate how happy they were before their big win; how happy they were at the present moment; and how happy they expected to be in the future. They were also asked to rate how much pleasure they derived from everyday activities such as talking with friends, watching TV, getting a compliment or shopping for clothes. For comparison, the same questions were asked of their neighbours who had not won the lottery. Not exactly losers, but not winners either. Despite their windfalls, the lottery winners were no happier than their neighbours but reported significantly less enjoyment in daily activities.

The lottery winner study, now forty years old, was so influential and counterintuitive that it continues to stimulate further research and controversy. The most recent study (published in 2018) of over 3,000 Swedish lottery players who had won significant amounts of money appears to contradict the original claim that money does not increase happiness.[59] When asked how life was for them at least five years after their windfall, they reported significantly higher levels of overall life satisfaction compared to those who had not won. This was mainly due to the fact their financial worries had been removed. However, as we noted earlier in Kahneman's study of rising salaries, satisfaction is not the same as happiness. In terms of happiness and mental health, there were no significant increases as a result of winning a large amount of money.

Gambling also reveals something interesting about the ownership of choices. People are reluctant to change their minds if they are the ones making the decision. Just after placing bets, racing punters are more confident of their horse's chances than they are immediately before laying their bets.[60] Choices generate an illusion of control,[61] where participants are reluctant to exchange lottery tickets that they have selected compared to ones that have been allocated. They believe they are more likely to win if they have made the choice. Even when players are offered a bonus for exchanging tickets, they don't.[62] It's not so much that they magically think they have luck, but rather they report that they would feel much worse if they swapped a ticket and lost than if they stuck with it and lost.[63] Again, emotions are ruling the decision.

Most of us do not like to take risks because of our fear of losing. It's not just humans who are risk averse. When the stakes are high, even the simplest organisms develop strategies to avoid risk. Deep in our evolutionary history, we developed a bias against taking chances. For most animals, the proverbial bird in the hand is worth more than two in the bush. However, avoiding all risks is also not a good strategy. Just like in the economic games we encountered earlier, you need to balance risk against the potential advantage of gains, so strategies have to evolve to be flexible enough to be passed on to future generations as adaptations.

Using computer simulations to model the reproductive success of risky behaviours over a thousand generations, it turns out that a preference for risk aversion only evolves in small populations, and especially in groups of 150 or fewer.[64] This figure will be familiar to readers of evolutionary psychology as it coincides with Dunbar's Number, named after evolutionary psychologist Robin Dunbar who calculated that 150 was the optimum size of a group of hominids living together.[65] Moreover, the size of the loss aversion bias (the minimum number of birds in the bush there needs to be before you let go of the one in your hand) derived from mathematical models turns out to be 2.2 – a value that is remarkably close to the $20 most of us require in order to accept a bet with a potential loss of $10.

Not everyone is risk averse. Twin studies from Sweden, comparing up to 30,000 identical and non-identical twins raised together and separately, enabled researchers to establish to what extent behaviours were shaped by environments and childhood experiences and to what extent they were predicted by genes.[66] When it comes to financial decisions that involve risk, such as investing in the stock market, these twin studies reveal that around a third (30 per cent) of the variation in risk-taking behaviour is related to our biology. Impressive as this may sound, it does mean that the major influence on risky behaviours (the remaining 70 per cent) is not controlled by our genes. Rather, it comes down to life experiences which interact with our biology.

Important choices regarding ownership are not simply System 2 mathematical equations we coldly calculate in our heads, but also System 1 activity that fires the emotional centres of our brains.[67] To make decisions, our brains weigh up the likelihood of losses versus gains and these two sides of the same coin are processed in different circuitry. We may punch the air and feel the jubilant elation of a win, but that does not compare with the dull, sickening pain of loss that churns in our guts and seems to linger longer because remorse is a more powerful emotion than joy. When we anticipate making acquisitions at bargain prices, the reward centres of a region deep within our brain known as the ventral striatum light up, much as they do in anticipation of other positive experiences.[68] However, faced with the prospect of a loss on a deal, the punishment and pain circuitry, including the insula and amygdala, usually associated with painful experiences, is triggered.

Unless we are professional traders who cannot afford to get emotionally connected, then each decision we make is a neural trade-off in our brain between the potential pleasure of acquisition and the pain of paying for it. This explains why taking painkillers reduces the price that owners request when selling something.[69] Brain imaging can even predict those who are more risk averse by the higher neural responses generated by prospective losses compared to gains.[70] This emotional battle is exactly what traders are relying on as they try to sell us stuff that we really don't need, which is why they know that purchases that appeal to the heart rather than the head are more likely to be successful.

Wanting is different from needing because it is more to do with the psychological fulfilment we seek through what we can own. But it is what we could lose that seems to be the dominant force in our decision-making. And when it comes to the things we own, then this loss is all the more potent for possessions that say something about us.

7
Letting Go

A BIRD IN THE HAND

As a young economics graduate in the early 1970s, Richard Thaler noted how one of his professors, a wine connoisseur, had two rules when it came to buying and selling. First, he would never pay more than $35 for a bottle of wine; and second, he would not sell a bottle unless he got more than $100. This strategy meant he was always going to make a profit, but it was also illogical. If you buy a bottle for $35 then you should sell it for any amount over your original purchase price, taking into consideration all the other factors that may have contributed to a change in valuation such as transport, inflation and so on. However, as Thaler observed, time after time, people put a much greater value on their possessions than others are willing to pay. This may seem obvious, but Thaler's observation was to mark the beginning of the new field of behavioural economics, for which he would eventually be awarded a Nobel prize in 2017.

Behavioural economics is the application of psychological biases to economic decisions and it overturned the standard models of commerce by introducing the vagaries of human decision-making. In their 'prospect theory', Kahneman and Tversky articulated a set of psychological principles that shape the way that we reason when it comes to decision-making.[1] Just like when calculating our social status and the time-limited joy we gain from purchases, our brains are biased. First, as discussed previously, evaluating any change in our circumstances is relative to some point. Whether we stand to gain or lose something depends on what we have had in the past. Our experiences are shaped by past events, from the sweetness of a drink to the boredom of watching a play for the umpteenth time. Remember the hedonic adaptation that we all succumb to? We compare all experiences against what we are used to. The second principle Kahneman and Tversky described is that any change is relative to the current value you have. So not only are past experiences relevant but so is your current position. A starving man is going to accept any handout even though he may have been rich in the past. Finally, and most importantly, the prospect of loss weighs more heavily in our minds than the prospect of gain. We want at least two birds in our bush before we let go of the one in our hand.

When Thaler read about prospect theory, suddenly much of human economic behaviour made more sense. People are not rational when it comes to ownership. They have an inherent bias to overvalue their possessions and it can be explained by loss aversion, as prospect theory predicted. Just like the simple gamble on the toss of a coin, on average, people must be paid twice as much to give up a possession than they are willing to pay to acquire it.[2] This may seem to make good business sense – buyers and sellers both try to maximize their gains from a transaction – but the main reason comes down to ownership and the over-inflated sense of personal loss by the seller.

We overvalue things as soon as they come into our possession. This bias, known as the 'endowment effect',[3] is one of the most robust phenomena in behavioural economics. In short, we expect more money for selling an item than we would be willing to pay for acquiring the same item. There is always an imbalance between the vendor and the buyer, but more so if the item for sale is a personal possession.

Many manipulations can induce endowment effects. Bidding at an auction on an item that you have not yet acquired is more likely to lead to further bids – a ploy that most auction houses appreciate will lead to a bidding frenzy.[4] Simply holding or touching a potential purchase is sufficient to trigger endowment.[5] When the salesperson asks you just to try on a suit or go for a spin in the car, they are relying on the endowment effect – the first taste of ownership – to overcome the toughest barrier to a purchase.

Although common, the endowment effect is not universal. When researchers started to look at different societies and cultures, something remarkable was discovered: the individualist–collectivist dimension influenced the power of the endowment effect. In one remarkable cross-cultural study, social psychologist William Maddux and a team of international collaborators studied college students from Western and Eastern backgrounds in the US, Canada, China and Japan.[6] Students were assigned to be either 'buyers' or 'sellers'. The sellers were given a mug with their school's logo on it and told that they owned it but to choose a price between $0 and $10 that they would be willing to sell it at. Buyers were asked how much they would pay for the same mug. As predicted, the sellers' average price of $4.83 was twice the buyers' average offer of $2.34. However, when the researchers looked at the cultural backgrounds of the students separately, sellers from Western backgrounds asked for more ($5.02) compared to the average buyer's offer ($1.78). In contrast, students from Eastern backgrounds were much closer in what sellers requested ($4.68) to what buyers offered ($3.08).

Then, with another group of Chinese students, the experimenters manipulated the participants' self-construal before the transaction. They asked the Eastern students to write either a brief essay about their friendships and camaraderie with other people, or an essay about their unique character and skills and how they might stand out compared with other people. When the students wrote about other people, the endowment effect was reduced, but if they wrote about themselves it was increased. Finally, the researchers manipulated the relationship between owners and their mugs by getting Eastern and Western students to write about how important the mug was to them, or how unimportant. In Western students, this meaningful manipulation increased the endowment effect compared to Eastern students, which produced the opposite effect. In other words, forcing Western students to focus on their possession made them value it more, whereas Eastern students valued it comparatively less. Clearly, the endowment effect is not inevitable but rather reflects the way we consider our possessions in relation to our self-construal, which is shaped by cultural norms of individualism or collectivism.

If the endowment effect is shaped by culture, can we show the seeds of this effect in children before culture kicks in? We decided to investigate the development of the endowment effect in very young children using priming of the self or others in how they value toys. Normally, the endowment effect is not observed in Western children until they are around five to six years old,[7] so we targeted three- to four-year-olds. At this age, the concept of value is beyond the grasp

Smiley scale used to elicit relative evaluations of toys by pre-schoolers

of children, but if they place one toy on a smiley face on a scale and another on a face with a frown then we can assume the children prefer one toy more than the other, which is a kind of relative value.

Sandra Weltzien and I began by getting the toddlers to place different toys on the smiley scale to show that they understood the game, and then gave them two identical spinning-top toys. If they placed them on the same smiley face, then it meant they thought they were of the same value. Sandra then gave the children one of the tops and asked them to draw a picture either of themselves, their friend or a farm scene. Afterwards she asked the children to rate the toys again, including the two spinning tops. Just like Maddux's adults, those children asked to draw themselves valued their spinning top more than the identical top that did not belong to them. In this experiment, therefore, we were able to induce an endowment effect at an age when it is not normally found by getting children to focus on their selves.[8]

If the bias to overvalue possession is related to self-construal, then the recent discovery that individuals with autism lack an endowment effect is consistent with this account.[9] Their expression of self-construal differs from typical individuals. High-functioning individuals with autism spectrum disorder without language impairments have difficulty using the first-person pronouns 'I' and 'me'[10] and have impaired autobiographical memory.[11] Maybe this different awareness of their psychological self is why they do not overvalue their possessions as most of us do.

The difference in self-construal across the independent–collectivist divide can also explain the cultural variations in the endowment effect. Consider again the Hazda tribe of Northern Tanzania, one of the last hunter-gather societies left in the world. As we saw in previous chapters, they tend to have few possessions and operate a demand-sharing policy whereby members of the tribe take things they need if they are not being used. It is no surprise, then, that when tested with trading experiments using culturally appropriate items, many of the Hazda do not show the endowment effect.[12] Why is this?

One reason is that hunter-gatherers have few possessions other than those that are necessary to maintain their nomadic lifestyle. They simply cannot carry much stuff around and so possessions are not a priority for them. This is why they developed demand-sharing as a way of optimizing the amount of materials and resources they need to carry among themselves. However, there is one interesting exception to this – the Hazda who have been exposed to Western influence. When anthropologists studied this subgroup, they discovered evidence of the endowment bias in those who interacted frequently with tourists or had the experience of trading at markets. When forced to trade with Westerners, the Hazda develop biases too.

Successful traders cannot afford to have a strong endowment effect. If they were always to ask twice what people were willing to pay for items, then they would soon be out of business. This explains why experience as a trader reduces the endowment effect in that their asking prices are more closely matched to those the consumer's willing to pay.[13] Again, imaging studies point to the reduction in the pain of loss. Experienced traders show lower activation of the negative loss centres of the insula compared to inexperienced traders who are still treating sales as a loss.[14] However, it remains uncertain as to whether experience as a trader diminishes the endowment effect over time or rather that those individuals who become successful traders are less attached to possessions in the first place. The endowment effect may be a System 1 bias to avoid losses, but it can be overridden by the cultural context of the value we put on possessions as well as goals to make a profit.

THE THRILL OF THE CHASE

What compels us to acquire in the first place? Why do some people describe themselves as shopaholics? You might imagine it is the acquisition that is so satisfying but, as many hardcore shoppers will attest, it is the anticipation of the acquisition that is so powerful. People can work themselves up into a frenzy. Law-abiding citizens can become lawless mobs – as witnessed by the growing phenomenon of 'Black Friday', where shoppers fight over shopping bargains, fuelled by the prospect of gain. People have even been killed in the stampede to get a bargain.[15]

Jean-Paul Sartre, in a twist on William James's quote about 'a man's Self is the sum total of all that he CAN call his', wrote: 'Man is not the sum of what he has already, but rather the sum of what he does not yet have, of what he could have.' For Sartre, it is the pursuit of goals, rather than acquisition, that defines who we are. His insight is consistent with the neuroscience of motivation. In the brain there are different mechanisms operating depending on whether you already own something or whether you desire ownership.[16] Objects already perceived as extensions of the self are incorporated into the neural networks that generate the sense of self. In contrast, objects that you desire may appeal to your sense of self, but they also trigger systems that respond to novelty and the thrill of the chase. This is the 'must have' feeling you get when you see the latest Apple product if you happen to be an Apple groupie. Several years back, I went through a period of collecting old movie posters that I bid for on eBay. I would log on to auctions to buy posters, but the anticipation was more exciting than actually acquiring the purchase when it arrived in the post. I collected well over fifty posters before I finally realized that I could not display them all and the thrill of the chase had worn off.

If you think about it, we spend a lot more time pursuing pleasures than consuming them. Common to most pleasurable experiences is novelty – remember the Coolidge effect? As the Stanford University neuroscientist Brian Knutson points out, a long tradition of human exploration, from crossing the oceans to climbing mountains and stepping on the moon, is testimony to the motivating force of novelty.[17] It is also a form of ownership to be the first, which is why we celebrate and remember these individuals. Goals that are easily obtained are less rewarding than achievements that take time and effort. Why is this?

One explanation comes from the way we are motivated to achieve goals by different systems in the brain. Nestled deep within a bend of the brainstem – the oldest part of the brain that supports all the vital functions – is the ventral tegmental area (VTA). This contains dopamine neurons responsible for activating the motivational systems of the brain that respond to novelty and reward. One of these areas sitting atop the brainstem is the striatum, an interconnected set of systems that control our behaviours in relation to punishments and rewards. In 1954, Canadian psychologists James Olds and Peter Milner, from McGill University, were conducting research on brain learning mechanisms in rats using electrodes to stimulate different areas when they stumbled upon what was, literally, an *exciting* finding.[18] Rats with an electrode implanted in their septal (the rat equivalent of the human striatum) would repeatedly push a lever to deliver a brief electric shock directly to their brain even at the expense of drinking and eating. They had become addicted to self-stimulation because it was so exciting. VTA dopaminergic neurons also project to the prefrontal cortex where executive decisions are made. This is where we get our passion to pursue. Together the VTA, striatum and prefrontal cortex represent the motivational circuits that identify our goals, and then set about pursuing them.

Subsequent research since the original discovery of pleasure centres in the brain has confirmed that VTA dopaminergic neurons are activated by a range of addictive human pursuits including sex, drugs and rock'n'roll.[19] To that list you can add shopping. In one study of patients who were administered drugs that alter dopaminergic activity for the control of their Parkinson's disease, one of the side-effects was an increase in gambling, sex addiction and compulsive shopping.[20] Each of these is associated with anticipatory pleasure. As the character Dr Frank-N-Furter in *The Rocky Horror Picture Show* teases us, it is the anticipation, not the conquest, that is so pleasurable. In the case of shopping, Knutson and his colleagues demonstrated that the anticipation of a bargain activates the VTA, whereas high prices or a financial loss register in the disgust centres of the insula region of the brain.[21]

We assume consumerism is motivated by the pleasure of acquisition, but in fact it is the pursuit that really compels us to constantly fill our lives with stuff. When we are motivated to acquire, we have a goal that is intrinsically rewarding. We may feel disappointed or thwarted if we fail to achieve that goal but, equally, we are not satiated by success because acquisitions rarely deliver the expected pleasures we anticipate. Even if our acquisitions do provide us with pleasure, that emotion easily habituates and so we set off again to seek out the next must-have thing.

Before we even take possession, our brains are savouring the prospects of gain. Once we own them, we endow our possessions with excessive value because they are an extension of our self. The problem is that many of us quickly habituate to them and then set off again for the next conquest. These are powerful emotional drives that are not easily satiated by possession. Some people simply never stop acquiring, which eventually can take over their lives and they can literally be smothered by ownership.

UNABLE TO LET GO

One of the most extreme forms of abnormal ownership manifests as hoarding disorder, a condition of peculiar interest to the general public. A television show on American cable network A&E called *Hoarders* generated record numbers of viewers. Then there were related spin-off shows – *Hoarder SOS, The Hoarder Next Door, Britain's Biggest Hoarders* and even *Hoarding – Buried Alive*. It turns out many people take a voyeuristic pleasure in watching a show about hoarders, perhaps because many people love to marvel at the dysfunctional lives of others.

Hoarding has deep roots. Many animals hoard. Insects, birds and mammals stockpile food. Hoarding disorder could be considered a normal foraging behaviour that has got out of hand. Every Christmas and New Year when supermarkets are closed only for a couple of days, shelves empty as the general public regresses to a frenzy of panic buying to ensure that they will be safely fed over the festive period. Even in good times, when resources are abundant, every household has a stock of food in the fridge or tins in the larder. It's a good strategy to make provision for lean times, but humans are different in that some stockpile items of no intrinsic value that prevent them from living healthy lives.

Hoarding disorder is a specific form of pathological collecting where the sufferer is unable to discard objects to the extent that their homes become so cluttered that they are unable to move around freely. These houses often draw the attention of local authorities when they become infested firetraps. Unlike obsessive collectors who seek out specific items to acquire, the hoarder collects almost anything. The most common items are newspapers and magazines, but a true hoarder throws away very little.

Around 1 in 50 members of the general public have a hoarding problem in that they accumulate excessive amounts of items that eventually affect their lives. It can start in childhood but the incidence of hoarding increases with age, with a 20 per cent increase with every five additional years.[22] The volume of stuff presents a risk to health and, in some rare cases, death when the owner has been crushed by the collapsing weight.[23] Australia's Melbourne Fire Brigade estimates that one-quarter of preventable fire-related deaths in the over fifties are due to hoarding.[24]

There are a number of reasons that hoarding disorder arises, including a genetic component as the incidence runs in families.[25] It has a multitude of associated risk factors including anxiety, depression, negative life events, disrupted childhoods and various cognitive dysfunctions related to suppressing urges and controlling thoughts. Hoarders often talk about their possessions in terms of their potential to be useful but the one thing that is common to hoarding is the fear of loss. Hoarders typically rationalize their behaviour with the assertion that things are valuable or potentially valuable and can be re-used or that they are part of their identity. In all these cases, hoarding seems to provide a sense of comfort and familiarity.[26]

Hoarding used to be considered a subtype of obsessive-compulsive disorder but is now regarded as a disorder in its own category. There is even some evidence that hoarding activates distinct brain areas. Hoarders and those with obsessive-compulsive disorder had their brains scanned as they watched either their mail or letters belonging to someone else being shredded.[27] When they had to decide whether to keep or shred their post, hoarders experienced heightened anxiety, indecisiveness, sadness and regret compared to those with obsessive-compulsive disorder. These emotions were associated with circuitry in the frontal regions of the brain that are usually associated with inhibition and evaluating risky situations.[28] Moreover, the extent of brain activation predicted the severity of their hoarding disorder and self-report measures of the discomfort they experienced when faced with the prospect of discarding possessions. They literally felt sick at the prospect of losing something.

It may be no coincidence then that these are the very same brain regions activated by the endowment effect where there is an over-valuation of personal possessions.[29] In a sense, the hoarder exhibits the extreme form of the extended self, as it is only when possessions become owned that the disorder manifests. Everything we own is registered in the brain as 'ours' as opposed to someone else's, but whereas most individuals can readily update, replace, renew or discard their extended material identity, the hoarder cannot let go for fear of self-loss. They may rationalize their actions as prudent foresight but, on balance, the price they pay in terms of mental and physical health – as well as the cost to relationships – simply does not add up.

Some possessions are more personal, and hence considered more a part of us, than others. For most people, their home is perhaps the clearest extension of their self since our identities are intricately linked to the place where we spend most of our time. When we say something or someone is 'homely', we are describing a set of attributes that are comforting, safe and reassuring. 'Homemade' and 'home-baked' are descriptions that evoke the personal touch. We talk of homes having hearts and souls as if they were living entities. Some of our strongest feelings are for things that we associate with our homes, which is why we defend the right to retain ownership of them so vehemently.

Faced with the loss of their property, some people take extreme measures to prevent anyone easily taking away what they perceive they own. Or they deliberately sabotage the property. Apparently, every estate agent has a horror story to tell.[30] People will foul, booby-trap or destroy homes when faced with repossession. However, the worst spiteful acts are not against property but against people who are considered the property of others.

The leading cause of death around the world in women of reproductive age is murder by a current or former partner.[31] In many instances, this violence results from separation or the threat of losing someone. In the ultimate act of self-destruction when faced with loss, some deranged partners – and it is usually men with no previous criminal record – will annihilate their families and possessions before killing themselves.[32] Why else would people commit such destruction if not because of a distorted sense of self and ownership?

The flipside of family annihilations in Western culture is the corresponding crime of so-called 'honour' killings in Asian cultures, which typically involve the murder of daughters and wives who are believed to have brought shame on the family. Although predominantly associated with Middle Eastern and South Asian countries, 'honour' killings are found around the world. In both tragic scenarios of family annihilations and 'honour' killings, the integrity of self-identity, albeit as an individual in the West or as a family in Asian cultures, is judged to have been violated. Such horrendous crimes are a distortion of what many regard as normal attitudes about ownership. We naturally consider spouses and family members as an extension of ourselves. We will all experience the death of loved ones, which is why the condolence 'I am sorry for your loss' captures this ownership relationship so aptly. However, these personal relationships do not entitle the ultimate act of ownership – *jus abutendi*, to treat property as we wish, even to the point of destruction.

HOME IS WHERE THE HEART IS

In 1997, Susette Kelo, a nurse with a life-long passion to live in a traditional house overlooking water, had her dream come true when she purchased a Victorian clapboard house in need of renovation that looked out over the Thames River in Fort Trumbull, a working-class neighbourhood of New London, Connecticut. Susette loved her house and threw herself into restoring the property. She decided to paint it pink – 'Odessa Rose' from Benjamin Moore's historic collection. It was in a run-down part of town, but it was hers.

Less than a year later, her world was thrown into turmoil. Susette was not the only person looking to find a prime waterside property. To revitalize the area and bring in investment to create new jobs, the New London Development Corporation (NLDC) planned to redevelop Fort Trumbull into a prime waterside area tailored to the recent arrival of the multinational pharmaceutical giant Pfizer.

Seven months after moving in, Susette received notification from the NLDC that her house, along with around ninety other properties, was subject to a compulsory purchase order under the power of a legal manoeuvre known as 'eminent domain'. Not every resident wanted to move. Some of these residents had been in their houses for generations. Susette's neighbour, Mrs Wilhelmina Dery, had been born in the house she occupied and wanted to live out her remaining days there. Money was not enough compensation for that wish. For Susette Kelo, who became the lead named plaintiff in the subsequent court case, it was not the money, but the principle.

The legal battles in the courts raged on for nearly ten years until Kelo v. The City of New London eventually ended up at the US Supreme Court in 2005. The City argued that the redevelopment was for public use because it would bring economic growth to a deprived area. In spite of widespread public outrage in this David and Goliath confrontation between humble homeowners and the might of 'big pharma', the Supreme Court judges, in a five to four split, ruled in favour of the City of New London. The properties at Fort Trumbull would be compulsorily purchased and then bulldozed to the ground to make way for the new urban village that Pfizer wanted.

The fallout from the Kelo v. The City of New London case was tumultuous and led to debates at the national level. The public disapproval rating for the Kelo decision was around 80–90 per cent, a figure higher than for many other controversial US Supreme Court cases. Others were more pragmatic. Both the *Washington Post* and the *New York Times* welcomed the decision as common sense, and for the greater good to act in the public's interest. Libertarians were outraged. In a country where private property is privileged to the extent that you are entitled to defend it with considerable, and sometimes lethal, force this ruling meant that any private property could be taken away in the interests of commercial gain.

Why were people so outraged? Why were Susette and her neighbours so reluctant to move for the potential economic benefit that redevelopment would bring to the community? Were they not being selfish in refusing to budge when so many desperately need the jobs that the new development would bring? Jeremy Bentham advocated that utilitarianism compels us to take decisions which are in the best interests to most. Or as Spock says, in his much-lauded death scene from *Star Trek II: The Wrath of Khan* (1982), 'The needs of the many outweigh the needs of the few.'

Why all the complaints, when property owners were adequately compensated? To investigate the psychology behind the Kelo v. The City of New London case, two lawyers at Northwestern University in Chicago conducted a study to determine just how much compensation should have been offered for a hypothetical property and whether it really mattered who ended up with the land.[33] Using an online survey of adults, they presented differing eminent domain scenarios, including whether a property had been in the family for two years or a hundred years. They also varied the intended use of the acquired land, for building a) a children's hospital, b) a shopping mall, or c) for some unspecified use. Respondents were told that the property under consideration was valued at $200,000 by an independent appraiser and that they would be paid all relocation expenses. How much would these adults be willing to accept for the property?

The lawyers found that the intended use of the land did not really play a major role in people's decisions but rather the length of occupation was the most significant factor. Around 20 per cent were willing to accept the $200,000 offer on the table, but 80 per cent wanted more. Over a third wanted another $100,000 and around 10 per cent overall said they would refuse to sell at any price: they felt it would be morally wrong if their family had lived in the house for a hundred years. However, this nostalgic attitude is not shared universally across cultures. With the Hong Kong territories reverting to Chinese rule in 1997, Hong Kong businessmen bought up historic properties in Vancouver during the 1990s. Rather than valuing the provenance of these historic buildings, they began tearing them down to erect so-called 'monster houses' that occupied most of the plots of land, much to the consternation of the local residents.[34] This was partly an economic decision to maximize the use of land, but it also reflected a cultural difference. When it comes to buying houses, the Chinese typically prefer brand-new properties. A survey of Chinese potential property buyers looking for houses in the US revealed that they not only prefer new houses but the least important factor when it comes to buying a property is the character and uniqueness of the home, in comparison to Westerners who preferentially look for older buildings with charm.[35] How odd it must seem to Eastern eyes when homeowners pay large amounts of money to reclamation yards to acquire and re-install second-hand original features taken from demolished houses!

Back in New London, the City Hall officials were not so sentimental. Susette Kelo eventually sold her house and moved to a new location in Connecticut. She is still bitter and feels her home was stolen. Despite the Supreme Court decision, her neighbour Mrs Dery was able to spend her remaining time in her home, dying in March 2006, eight months after the court ruling but before she was to have been removed forcibly. She died just a few feet away from where she was born the year the First World War ended.

Kelo's little pink house did not eventually succumb to the wrecker's ball. A local builder, Avner Gregory, purchased the house for $1 from the developers, dismantled it and reassembled it in downtown New London. He offered Susette the opportunity to rent it, but she turned down the invitation. She wanted to move on. Ironically, the little pink house has now become a visitor attraction, listed as one of Connecticut's historic buildings at 36 Franklin Street.

As for the influx of wealth and redevelopment promised by the NLDC plan, the project collapsed after Pfizer decided to relocate with a loss of 1,400 jobs. The city spent $78 million bulldozing homes and preparing the area for development, and yet the land still stands empty save for a colony of feral cats that has taken up residency. Money had prevailed over sentimental attachment.

SHAKY FOUNDATIONS

Owning your own home is not just an economic statement but a psychological affirmation of identity. It is not uncommon for survivors of natural disasters, where homes have been demolished, to return even when they are housed in temporary accommodation. In 2016, the historic town of Amatrice in Italy's Apennine mountain range was hit by a powerful earthquake and was almost completely flattened. At the epicentre of devastation, aerial photographs show only one modern building amid the rubble of the neighbouring medieval premises. Almost a hundred years earlier, the city of L'Aquila, near to Amatrice, lost around 30,000 lives following an earthquake in 1915. In 2009, L'Aquila was hit again with a loss of 300 lives. You might think that people would learn. The Apennines, like all mountain ranges, were formed by the constant clash of tectonic plates in the Earth's upper crust, forcing the land mass to buckle and sheer upwards. This region sits atop the African and Eurasian continental plates. There have, and always will be, powerful earthquakes and eruptions – 'geohazards' – in Italy and yet the Italians are reluctant to move or reconstruct their villages with modern buildings designed to withstand earthquakes. It seems foolhardy.

There is an obvious financial incentive to keep the historic buildings that form a major part of Italy's tourism industry, worth $180 billion annually, but there are also deeper issues of ownership that figure in the Italian psyche. Marco Cusso, an Italian structural engineer who specializes in earthquake damage, pointed out: 'Our approach is not to demolish what is unsafe. We always try to fix or strengthen in order to keep it because most of these things are part of our identity. I don't know if it's right or not but it's like that.'[36]

When people have occupied, lived and died in a particular area of land for generations, one can imagine their identity seeping into the land. To readily give it up or to sell it would be considered taboo as it would be a violation of its sacred value. People are willing to sacrifice their lives for their homeland even if they are offered alternatives that are much more useful in terms of fertility and resources. How else can we understand the conflict over land in Israel that to many outsiders looks like nothing more than barren desert?

Psychologist Paul Rozin looked at attitudes to swapping land among Israeli Jewish college students.[37] In response to the question, 'Is there any piece of land in Israel that you would never be willing to trade under any circumstance?', 59 per cent answered 'Jerusalem'. In response to the prospect of trading Har Herzl, Israel's national cemetery in Jerusalem, which holds the remains of some major historical figures, 83 per cent of Israelis agreed that they 'would never trade it for other land or anything else'.

Jerusalem is a fascinating, sacred city at the centre of the ancient world. Everywhere you turn, you encounter some holy site or ancient relic. It is also one of the most passionate places on the planet where conflicts and tensions over ownership, territory and control are constantly balanced on a knife edge. The Old City is carved up into four different quarters under the control of distinct religious groups – Armenian, Jewish, Christian and Muslim. Even the Church of the Holy Sepulchre is divided into different sections under the control of separate factions of the Christian faith. Depending on who you are, there are certain places you can and cannot go.

The Middle East is a complex cauldron of conflict where there does not appear to be any long-lasting co-operation and co-existence. Modern civilization began here in the Fertile Crescent over 7,000 years ago with the development of agriculture. With settlement and the accumulated wealth from agriculture and associated trade came the inevitable disputes over ownership. Ever since, there has been conflict in the region between warring factions, each with some historical claim. The Israeli–Palestinian situation is just another in a long line of bitter disputes. The State of Israel was created in 1948 for the surviving European Jews after the Second World War, but this involved taking over territory previously held by Palestinian Arabs. From the Palestinian perspective, this was theft of their land.

The word '*intifada*' is an Arabic word derived from a verb meaning 'to shake off' and has come to refer to the Palestinian uprising against Israeli oppression. In 1987, the first Palestinian intifada took place to shake off the Israeli occupation of the West Bank and Gaza strip. Much of the disputed territories are poor quality land but their symbolic value is priceless. The second intifada, in 2000, was triggered by Ariel Sharon, an Israeli politician, visiting the Temple Mount in Jerusalem – one of the holiest sites in Islam. As a Jew, his visit to this sacred Muslim site was considered provocative and started a riot. What is remarkable is that, like much of Jerusalem, the Temple Mount is also venerated by Jews and Christians. Many of the holy sites in this ancient city are associated with historical events or individuals from the different religions and have changed hands multiple times over the centuries following various invasions and conflicts. Each side argues over the rightful ownership.

The wars in the Middle East might seem to be based on religious differences, but they are also all about control. However, because the conflict is framed in terms of religion and sacred values, each side is motivated by a deeper sense of ownership. You cannot trade identity. Negotiating a settlement will have to take into consideration the sacred value of the land under dispute. It would be naive to offer financial compensation or alternative relocations, because this would fail to take into consideration the emotional connection with the land. Indeed, any financial settlement would be regarded as sacrilegious by putting a price on something which should be priceless. So, each side is forced to continue fighting.

DOES OWNERSHIP MAKE US HAPPIER?

We extend our individual selves into the world through the power of ownership, and we signal our identity and status to others through our possessions. It is not so much the value of possessions we lose that affects us but the extent to which they represent who we are. This relationship varies individually as well as from culture to culture, but we all construct a sense of self to some extent through ownership. It explains our motivations to acquire more but also our reluctance to let go of what we have. If we are going to tackle territorial disputes, let alone the problem of relentless materialism and consumerism, then we need to understand this peculiar relationship that humans have with their stuff.

Our irrational behaviour arises because we identify too closely with what we think we own. There is an inherent irony operating here though. We overvalue what we have and are reluctant to let it go because it represents who we are, but we also easily get used to most of our possessions. We set out to acquire more stuff in a relentless, yet ultimately unfulfilling, quest to enhance who we are. This may lead us to feel more successful, but the paradox is that in accumulating more stuff, we are increasingly less satisfied.

No doubt, many readers will reject the claim that materialistic goals are unsatisfying. In fact, they may regard the underlying warning message of this book as not relevant to them at all. Many are convinced that they will be satisfied with owning more than they need as their whole motivation in life is premised on this belief. Ownership is central to our morality, politics and worldview, but the only way to settle the argument is to look at the data – not from one or two WEIRD studies but from as many studies by as many people as you can find investigating the link between materialism and well-being.

Such studies of all the available research are known as meta-analyses, which are the gold standard in science because, rather than relying on any one study, research group or individual scientist who may be biased to find a particular outcome, meta-analyses average results across large numbers of studies, thereby providing a much more balanced and accurate assessment of the field. And the jury is in. To date, the most recent and comprehensive meta-analysis – by Helga Dittmar and her colleagues from the University of Essex of over 750 measures from over 250 independent studies – demonstrates 'a clear, consistent negative association between a broad array of types of personal well-being and people's belief in and prioritization of materialistic pursuits in life'.[38] This holds true irrespective of culture, age and gender. Some factors reduce the relationship but in no instance did the researchers find a positive relationship.

If we were content with ownership, then we would stop acquiring more stuff. But the combination of the thrill of the chase, the need for status and the crippling sense at the prospect of loss reveal that ownership is one of the strongest human urges and does not easily respond to reason. Of course, most of us think we are the exception, but then, that is why we are possessed.

Epilogue

RACE TO THE END

'A person who owns a nice home, a new car, good furniture, the latest appliances, is recognized by others as someone who has passed the test of personhood in our society.'

Mihaly Csikszentmihalyi[1]

For many people, our possessions prove our worth to society: the more we have the more worthwhile we are. This is wrong for a number of reasons, if not for the simple fact that ownership comes at a cost to society. If we value ownership simply for the sake of accumulated possessions we have, then we are validating behaviour which is ultimately harmful to others. The more we possess, the more inequality that creates. Not only is this morally questionable, environmentally disastrous and politically disruptive, but the science tells us that the relentless pursuit of possessions is unfulfilling and, for some, more miserable in the long run. We should live simpler, less cluttered, less competitive lives. Unfortunately, for most of us, it's only at the end of our lives that we come to this realization.

But we can't live without ownership either, as it is the basis for what holds our society together. Ownership is an incentive. We strive to improve our lot in life. People like success and are spurred on by ownership as reward for that effort. Innovation and progress are mostly the consequence of competition. When it comes to beating our rivals, we up our game and we expect the spoils of success. Nor are all the world's most successful individuals blindly accumulating wealth just to sit on the biggest pile of money. The Giving Pledge, set up by Bill and Melinda Gates with Warren Buffett in 2010, which so far has 187 billionaires willing to give away their wealth, is an antidote to the cynical view that humans are incapable of changing their possessive nature. Many of these individuals realize that not only is inherited wealth unfair, but it can be a curse to their children by removing the motivation for individual self-fulfilment and achievement.

At both the individual and group level, ownership provides a mechanism for human progress, but it also harbours the potential seeds of destruction. We behave as if we are possessed – as if there is some external influence that is controlling us. This controlling influence has its roots in biology. We have seen how ownership emerged from a competitive drive that is inherent to all life on Earth. All animals compete, but those that live in social groups have evolved strategies to protect and share resources. Co-operation and sharing are found in other animals but ownership is a social contract that is uniquely human, since it requires brains capable of theory of mind, detailed communication of intent, predicting the future, remembering the past and understanding concepts of reciprocity, convention, inheritance, laws and justice. Non-humans may exhibit some of these skills in rudimentary form but only humans possess the full repertoire of components necessary for establishing the concept of ownership.

Ownership may be a mere human concept, as Bentham surmised, but it is a powerful enough idea to have enabled stable societies to emerge. Many other animals live in social groups, but they do not operate with the principles of ownership that enable legacies. In non-human societies, hierarchies are constantly shifting as each new generation battles for dominance. In human society, ownership provides mechanisms for relative continuity from one generation to the next when it comes to the distribution of limited resources. This stability within human societies is how our species transformed ourselves from nomadic hunter-gatherers into settled communities where agriculture, technology and education could thrive. In short, ownership enabled human civilization to become the establishment. But therein lies the problem. Establishments are resistant to change, which is why the inequality that ownership creates is so entrenched.

In 2017, a video called the '$100 race' went viral with over 50 million views on social media.[2] It dramatically illustrated how inherited wealth and privilege provided an unfair advantage in life. One hundred US teenagers were told to line up to race for a $100 banknote, but before they got started, the referee introduced a few conditions. If they answered 'yes' then they could take two steps forward. If the condition did not apply, they remained where they stood. Runners were told to take two steps forward if their parents were still both married. Take two steps forward if they had private education. Take two steps forward if they did not have to worry about money, and so on. After about ten such instructions, before the race even got started, the leaders out in front were predominantly white males, whereas those left back at the starting line were mostly people of colour. Despite their best efforts, the race was effectively over for them before it had begun. All the advantages that the leaders were given had nothing to do with aptitudes, abilities, individual choices or decisions. They were mostly to do with inherited wealth and all the opportunities and benefits it provides. How can those without these privileges pass the test of personhood when the odds are stacked so much against them? That's why ownership perpetuates unfair societies.

Since the beginning of civilization itself, we have been considering the morality of ownership, and worrying about its costs. But I hope to have opened your eyes to the personal reasons why we are possessed. Ownership is not simply a moral and political issue. Rather, the psychology of ownership reveals something about what motivates us at our core. Possessions are a means of broadcasting our success. Like other animals, we signal in order to increase our chances of reproducing our genes, but our possessions satisfy a much deeper need to be valued by others beyond the family circle. Emotional attachment to immediate family is not uncommon in the animal kingdom but we humans uniquely seek emotional sustenance from society at large. We want strangers to notice us too. As Adam Smith pointed out, rich men glory in their ownership because they draw upon themselves the attention of the world. But not everyone can be rich, and so this creates distorted conditions of competition that no longer serve the biological imperative. Ownership has become a drive for recognition in its own right.

Our sense of self-worth is almost entirely defined by how we evaluate ourselves relative to others. As we noted, such comparison is a fundamental component in that our brains operate by calculating relative status as the most meaningful metric in life. A spike of electrical activity by a neuron is only meaningful in relation to its previous activity and that of its connected neighbours. This principle applies at every level, from the basic sensory processing of nerve cells all the way up the nervous system to the comparisons we make with others and the emotional lives we lead. If others praise us, we feel happy. If they ignore us, we feel despair.

This social comparison is foolish because we overestimate the importance of other people's opinions. We are also very inaccurate when it comes to judging others. Not only are other people less interested in us than we imagine, but their opinions are often superficial, guided by prejudices and full of errors. As the philosopher Arthur Schopenhauer warned in 1851, 'Whoever attaches a lot of value to the opinions of others, pays them too much honour.'[3] And yet, who is immune to the opinions of others?

The popularity and influence of modern social media such as Facebook and Instagram have amplified our dependency on approval. Social comparisons fuel our feelings of inadequacy when we compare our successes to others. As novelist Gore Vidal quipped, 'Every time a friend succeeds, I die a little.' We are constantly reminded that others seem to be doing better and leading much more fulfilling lives than ours. We endorse the value of other people's posts by our 'likes'. We re-tweet their opinions. We experience FOMO – 'fear of missing out' – and think that we are ignored while everyone else has been invited to the best parties. Like false prophets, we desperately seek followers to justify our self-worth. We are human meerkats, always on the look-out, but rather than surveying the area for potential threats in order to protect the group, we are socially peacocking in an effort to be recognized – desperately seeking approval. But the hedonic treadmill of social comparison is a never-ending perpetual motion machine.[4] You can never have enough adulation.

In a world where everyone wants to be celebrated, social mobility provides a way to reach the top. But it also creates an unrealistic expectation that everyone can be a winner. This is typical of hierarchical societies that champion individualism and meritocracy. Those who have succeeded strive to hang on to their position of dominance, whereas those below are constantly struggling to displace them. Rather than levelling the playing field to allow everyone a chance to rise, meritocracy perpetuates the problem because we justify the inequalities that emerge in society. We admire the successful, aspire to be like them and generally think that if we make it, then we too should be able to enjoy the fruits of our labour.

But we must re-evaluate our time on this planet. The term 'rat race' originated with early psychological studies of rats running in mazes, but it came to mean the pointless and relentless pursuit of goals, as encouraged by modern working practices, with a corresponding failure to appreciate non-materialistic pursuits. As we noted earlier, once you get past the basic provisions to make life comfortable, accumulating more possessions does not make you happier, just more affirmed in your success; more assured that you are justified in your accumulation of wealth. Our systems of inheritance reassure us that we can leave our wealth to our children in the knowledge that they will be better equipped for their own race, but really, what kind of personal satisfaction can they achieve if you have already given them a head start?

Not only do possessions fail to generate the levels of happiness we expect, but the whole issue of happiness needs reconsideration. In the modern era, we have come to expect happiness as a basic human right. The 'pursuit of happiness' is enshrined in the US Declaration of Independence and the individualism that underpins the ownership culture tells us that we are responsible for our well-being. If you are unhappy, then it is your fault and you need to do something about it. As I said at the very beginning and have reiterated throughout this book, we think that possessions lead to happiness – hence the need for 'retail therapy' when you feel unhappy. While it is true that possessions may provide moments of hedonic pleasure, these eventually subside. For this reason, ownership cannot provide ever-lasting happiness – but then, such a state would be suspiciously peculiar and not natural. We all habituate to experiences and need the highs and lows of daily existence in order to recognize the good and bad times. If everything stayed at the same level, eventually you would not notice anything.

There is also something inherently wrong about the assumption that we need to be constantly happy. Today's marketing and self-help industries make us feel guilty if we are not happy, and thus we become increasingly dissatisfied, looking for ways to make ourselves better through our purchases. In the past, however, when life was 'nasty, brutish and short' – as Thomas Hobbes famously observed – unhappiness was considered a normal state of life. Indeed, some religious types, such as Protestant Puritans, took the words of Jesus, 'Blessed are ye that weep now: for ye shall laugh', as a literal command to lead a sombre life on Earth to ensure a happy afterlife. They actively discouraged earthly pleasures that could bring happiness. These extreme puritanical views are no longer common, but the modern ideal that we should always be happy is equally absurd. This expectation can only make us feel constantly inadequate, which leads us to strive for perfection.

Striving for success in the rat race seems to be the answer as it provides observable rewards. These rewards may attract the attention and aspiration of others, but equally they inspire negative emotions. Envy rears its ugly head when we compare ourselves to others, and what better focus than the material possessions we show off? Sometimes, however, people react against such displays. Vandalism is often motivated by envy of those with possessions. Negative emotions can range from benign emulation, where we want to be like another, to malicious immolation where we would prefer to see our competitors destroyed. But just like with benign or malignant tumours, you would be better without either.[5]

Added to these unrealistic expectations is a belief that we are never truly valued, which means we are never really going to be satisfied. Very few of us say 'I think I am receiving the full credit that I am due' or 'I am very fortunate', at least not unless we have had a wake-up call due to some life-threatening event such as a car crash or illness. Rather we justify our success as deserved and then set off to achieve the next goal we think will bring us the validation we seek. We may have moments of gratitude, but these are so easily overwhelmed by our constant comparisons. Clearly the question is not how to acquire more but, rather, how to be happy with what we have. This is why contemplation, meditation, mindfulness or simple reflection provide brief respites of happiness, because we get to savour the moment before the competitive urge takes hold again.

What we need is not more stuff but more time to appreciate what we have. This is where technology may ultimately liberate us from relentless material consumerism. But there may be future dangers to consider. As Professor of Innovation at Northwestern University's Kellogg School of Management, Robert Wolcott points out that throughout history the vast majority of humans have worked because they have had to.[6] But ever since the industrial revolution and, more recently, in the information age, jobs are fast disappearing as technology and artificial intelligence transform the working landscape. Today around 10 per cent of the US workforce are employed in the transport industry.[7] Within one generation, automation is likely to make this occupation obsolete in the same way that the armies of farm labourers no longer exist in industrialized countries.

Scientific advances could create technological unemployment. If in the future there is less work for all of us to do, how will we occupy our time? I posed this question to Sherry Turkle, an MIT sociologist, who replied that technological unemployment was a myth because, even if we do build the machines that remove the need for us to work, we will still grow old and infirm and need human contact and support. Despite the best innovations in robotics and artificial intelligence, we are never really going to build artificial people who can replace real humans. Even if we can produce replicants that are indistinguishable from humans, we'll always be checking to see if they are real. Only authentic individuals with their essential qualities will satisfy our basic emotional need to connect with other *people*.

What the technology will eventually provide, however, is more time for everyone; and given this is the most precious thing we all have, to a greater or lesser degree, then it is our duty to spend it wisely rather than in chasing possessions. Technology and increased life expectancy mean we will be spending more time looking after each other and, hopefully, the planet that we share. We need to turn away from individual ownership because it separates us as humans and sets us against each other in a foolish quest to acquire as much as possible and more than we need. Ownership may be in our nature, but it is not in our best interests. We need to exorcise this possession.

Acknowledgements

I have been conducting experiments on the development of ownership and sharing in children for some years now, and so I thought *Possessed* would be an easy book to write. However, it turned out to be much harder than I anticipated because, once you drill down into the topic, you find it touches just about every facet of human existence. The reach of the book is deliberately wide and I know that I have overstretched into domains that are beyond my areas of expertise. That said, these topics are all interrelated, and I hope I have managed to provide a framework that brings them together in a way that readers find as fascinating as I do.

The book was conceived and written during the political turmoil that began in 2016, and so it unintentionally ended up addressing how ownership relates to the current situation in Europe and the US. President Donald Trump is the focus of much criticism and it remains to be seen whether he is still in power when this book is published. I am adamant that his worldviews are not the way for humanity to prosper in the long run.

I am glad to have had the benefit of two editors – Laura Stickney of Allen Lane and Joan Bossert from Oxford University Press – who both brought enormous expertise and wisdom to bear upon a book that was in real danger of becoming unfocused and losing its message. I would also like to thank my copy editor Charlotte Ridings, who did a wonderful job. I am indebted to my agent, Katinka Matson, who supported this idea from the very start.

Finally, I would also like to thank colleagues and students who have shaped my thinking, and to mention a few specifically. Paul Bloom is not only a good friend but a constant source of inspiration.

When he first heard about my plans for this book at a meeting in New Orleans, he was tremendously enthusiastic, but there again, he always is. Many of his ideas are scattered across these pages. So too is the work of Robert Frank, Ori Friedman, Russell Belk and Daniel Kahneman. I would particularly like to thank Laurie Santos for her ideas and inspiration in understanding what makes us happy. There are a number of others I would like to thank, including Patricia Kanngiesser, Anna Kirsch, Susan Kucera, Gawain Bantle and Ashley Lee, who have provided support, great ideas and feedback. Patricia, in particular, provided original and valuable ideas that form much of the basis of the book. Finally, I would like to thank Sandra Weltzien, who not only undertook much of the research on children but has been a wonderful student and friend. She taught me about the Law of Jante and *hygge*. And, of course, I must thank my long-suffering family who have been so tolerant of me.

References

PROLOGUE

1 Gilbert, D. T. and Wilson, Timothy D. (2000), 'Miswanting: some problems in the forecasting of future affective states'. In J. P. Forgas, ed., *Thinking and Feeling: The Role of Affect in Social Cognition*. Cambridge: Cambridge University Press.

2 'Terrified grandad feared he would die while clinging to van as thief drove off', http://www.barrheadnews.com/news/trendingacrossscotland/14717683.Terrified_grandad_feared_he_would_die_while_clinging_to_van_as_thief_drove_off/.

3 'Mother clung to her car bonnet for 100 yards before being flung off into a lamppost as thief drove off with it', http://www.dailymail.co.uk/news/article-2549471/Mother-clung-car-bonnet-100-yards-flung-lamppost-thief-drove-it.html.

4 Stephenson, J., et al. (2013), 'Population, development and climate change: links and effects on human health', *Lancet*, published online 11 July 2013.

5 http://www.worldwatch.org/sow11.

6 https://yougov.co.uk/topics/politics/articles-reports/2016/01/08/fsafasf. Only 11% of respondents in this 2016 poll thought the world was getting better, compared to 58% who thought it was getting worse.

7 Pinker, S. (2018), *Enlightenment Now*. London: Allen Lane.

1. DO WE REALLY OWN ANYTHING?

1 *Finders Keepers* (2015), directed by Bryan Carberry and Clay Tweel. Firefly Theater and Films.

2   Van de Vondervoort, J. W. and Friedman, O. (2015), 'Parallels in pre-schoolers' and adults' judgments about ownership rights and bodily rights', *Cognitive Science*, 39, 184–98.

3   Bland, B. (2008), 'Singapore legalises compensation payments to kidney donors', *British Medical Journal*, 337: a2456, doi:10.1136/bmj.a2456.

4   Sax, J. L. (1999), *Playing Darts with a Rembrandt: Public and Private Rights in Cultural Treasures*. Ann Arbor, MI: University of Michigan Press.

5   Howley, K. (2007), 'Who owns your body parts? Everyone's making money in the market for body tissue except the donors', http://reason.com/archives/2007/02/07/who-owns-your-body-parts/print.

6   DeScioli, P. and Karpoff, R. (2015), 'People's judgments about classic property law cases', *Human Nature*, 26, 184–209.

7   Hobbes, T. (1651/2008), *Leviathan*. Oxford: Oxford University Press.

8   Locke, J. (1698/2010), *Two Treatises of Government*. Clark, NJ: The Lawbook Exchange.

9   Taken from transcripts for the Poomaksin case study, supra note 6. Knut-sum-atak circle discussion no. 2 (3 December 2003), Oldman River Cultural Centre, Brocket, Alberta. Cited in Noble, B. (2008), 'Owning as belonging/owning as property: the crisis of power and respect in First Nations heritage transactions with Canada'. In C. Bell and V. Napoleon, eds., *First Nations Cultural Heritage and Law, vol. 1: Case Studies, Voices, Perspectives*. Vancouver: University of British Columbia Press, pp. 465–88.

10 http://www.hedgehogcentral.com/illegal.shtml.

11 Buettinger, C. (2005), 'Did slaves have free will? Luke, a Slave, v. Florida and crime at the command of the master', *Florida Historical Quarterly*, 83, 241–57.

12 Morris, T. D. (1996), *Southern Slavery and the Law 1619–1860*. Chapel Hill, NC: North Carolina University Press.

13 http://www.ilo.org/global/topics/forced-labour/lang--en/index.htm.

14 Global Slavery Index, https://www.globalslaveryindex.org/findings/.

15 https://www.theguardian.com/technology/2017/jun/18/foxconn-life-death-forbidden-city-longhua-suicide-apple-iphone-brian-merchant-one-device-extract.

16 'Global Estimates of Modern Slavery: Forced Labour and Forced Marriage', International Labour Office (ILO), Geneva, 2017.

17 Coontz, S. (2006), *Marriage, a History: How Love Conquered Marriage*. London: Penguin.

18 http://wbl.worldbank.org/.

19 Zajonc, R. B. (1968), 'Attitudinal effects of mere exposure', *Journal of Personality and Social Psychology*, 9, 1–27.

20 Marriage and Divorce Statistics: Statistics explained, http://ec.europa. eu/eurostat/statisticsexplained/.

21 Foreman, A. (2014), 'The heartbreaking history of divorce', *Smithsonian Magazine*, https://www.smithsonianmag.com/history/heartbreaking-history-of-divorce-180949439/.

22 Jenkins, S. P. (2008), 'Marital splits and income changes over the longer term', Institute for Social and Economic Research, https://www.iser. essex.ac.uk/files/iser_working_papers/2008-07.pdf.

23 https://www.gov.uk/government/publications/the-royal-liverpool-childrens-inquiry-report.

24 'Are our children now owned by the state?' Nigel Farage discusses why Alfie's life matters on *The Ingraham Angle*, http://video.foxnews.com/ v/5777069250001/?#sp=show-clips.

25 Health Care Corporation of America v. Pittas, http://caselaw.findlaw. com/pa-superior-court/1607095.html.

26 '24,771 dowry deaths reported in last 3 years', *Indian Express*, http:// indianexpress.com/article/india/india-others/24771-dowry-deaths-reported-in-last-3-years-govt/, retrieved 21 December 2016.

27 Stubborn Son Law Act of the General Court of Massachusetts in 1646: 'If a man have a stubborn or rebellious son, of sufficient years and under-standing, viz. sixteen years of age, which will not obey the voice of his Father or the voice of his Mother, and that when they have chastened him will not harken unto them: then shall his Father and Mother being his natural parents, lay hold on him, and bring him to the Magistrates assembled in Court and testify unto them, that their son is stubborn and rebellious and will not obey their voice and chastisement . . . such a son shall be put to death.' States that followed were Connecticut (1650), Rhode Island (1668) and New Hampshire (1679).

28 Norenzayan, A., et al. (2016), 'The cultural evolution of prosocial reli-gions', *Behavioral and Brain Sciences*, 39, E1, doi:10.1017/S0140525 X14001356.

29 Pape, R. A. (2003), 'The strategic logic of suicide terrorism', *American Political Science Review*, 97, 343–61.

30 http://www.oxfordtoday.ox.ac.uk/interviews/trump-no-hitler-%E2%80% 93he%E2%80%99s-mussolini-says-oxford-historian.

31 https://www.bbc.co.uk/news/world-europe-36130006.

32 Stenner, K. and Haidt, J. (2018), 'Authoritarianism is not a momentary madness'. In C. R. Sunstein, ed., *Can It Happen Here?* New York: HarperCollins.

33 Hetherington, M. and Suhay, E. (2011), 'Authoritarianism, threat, and Americans' support for the war on terror', *American Journal of Political Science*, 55, 546–60.

34 Adorno, T. W., et al. (1950), *The Authoritarian Personality*. New York: Harper & Row.

35 Kakkara, H. and Sivanathana, N. (2017), 'When the appeal of a dominant leader is greater than a prestige leader', *Proceedings of the National Academy of Sciences*, 114, 6734–9.

36 Inglehart, R. F. (2018), *Cultural Evolution: People's Motivations are Changing, and Reshaping the World*. Cambridge: Cambridge University Press.

37 Stenner, K. and Haidt, J. (2018), 'Authoritarianism is not a momentary madness'. In C. R. Sunstein, ed., *Can It Happen Here?* New York: HarperCollins.

38 https://yougov.co.uk/topics/politics/articles-reports/2012/02/07/britains-nostalgic-pessimism.

39 https://yougov.co.uk/topics/politics/articles-reports/2016/01/08/fsafasf.

40 Inglehart, R. F. and Norris, P. (2016), 'Trump, Brexit, and the rise of Populism: Economic have-nots and cultural backlash (July 29, 2016)'. Harvard Kennedy School Working Paper No. RWP16-026, https://ssrn.com/abstract=2818659.

41 Ibid.

42 Olson, K. R. and Shaw, A. (2011), ' "No fair, copycat!" What children's response to plagiarism tells us about their understanding of ideas', *Developmental Science*, 14, 431–9.

43 Vivian, L., Shaw, A. and Olson, K. R. (2013), 'Ideas versus labor: what do children value in artistic creation?' *Cognition*, 127, 38–45.

44 Shaw, A., Vivian, L. and Olson, K. R. (2012), 'Children apply principles of physical ownership to ideas', *Cognitive Science*, 36, 1383–403.

45 https://www.forbes.com/sites/oliverchiang/2010/11/13/meet-the-man-who-just-made-a-cool-half-million-from-the-sale-of-virtual-property/#5cc281621cd3.

46 Kramer, A. D. I., Guillory, J. E. and Hancock, J. T. (2014), 'Experimental evidence of massive scale emotional contagion through social networks', *Proceedings of the National Academy of Sciences*, 111, 8788–90.

47 https://www.inc.com/melanie-curtin/was-your-facebook-data-stolen-by-cambridge-analytica-heres-how-to-tell.html.

48 Rokka, J. and Alrodi, M. (2018), https://theconversation.com/cambridge-analyticas-secret-psychographic-tool-is-a-ghost-from-the-past-94143?fbclid=IwARoyfeEo2an4Bpogh8d1b8F2yabbsD9y_9ShQKLezCntUP D1S_kGrT1JlAA.

49 Packard, V. (1957), *The Hidden Persuaders*. New York: Pocket Books.

50 Lilienfeld, S. O., et al. (2010), *50 Great Myths of Popular Psychology*. Oxford: Wiley-Blackwell.

51 Bentham, Jeremy (1838–1843), *The Works of Jeremy Bentham, published under the Superintendence of his Executor, John Bowring*. Edinburgh: William Tait, 11 vols. Vol. 1, http://oll.libertyfund.org/titles/2009.

52 Pierce, J. L., Kostova, T. and Dirks, K. T. (2003), 'The state of psychological ownership: integrating and extending a century of research', *Review of General Psychology*, 7, 84–107.

2. NON-HUMANS POSSESS, BUT ONLY HUMANS CAN OWN

1 Triplett, N. (1898), 'The dynamogenic factors in pacemaking and competition', *American Journal of Psychology*, 9, 507–33.

2 Clark, A. E. and Oswald, A. J. (1996), 'Satisfaction and comparison income', *Journal of Public Economics*, 61, 359–81.

3 Smith, D. (2015), 'Most people have no idea whether they are paid fairly', *Harvard Business Review*, December issue, https://hbr.org/2015/10/most-people-have-no-idea-whether-theyre-paid-fairly.

4 Mencken, H. L. (1949/1978), 'Masculum et Feminam Creavit Eos', in *A Mencken chrestomathy*. New York: Knopf, pp. 619–20.

5 Neumark, D. and Postlewaite, A. (1998), 'Relative income concerns and the rise in married women's employment', *Journal of Public Economics*, 70, 157–83.

6 Hofmann, H. A. and Schildberger, K. (2001), 'Assessment of strength and willingness to fight during aggressive encounters in crickets', *Animal Behaviour*, 62, 337–48.

7 Davies, N. B. (1978), 'Territorial defence in the speckled wood butterfly (*Pararge aegeria*): the resident always wins', *Animal Behaviour*, 26, 138–47.

8 Lueck, D. (1995), 'The rule of first possession and the design of the law', *Journal of Law and Economics*, 38, 393–436.

9 Harmand, S., et al. (2015), '3.3-million-year-old stone tools from Lomekwi 3, West Turkana, Kenya', *Nature*, 521, 310–15.

10 Mann, J. and Patterson, E. M. (2013), 'Tool use by aquatic animals', *Philosophical Transactions of the Royal Society B: Biological Sciences*, 368 (1630), https://doi.org/10.1098/rstb.2012.0424.

11 https://anthropology.net/2007/06/04/82000-year-old-jewellery-found/.

12 Brosnan, S. F. and Beran, M. J. (2009), 'Trading behavior between conspecifics in chimpanzees, *Pan troglodytes*', *Journal of Comparative Psychology*, 123, 181–94.

13 Kanngiesser, P., et al. (2011), 'The limits of endowment effects in great apes (*Pan paniscus, Pan troglodytes, Gorilla gorilla, Pongo pygmaeus*)', *Journal of Comparative Psychology*, 125, 436–45.

14 Radovčić, D., et al. (2015), 'Evidence for Neandertal jewelry: modified white-tailed eagle claws at Krapina', *PLoS ONE*, 10 (3), e0119802, doi:10.1371/journal.

15 Lewis-Williams, D. (2004), *Mind in the Cave: Consciousness and the Origins of Art*. London: Thames & Hudson.

16 Gomes, C. M. and Boesch, C. (2009), 'Wild chimpanzees exchange meat for sex on a long-term basis', *PLoS ONE*, 4 (4), e5116, doi:10.1371/journal.pone.0005116.

17 HSBC Report (2013), 'The Future of Retirement: Life after Work', https://investments.hsbc.co.uk/myplan/files/resources/130/future-of-retirement-global-report.pdf.

18 https://www.pru.co.uk/press-centre/inheritance-plans/.

19 https://www.legalandgeneral.com/retirement/retirement-news/2018/bank-of-mum-and-dad-report-2018.pdf.

20 Trivers, R. L. and Willard, D. E. (1973), 'Natural selection of parental ability to vary the sex ratio of offspring', *Science*, 179, 90–92.

21 Smith, M. S., Kish, B. J. and Crawford, C. B. (1987), 'Inheritance of wealth as human kin investment', *Ethological Sociobiology*, 8, 171–82.

22 Song, S. (2018), 'Spending patterns of Chinese parents on children's backpacks support the Trivers–Willard hypothesis', *Evolution & Human Behavior*, 39, 339–42.

23 Judge, D. S. and Hrdy, S. B. (1992), 'Allocation of accumulated resources among close kin: inheritance in Sacramento, California, 1890–1984', *Ethological Sociobiology*, 13, 495–522.

24 http://www.bloomberg.com/news/articles/2013-07-02/cheating-wives-narrowed-infidelity-gap-over-two-decades.

25 Walker, R. S., Flynn, M. V. and Hill, K. R. (2010), 'Evolutionary history of partible paternity in lowland South America', *Proceedings of the National Academy of Sciences*, 107, 19195–200.

26 Michalski, R. L. and Shackelford, T. K. (2005), 'Grandparental invest-
    ment as a function of relational uncertainty and emotional closeness
    with parents', *Human Nature*, 16, 293–305.

27 Gray, P. B. and Brogdon, E. (2017), 'Do step- and biological grandpar-
    ents show differences in investment and emotional closeness with their
    grandchildren?', *Evolutionary Psychology*, 15, 1–9.

28 Gaulin, S. J. C., McBurney, D. H. and Brakeman-Wartell, S. L. (1997),
    'Matrilateral biases in the investment of aunts and uncles: a conse-
    quence and measure of paternity uncertainty', *Human Nature*, 8,
    139–51.

29 Rousseau, J.-J. (1754/1984), *A Discourse on Inequality*. Harmonds-
    worth: Penguin.

30 Strassmann, J. E. and Queller, D. C. (2014), 'Privatization and prop-
    erty in biology', *Animal Behaviour*, 92, 305–11.

31 Riedl, K., Jensen, K., Call, J. and Tomasello, M. (2012), 'No third-party
    punishment in chimpanzees', *Proceedings of the National Academy of
    Sciences*, 109, 14824–9.

32 Rossano, F., Rakoczy, H. and Tomasello, M. (2011), 'Young children's
    understanding of violations of property rights', *Cognition*, 121, 219–27.

33 Slaughter, V. (2015), 'Theory of mind in infants and young children: a
    review', *Australian Psychologist*, 50, 169–72.

34 Guala, F. (2012), 'Reciprocity: weak or strong? What punishment
    experiments do (and do not) demonstrate', *Behavioral and Brain Sci-
    ences*, 35, 1–15.

35 Lewis, H. M., et al. (2014), 'High mobility explains demand sharing
    and enforced cooperation in egalitarian hunter-gatherers', *Nature
    Communications*, 5, 5789.

36 https://www.youtube.com/watch?v=UGttmR2DTY8.

37 Tilley, N., et al. (2015), 'Do burglar alarms increase burglary risk? A
    counter-intuitive finding and possible explanations', *Crime Prevention
    and Community Safety*, 17, 1–19.

38 Fischer, P., et al. (2011), 'The bystander-effect: a meta-analytic review
    on bystander intervention in dangerous and non-dangerous emergen-
    cies', *Psychological Bulletin*, 137, 517–37.

39 Hardin, G. (1968), 'The tragedy of the commons', *Science*, 162, 1243–8.

40 Lloyd, W. F. (1833/1968), *Two Lectures on the Checks to Population*.
    New York: Augustus M. Kelley.

41 Crowther, T. W., et al. (2015), 'Mapping tree density at a global scale',
    Nature, 525, 201–5.

42 Gowdy, J. (2011), 'Hunter-gatherers and the mythology of the market', https://libcom.org/history/hunter-gatherers-mythology-market-john-gowdy.

43 Sahlins, M. (1972), *Stone Age Economics*. Chicago: Aldine Publishing.

44 http://www.rewild.com/in-depth/leisure.html.

3. ORIGINS OF OWNERSHIP

1 http://www.usatoday.com/story/news/nation-now/2015/10/01/banksy-mural-detroit-michigan-auction/73135144/.

2 https://www.corby.gov.uk/home/environmental-services/street-scene/enviro-crime/graffiti.

3 http://www.bristolpost.co.uk/banksy-s-bristol-exhibition-brought-163-15-million-city/story-11271699-detail/story.html.

4 http://news.bbc.co.uk/1/hi/uk/6575345.stm.

5 http://www.tate.org.uk/art/artworks/duchamp-fountain-t07573/text-summary.

6 Naumann, Francis M. (2003), 'Marcel Duchamp: money is no object. The art of defying the art market', *Art in America*, April.

7 Furby, L. (1980), 'The origins and early development of possessive behavior', *Political Psychology*, 2, 30–42.

8 White, R. W. (1959), 'Motivation reconsidered: the concept of competence', *Psychological Review*, 66, 297–333.

9 Fernald, A. and O'Neill, D. K. (1993), 'Peekaboo across cultures: how mothers and infants play with voices, faces and expressions'. In K. McDonald, ed., *Parent–Child Play: Descriptions and Implications*. Albany, NY: State University of New York Press.

10 Seligman, M. E. P. (1975), *Helplessness*. San Francisco: Freeman.

11 Goldstein, K. (1908), 'Zur lehre von de motorischen', *Journal für Psychologie und Neurologie*, 11, 169–87.

12 Finkelstein, N. W., et al. (1978), 'Social behavior of infants and toddlers in a day-care environment', *Developmental Psychology*, 14, 257–62.

13 Ibid.

14 Hay, D. F. and Ross, H. S. (1982), 'The social nature of early conflict', *Child Development*, 53, 105–13.

15 Dunn, J. and Munn, P. (1985), 'Becoming a family member: family conflict and the development of social understanding in the second year', *Child Development*, 56, 480–92.

16 Mueller, E. and Brenner, J. (1977), 'The origins of social skills and interaction among playgroup toddlers', *Child Development*, 48, 854–61.

17 Krebs, K. (1975), 'Children and their pecking order', *New Society*, 17, 127–8.

18 Vandell, D. (1976), 'Boy toddlers' social interaction with mothers, fathers, and peers'. Unpublished doctoral dissertation, Boston University.

19 Hay, D. F. and Ross, H. S. (1982), 'The social nature of early conflict', *Child Development*, 53, 105–13.

20 Burford, H. C., et al. (1996), 'Gender differences in preschoolers' sharing behavior', *Journal of Social Behavior and Personality*, 11, 17–25.

21 Whitehouse, A. J. O., et al. (2012), 'Sex-specific associations between umbilical cord blood testosterone levels and language delay in early childhood', *Journal of Child Psychology and Psychiatry*, 53, 726–34.

22 In 1994, Andrew De Vries, 28, from Aberdeen, was shot after he knocked on the back door of a house in Dallas, Texas, apparently seeking a taxi for himself and a Scottish colleague. The owner fired through the door. https://www.nytimes.com/1994/01/08/us/homeowner-shoots-tourist-by-mistake-in-texas-police-say.html.

23 https://www.inverse.com/article/18683-pokemon-go-not-license-trespass-get-off-my-lawn.

24 https://www.nps.gov/yell/planyourvisit/rules.htm.

25 Blake, P. R. and Harris, P. L. (2011), 'Early representations of ownership'. In H. Ross & O. Friedman, eds., *Origins of Ownership of Property*. New Directions for Child and Adolescent Development, 132. San Francisco: Jossey-Bass, pp. 39–51.

26 Friedman, O. and Neary, K. R. (2008), 'Determining who owns what: do children infer ownership from first possession?', *Cognition*, 107, 829–49.

27 Hay, D. F. (2006), 'Yours and mine: toddlers' talk about possessions with familiar peers', *British Journal of Developmental Psychology*, 24, 39–52.

28 Nelson, K. (1976), 'Some attributes of adjectives used by young children', *Cognition*, 4, 13–30.

29 Rodgon, M. M. and Rashman, S. E. (1976), 'Expression of owner-owned relationships among holophrastic 14- and 32-month-old children', *Child Development*, 47, 1219–22.

30 Friedman, O., et al. (2011), 'Ownership and object history'. In H. Ross & O. Friedman, eds., *Origins of Ownership of Property*. New Directions for Child and Adolescent Development, 132. San Francisco: Jossey-Bass, pp. 79–89.

31 Preissler, M. A. and Bloom, P. (2008), 'Two-year-olds use artist intention to understand drawings', *Cognition*, 106, 512–18.

32 Kanngiesser, P., Gjersoe, N. L and Hood, B. (2010), 'The effect of creative labor on property-ownership transfer by preschool children and adults', *Psychological Science*, 21, 1236–41.

33 Kanngiesser, P., Itakura, S. and Hood, B. (2014), 'The effect of labour across cultures: developmental evidence from Japan and the UK', *British Journal of Developmental Psychology*, 32, 320–29.

34 Kanngiesser, P. and Hood, B. (2014), 'Not by labor alone: considerations for value influences use of the labor rule in ownership judgments', *Cognitive Science*, 38, 353–66.

35 https://www.bloomberg.com/view/articles/2014-11-14/why-pay-15-million-for-a-white-canvas.

36 https://www.telegraph.co.uk/news/worldnews/northamerica/usa/7835931/Florida-heiress-leaves-3m-and-Miami-mansion-to-chihuahua.html.

37 Noles, N. S., et al. (2012), 'Children's and adults' intuitions about who can own things', *Journal of Cognition and Culture*, 12, 265–86.

38 Ibid.

39 Martin, C. L. and Ruble, D. (2004), 'Children's search for gender cues: cognitive perspectives on gender development', *Current Directions in Psychological Science*, 13, 67–70.

40 Kahlenberg, S. M. and Wrangham, R. W. (2010), 'Sex differences in chimpanzees' use of sticks as play objects resemble those of children', *Current Biology*, 20, 1067–8.

41 Miller, C. F., et al. (2013), 'Bringing the cognitive and social together: how gender detectives and gender enforcers shape children's gender development'. In M. R. Banaji and S. A. Gelman, eds., *Navigating the Social World: What Infants, Children, and Other Species Can Teach Us*. New York: Oxford University Press.

42 Malcolm, S., Defeyter, M. A. and Friedman, O. (2014), 'Children and adults use gender and age stereotypes in ownership judgments', *Journal of Cognition and Development*, 15, 123–35.

43 Winnicott, D. W. (1953), 'Transitional objects and transitional phenomena', *International Journal of Psychoanalysis*, 34, 89–97.

44 Lehman, E. B., Arnold, B. E. and Reeves, S. L. (1995), 'Attachment to blankets, teddy bears and other non-social objects: a child's perspective', *Journal of Genetic Psychology: Research and Theory on Human Development*, 156, 443–59.

45 Hong, K. M. and Townes, B. D. (1976), 'Infants' attachment to inanimate objects. A cross-cultural study', *Journal of the American Academy of Child Psychiatry*, 15, 49–61.

46 Passman, R. H. (1987), 'Attachments to inanimate objects: are children who have security blankets insecure?', *Journal of Consulting and Clinical Psychology*, 55, 825–30.

47 Hood, B. M. and Bloom, P. (2008), 'Children prefer certain individuals to perfect duplicates', *Cognition*, 106, 455–62.

48 Fortuna, K., et al. (2014), 'Attachment to inanimate objects and early childcare: a twin study', *Frontiers in Psychology*, 5, 486.

49 Gjersoe, N. L, Hall, E. L. and Hood, B. (2015), 'Children attribute mental lives to toys only when they are emotionally attached to them', *Cognitive Development*, 34, 28–38.

50 Hood, B., et al. (2010), 'Implicit voodoo: electrodermal activity reveals a susceptibility to sympathetic magic', *Journal of Culture & Cognition*, 10, 391–9.

51 Harlow, H. F., Dodsworth, R. O. and Harlow, M. K. (1965), 'Total social isolation in monkeys', *Proceedings of the National Academy of Sciences*, 54, 90–97.

4. IT'S ONLY FAIR

1 Shorrocks, A., Davies, J. and Lluberas, R. (2015), 'Credit Suisse Global Wealth Report', Credit Suisse.

2 Mishel, L. and Sabadish, N. (2013), 'CEO Pay in 2012 was Extraordinarily High Relative to Typical Workers and Other High Earners', Economic Policy Institute.

3 Norton, M. I. and Ariely, D. (2011), 'Building a better America – one wealth quintile at a time', *Perspectives on Psychological Science*, 6, 1–9.

4 Bechtel, M. M., Liesch, R. and Scheve, K. F. (2018), 'Inequality and redistribution behavior in a give-or-take game', *Proceedings of the National Academy of Sciences*, 115, 3611–16.

5 Somerville, J., et al. (2013), 'The development of fairness expectations and prosocial behavior in the second year of life', *Infancy*, 18, 40–66.

6 Olson, K. R. and Spelke, E. S. (2008), 'Foundations of cooperation in young children', *Cognition*, 108, 222–31.

7 Shaw, A. and Olson, K. R. (2012), 'Children discard a resource to avoid inequity', *Journal of Experimental Psychology: General*, 141, 383–95.

8 Shaw, A., DeScioli, P. and Olson, K. R. (2012), 'Fairness versus favoritism in children', *Evolution and Human Behavior*, 33, 736–45.

9 Starmans, C., Sheskin, M. and Bloom, P. (2017), 'Why people prefer unequal societies', *Nature Human Behaviour*, 1, 82, doi: 10.1038/s41562-017-0082.

10 Baumard, N., Mascaro, O. and Chevallier, C. (2012), 'Preschoolers are able to take merit into account when distributing goods', *Developmental Psychology*, 48, 492–8.

11 Norton, M. I. and Ariely, D. (2011), 'Building a better America – one wealth quintile at a time', *Perspectives on Psychological Science*, 6, 1–9.

12 Norton, M. I. (2014), 'Unequality: who gets what and why it matters', *Policy Insights from the Behavioral and Brain Sciences*, 1, 151–5.

13 Savani, K. and Rattam, A. (2012), 'A choice mind-set increases the acceptance and maintenance of wealth inequality', *Psychological Science*, 23, 796–804.

14 *Giving USA 2015: The Annual Report on Philanthropy for the Year 2014.* Chicago: Giving USA Foundation, p. 26; https://www.civilsociety.co.uk/.

15 Persky, J. (1995), 'Retrospectives: the ethology of Homo Economicus', *Journal of Economic Perspectives*, 9, 221–3.

16 Carter, G. G. and Wilkinson, G. S. (2015), 'Social benefits of non-kin food sharing by female vampire bats', *Philosophical Transactions of the Royal Society B: Biological Sciences*, 282, https://doi.org/10.1098/rspb.2015.2524.

17 Tomasello, M. (2009), *Why We Cooperate.* Cambridge, MA: MIT Press.

18 Carter, G. and Leffer, L. (2015), 'Social grooming in bats: are vampire bats exceptional?', *PLoS ONE*, 10 (10): e0138430, doi:10.1371/journal.pone.0138430.

19 Hemelrijk, C. K. and Ek, A. (1991), 'Reciprocity and interchange of grooming and support in captive chimpanzees', *Animal Behaviour*, 41, 923–35.

20 Batson, C. D., et al. (1997), 'In a very different voice: unmasking moral hypocrisy', *Journal of Personality and Social Psychology*, 72, 1335–48.

21 Diener, E. and Wallbom, M. (1976), 'Effects of self-awareness on antinormative behavior', *Journal of Research in Personality*, 10, 107–11.

22 Beaman, A. L., Diener, E. and Klentz, B. (1979), 'Self-awareness and transgression in children: two field studies', *Journal of Personality and Social Psychology*, 37, 1835–46.

23 Bering, J. M. (2006), 'The folk psychology of souls', *Behavioral and Brain Sciences*, 29, 453–98.

24 Darley, J. M. and Batson, C. D. (1973), 'From Jerusalem to Jericho: a study of situational and dispositional variables in helping behavior', *Journal of Personality and Social Psychology*, 27, 100–108.

25 Shariff, A. F., et al. (2016), 'Religious priming: a meta-analysis with a focus on prosociality', *Personality and Social Psychology Review*, 20 (1), 27–48.

26 Duhaime, E. P. (2015), 'Is the call to prayer a call to cooperate? A field experiment on the impact of religious salience on prosocial behaviour', *Judgement and Decision Making*, 10, 593–6.

27 Shariff, A. F. and Norenzayan, A. (2007), 'God is watching you: priming God concept increases prosocial behavior in an anonymous economic game', *Psychological Science*, 18, 803–9.

28 Merritt, A. C., Effron, D. A. and Monin, B. (2010), 'Moral self-licensing: when being good frees us to be bad', *Social and Personality Psychology Compass*, 4, 344–57.

29 Sachdeva, S., Iliev, R. and Medin, D. L. (2009), 'Sinning saints and saintly sinners: the paradox of moral self-regulation', *Psychological Science*, 20, 523–8.

30 Henrich, J., et al. (2005), ' "Economic man" in cross-cultural perspective: behavioral experiments in 15 small-scale societies', *Behavioral and Brain Sciences*, 28, 795–815.

31 Sanfey, A. G., et al. (2003), 'The neural basis of economic decision-making in the ultimatum game', *Science*, 300, 1755–8.

32 Blount, S. (1995), 'When social outcomes aren't fair: the effect of causal attributions on preferences', *Organizational Behavior & Human Decision Processes*, 63, 131–44.

33 Jensen, K., Call, J. and Tomasello, M. (2007), 'Chimpanzees are vengeful but not spiteful', *Proceedings of the National Academy of Sciences*, 104, 13046–50.

34 Nowak, M. (2012), *SuperCooperators: Altruism, Evolution, and Why We Need Each Other to Succeed*. New York: Free Press.

35 https://www.theguardian.com/science/head-quarters/2016/jul/05/deal-or-no-deal-brexit-and-the-allure-of-self-expression.

36 Yamagishi, Y., et al. (2012), 'Rejection of unfair offers in the ultimatum game is no evidence of strong reciprocity', *Proceedings of the National Academy of Sciences*, 109, 20364–8.

37 Yamagishi, Y., et al. (2009), 'The private rejection of unfair offers and emotional commitment', *Proceedings of the National Academy of Sciences*, 106, 11520–23.

38 Xiao, E. and Houser, D. (2005), 'Emotion expression in human punishment behavior', *Proceedings of the National Academy of Sciences*, 102, 7398–401.

39 Ong, Q., et al. (2013), 'The self-image signaling roles of voice in decision-making', https://econpapers.repec.org/paper/nanwpaper/1303.htm.

40 Hamann, K., et al. (2012), 'Collaboration encourages equal sharing in children but not in chimpanzees', *Nature*, 476, 328–31.

41 https://www.theguardian.com/commentisfree/2017/may/24/blood-donor-service-manchester-attack.

42 Li, Y., et al. (2013), 'Experiencing a natural disaster alters children's altruistic giving', *Psychological Science*, 24, 1686–95.

43 Andreoni, J. (1990), 'Impure altruism and donations to public goods: a theory of warm-glow giving', *The Economic Journal*, 100, 464–77.

44 Crumpler, H. and Grossman, P. J. (2008), 'An experimental test of warm glow giving', *Journal of Public Economics*, 92, 1011–21.

45 Titmuss, R. M. (1970), *The Gift Relationship*. London: Allen and Unwin.

46 Mellström, C. and Johannesson, M. (2008), 'Crowding out in blood donation. Was Titmuss right?', *Journal of the Economic Association*, 6, 845–63.

47 Ferguson, E., et al. (2012), 'Blood donors' helping behavior is driven by warm glow: more evidence for the blood donor benevolence hypothesis', *Transfusion*, 52, 2189–200.

48 Smith, A. (1759), 'Of Sympathy', in *The Theory of Moral Sentiments*. London: A Millar, pt 1, sec. 1, ch. 1.

49 Xu, X., et al. (2009), 'Do you feel my pain? Racial group membership modulates empathic neural responses', *Journal of Neuroscience*, 29, 8525–9.

5. POSSESSIONS, WEALTH AND HAPPINESS

1 Smith, A. (1759), *The Theory of Moral Sentiments*. London: A Millar, pt 1, sec. 3, ch. 2.

2 http://www.nytimes.com/2010/03/19/world/asia/19india.html.

3 Jaikumar, S. and Sarin, A. (2015), 'Conspicuous consumption and income inequality in an emerging economy: evidence from India', *Marketing Letters*, 26, 279–92.

4 https://www.independent.co.uk/news/world/americas/donald-trump-bill-gates-hiv-hpv-daughter-jennifer-looks-helicopter-a8357141.html.

5 Wallman, J. (2015), *Stuffocation: Living More with Less*. London: Penguin.

6 Trentmann, F. (2017), *Empire of Things: How We Became a World of Consumers, from the Fifteenth Century to the Twenty-First*. London: Penguin.

7 Beder, S. (2004), 'Consumerism: an historical perspective', *Pacific Ecologist*, 9, 42–8.

8   Zevin, D. and Edy, C. (1997), 'Boom time for Gen X', *US News and World Report*, 20 October.

9   Turner, C. (2015), 'Homes Through the Decades', NHBC Foundation, http://www.nhbc.co.uk/cms/publish/consumer/NewsandComment/HomesThroughTheDecades.pdf.

10 Veblen, T. (1899), *The Theory of the Leisure Class: An Economic Study of Institutions*. New York: Macmillan.

11 Loyau, A., et al. (2005), 'Multiple sexual advertisements honestly reflect health status in peacocks (*Pavo cristatus*)', *Behavioral Ecology and Sociobiology*, 58, 552–7.

12 Petrie, M. and Halliday, T. (1994), 'Experimental and natural changes in the peacock's (*Pavo cristatus*) train can affect mating success', *Behavioral Ecology and Sociobiology*, 35, 213–17.

13 Nave, G., et al. (2018), 'Single-dose testosterone administration increases men's preference for status goods', *Nature Communications*, 9, 2433, doi: 10.1038/s41467-018-04923-0.

14 http://www.bain.com/publications/articles/luxury-goods-worldwide-market-study-fall-winter-2016.aspx.

15 Nelissen, R. M. A. and Meijers, M. H. C. (2011), 'Social benefits of luxury brands as costly signals of wealth and status', *Evolution and Human Behavior*, 32, 343–55.

16 Gjersoe, N. L., et al. (2014), 'Individualism and the extended-self: cross-cultural differences in the valuation of authentic objects', *PLoS ONE*, 9 (3), e90787, doi:10.1371/journal.pone.0090787.

17 https://nypost.com/2016/06/21/trump-has-been-giving-out-fake-diamond-cuff-links-for-years/.

18 Schmidt, L., et al. (2017), 'How context alters value: the brain's valuation and affective regulation systems link price cues to experienced taste pleasantness', *Scientific Reports*, 7, 8098.

19 Gino, F., Norton, M. I. and Ariely, D. A. (2010), 'The counterfeit self: the deceptive costs of faking it', *Psychological Science*, 21, 712–20.

20 Bellezza, S., Gino, F. and Keinan, A. (2014), 'The red sneakers effect: inferring status and competence from signals of nonconformity', *Journal of Consumer Research*, 41, 35–54.

21 Ward, M. K. and Dahl, D. W. (2014), 'Should the Devil sell Prada? Retail rejection increases aspiring consumers' desire for the brand', *Journal of Consumer Research*, 41, 590–609.

22 http://www.dailymail.co.uk/femail/article-2822546/As-Romeo-Beckham-stars-new-ad-Burberry-went-chic-chav-chic-again.html.

23 Eckhardt, G., Belk, R. and Wilson, J. (2015), 'The rise of inconspicuous consumption', *Journal of Marketing Management*, 31, 807–26.

24 Smith, E. A., Bliege Bird, R. L. and Bird. D. W. (2003), 'The benefits of costly signaling: Meriam turtle hunters', *Behavioral Ecology*, 14, 116–26.

25 Frank. R. H. (1999), *Luxury Fever: Why Money Fails to Satisfy in an Era of Excess*. Princeton, NJ: Princeton University Press.

26 Whillans, A. V., Weidman, A. C. and Dunn, E. W. (2016), 'Valuing time over money is associated with greater happiness', *Social Psychological and Personality Science*, 7, 213–22.

27 Hershfield, H. E., Mogilner, C. and Barnea, U. (2016), 'People who choose time over money are happier', *Social Psychological and Personality Science*, 7, 697–706.

28 Nickerson, C., et al. (2003), 'Zeroing in on the dark side of the American Dream: a closer look at the negative consequences of the goal for financial success', *Psychological Science*, 14, 531–6.

29 Quartz, S. and Asp, A. (2015), *Cool: How the Brain's Hidden Quest for Cool Drives Our Economy and Shapes Our World*. New York: Farrar, Straus and Giroux.

30 Frank, R. H. (1985), *Choosing the Right Pond: Human Behavior and the Quest for Status*. New York: Oxford University Press.

31 Solnicka, S. J. and Hemenway, D. (1998), 'Is more always better? A survey on positional concerns', *Journal of Economic Behavior & Organization*, 37, 373–83.

32 Medvec, V. H., Madey, S. F. and Gilovich, T. (1995), 'When less is more: counterfactual thinking and satisfaction among Olympic medalists', *Journal of Personality and Social Psychology*, 69, 603–10.

33 de Castro, J. M. (1994), 'Family and friends produce greater social facilitation of food intake than other companions', *Physiology & Behavior*, 56, 445–55.

34 Doob, A. N. and Gross, A. E. (1968), 'Status of frustrator as an inhibitor of horn-honking responses', *Journal of Social Psychology*, 76, 213–18.

35 Holt-Lunstad, J., et al. (2015), 'Loneliness and social isolation as risk factors for mortality: a meta-analytic review', *Perspectives on Psychological Science*, 10, 227–37.

36 Festinger, L. (1954), 'A theory of social comparison processes', *Human Relations*, 7, 117–40.

37 Charles, K. K., Hurst, E. and Roussanov, N. (2009), 'Conspicuous consumption and race', *Quarterly Journal of Economics*, 124 (2), 425–67.

38 Jaikumar, S., Singh, R. and Sarin, A. (2017), ' "I show off, so I am well off": subjective economic well-being and conspicuous consumption in an emerging economy', *Journal of Business Research*, doi: 10.1016/j. jbusres.2017.05.027.

39 Charles, K. K., Hurst, E. and Roussanov, N. (2009), 'Conspicuous consumption and race', *Quarterly Journal of Economics*, 124 (2), 425–67.

40 Kaus, W. (2010), 'Conspicuous Consumption and Race: Evidence from South Africa', Papers on Economics and Evolution, No. 1003, Max-Planck-Institute für Ökonomik, Jena.

41 http://www.epi.org/publication/black-white-wage-gaps-expand-with-rising-wage-inequality/.

42 Zizzo, D. J. (2003), 'Money burning and rank egalitarianism with random dictators', *Economics Letters*, 81, 263–6.

43 Joseph, J. E., et al. (2008), 'The functional neuroanatomy of envy'. In R. H. Smith, ed., *Envy: Theory and Research*. Oxford: Oxford University Press, pp. 290–314.

44 van de Ven, N., et al. (2015), 'When envy leads to schadenfreude', *Cognition and Emotion*, 29, 1007–25.

45 van de Ven, N., Zeelenberg, M. and Pieters, R. (2015), 'Leveling up and down: the experiences of benign and malicious envy', *Emotion*, 9, 419–29.

46 van de Ven, N., Zeelenberg, M. and Pieters, R. (2015), 'The envy premium in product evaluation', *Journal of Consumer Research*, 37, 984–98.

47 Taute, H. A. and Sierra, J. (2014), 'Brand tribalism: an anthropological perspective', *Journal of Product & Brand Management*, 23, 2–15.

48 https://www.independent.co.uk/news/business/news/brexit-latest-news-fat-cat-pay-rethink-cipd-report-a7584391.html.

49 https://www.statista.com/statistics/424159/pay-gap-between-ceos-and-average-workers-in-world-by-country/.

50 https://www.usatoday.com/story/money/2017/05/23/ceo-pay-highest-paid-chief-executive-officers-2016/339079001/.

51 https://www.theguardian.com/media/greenslade/2016/aug/08/why-newspaper-editors-like-fat-cats-they-help-to-sell-newspapers.

52 http://www.dailymail.co.uk/tvshowbiz/article-4209686/Ruby-Rose-hints-tall-poppy-syndrome-Australia.html.

53 Nishi, C. L., et al. (2015), 'Inequality and visibility of wealth in experimental social networks', *Nature*, 526, 426–9.

54 Easterlin, R. A. (1974), 'Does economic growth improve the human lot?' In Paul A. David and Melvin W. Reder, eds., *Nations and Households in Economic Growth: Essays in Honor of Moses Abramovitz*. New York: Academic Press.

55 https://www.ft.com/content/dd6853a4-8853-11da-a25e-0000779e2340.

56 Diener, E. (2006), 'Guidelines for national indicators of subjective well-being and ill-being', *Journal of Happiness Studies*, 7, 397–404.

57 Kahneman, D. and Deaton, A. (2010), 'High income improves evaluation of life but not emotional well-being', *Proceedings of the National Academy of Sciences*, 107, 16489–93.

58 Gilovich, T. and Kumar, A. (2015), 'We'll always have Paris: the hedonic payoff from experiential and material investments', *Advances in Experimental Social Psychology*, 51, 147–87.

59 Nawijn, J., et al. (2010), 'Vacationers happier, but most not happier after a holiday', *Applied Research in Quality of Life*, 5, 35–47.

60 Loftus, E. (1979), 'The malleability of human memory', *American Scientist*, 67, 312–20.

61 Matlin, M. W. and Stang, D. J. (1978), *The Pollyanna Principle: Selectivity in Language, Memory, and Thought*. Cambridge, MA: Schenkman Publishing Co.

62 Oerlemans, W. G. M. and Bakker, A. B. (2014), 'Why extraverts are happier: a day reconstruction study', *Journal of Research in Personality*, 50, 11–22.

63 Matz, S. C., Gladston, J. J. and Stillwell, D. (2016), 'Money buys happiness when spending fits our personality', *Psychological Science*, 27, 715–25.

64 Lee, J. C., Hall, D. L. and Wood, W. (2018), 'Experiential or material purchases? Social class determines purchase happiness', *Psychological Science*, https://doi.org/10.1177/0956797617736386.

65 https://www.ons.gov.uk/peoplepopulationandcommunity/leisureand tourism/articles/traveltrends/2015#travel-trends-2015-main-findings.

66 https://www.forbes.com/sites/deborahweinswig/2016/09/07/millennials-go-minimal-the-decluttering-lifestyle-trend-that-is-taking-over/#1d955a583755.

67 https://www.mewssystems.com/blog/why-hotels-are-so-wasteful-and-how-they-can-stop.

68 Lenzen, M., et al. (2018), 'The carbon footprint of global tourism', *Nature Climate Change*, 8, 522–8.

6. WE ARE WHAT WE OWN

1 https://www.caba.org.uk/help-and-guides/information/coping-emotional-impact-burglary.

2 http://www.huffingtonpost.com/2015/04/21/self-storage-mcdonalds_n_7107822.html.

3 James, W. (1890), *Principles of Psychology*. New York: Henry Holt & Co.

4 Sartre, J.-P. (1943/1969), *Being and Nothingness: A Phenomenological Essay on Ontology.* New York: Philosophical Library/London: Methuen.

5 McCracken, G. (1990), *Culture and Consumption.* Bloomington, Ind.: Indiana University Press.

6 Shoumatoff, A. (2014), 'The Devil and the art dealer', *Vanity Fair*, April, https://www.vanityfair.com/news/2014/04/degenerate-art-cornelius-gurlitt-munich-apartment.

7 Prelinger, E. (1959), 'Extension and structure of the self', *Journal of Psychology*, 47, 13–23.

8 Dixon, S. C. and Street, J. W. (1975), 'The distinction between self and non-self in children and adolescents', *Journal of Genetic Psychology*, 127, 157–62.

9 Belk, R. (1988), 'Possessions and the extended self', *Journal of Consumer Research*, 15, 139–68.

10 https://www.theguardian.com/music/2017/jan/03/record-sales-vinyl-hits-25-year-high-and-outstrips-streaming.

11 Marx, K. (1867/1990), *Capital.* London: Penguin Classics.

12 Nemeroff, C. J. and Rozin, P. (1994), 'The contagion concept in adult thinking in the United States: transmission of germs and of interpersonal influence', *Ethos: Journal of the Society for Psychological Anthropology*, 22, 158–86.

13 Lee, C., et al. (2011), 'Putting like a pro: the role of positive contagion in golf performance and perception', *PLoS ONE*, 6 (10), e26016.

14 Damisch, L., Stoberock, B. and Mussweiler, T. (2010), 'Keep your fingers crossed! How superstition improves performance', *Psychological Science*, 21, 1014–20.

15 Vohs, K. (2015), 'Money priming can change people's thoughts, feelings, motivations, and behaviors: an update on 10 years of experiments', *Journal of Experimental Psychology: General*, 144, 8693.

16 Belk, R. (1988), 'Possessions and the extended self', *Journal of Consumer Research*, 15, 139–68.

17 Belk, R. W. (2013), 'Extended self in a digital world', *Journal of Consumer Research*, 40, 477–500.

18 Vogel, E. A., et al. (2015), 'Who compares and despairs? The effect of social comparison orientation on social media use and its outcomes', *Personality and Individual Differences*, 86, 249–56.

19 Hood, B. (2012), *The Self Illusion.* New York: Oxford University Press.

20 Evans, C. (2018), '1.7 million U.S Facebook users will pass away in 2018', The Digital Beyond, http://www.thedigitalbeyond.com/2018/01/1-7-million-u-s-facebook-users-will-pass-away-in-2018/.

21 Öhman, C. and Floridi, L. (2018), 'An ethical framework for the digital afterlife industry', *Nature Human Behavior*, 2, 318–20.

22 Henrich, J., Heine, S. J. and Norenzayan, A. (2010), 'The weirdest people in the world?', *Behavioral and Brain Sciences*, 33, 61–135.

23 Nisbett, R. E. (2003), *The Geography of Thought*. New York: Free Press.

24 Rochat, P., et al. (2009), 'Fairness in distributive justice by 3- and 5-year-olds across 7 cultures', *Journal of Cross-Cultural Psychology*, 40, 416–42.

25 Weltzien, S., et al. (forthcoming), 'Considering self or others across two cultural contexts: how children's prosocial behaviour is affected by self-construal manipulations', *Journal of Experimental Child Psychology*.

26 Best, E. (1924), *The Maori, Vol. 1*. Wellington, New Zealand: H. H. Tombs, p. 397.

27 Masuda, T. and Nisbett, R. E. (2001), 'Attending holistically vs analytically: comparing the context sensitivity of Japanese and Americans', *Journal of Personality & Social Psychology*, 81, 922–34.

28 Kitayama, S., et al. (2003), 'Perceiving an object and its context in different cultures', *Psychological Science*, 14, 201–6.

29 Gutchess, A. H., et al. (2006), 'Cultural differences in neural function associated with object processing', *Cognitive Affective Behavioral Neuroscience*, 6, 102–9.

30 Hedden, T., et al. (2008), 'Cultural influences on neural substrates of attentional control', *Psychological Science*, 19, 12–17.

31 Tang, Y., et al. (2006), 'Arithmetic processing in the brain shaped by cultures', *Proceedings of the National Academy of Sciences*, 103, 10775–80.

32 Zhu, Y., et al. (2007), 'Neural basis of cultural influence on self representation', *NeuroImage*, 34, 1310–17.

33 Kobayashi, C., Glover, G. H. and Temple, E. (2006), 'Cultural and linguistic influence on neural bases of theory of mind: an fMRI study with Japanese bilinguals', *Brain & Language*, 98, 210–20.

34 Gardner, W. L., Gabriel, S. and Lee, A. Y. (1999), ' "I" value freedom, but "we" value relationships: self-construal priming mirrors cultural differences in judgment', *Psychological Science*, 10, 321–6.

35 Kiuchi, A. (2006), 'Independent and interdependent self-construals: ramifications for a multicultural society', *Japanese Psychological Research*, 48, 1–16.

36 Han, S. and Humphreys, G. (2016), 'Self-construal: a cultural framework for brain function', *Current Opinion in Psychology*, 8, 10–14.

37 Bruner, J. S. (1951), 'Personality dynamics and the process of perceiving'. In R. R. Blake and G. V. Ramsey, eds., *Perception: An Approach to Personality*. New York: Ronald Press.

38 Mumford, L. (1938), *The Culture of Cities*. New York: Harcourt, Brace and Company.

39 Turner, F. J. (1920), *The Frontier in American History*. New York: Henry Holt & Co.

40 Vandello, J. A. and Cohen, D. (1999), 'Patterns of individualism and collectivism across the United States', *Journal of Personality and Social Psychology*, 77, 279–92.

41 Kitayama, S., et al. (2006), 'Voluntary settlement and the spirit of independence: evidence from Japan's "northern frontier"', *Journal of Personality and Social Psychology*, 91, 369–84.

42 Santos, H. C., Varnum, M. E. W. and Grossmann, I. (2017), 'Global increases in individualism', *Psychological Science*, 28, 1228–39.

43 Yu, F., et al. (2016), 'Cultural value shifting in pronoun use', *Journal of Cross-Cultural Psychology*, 47, 310–16.

44 Grossmann, I. and Varnum, M. E. W. (2015), 'Social structure, infectious diseases, disasters, secularism, and cultural change in America', *Psychological Science*, 26, 311–24.

45 Piaget, J. and Inhelder, B. (1969), *The Psychology of the Child*. New York: Basic Books.

46 Rodriguez, F. A., Carlsson, F. and Johansson-Stenman, O. (2008), 'Anonymity, reciprocity, and conformity: evidence from voluntary contributions to a national park in Costa Rica', *Journal of Public Economics*, 92, 1047–60.

47 Gächter, S. and Herrmann, B. (2009), 'Reciprocity, culture, and human cooperation: previous insights and a new cross-cultural experiment', *Philosophical Transactions of the Royal Society B: Biological Sciences*, 364, 791–80.

48 Cunningham, S., et al. (2008), 'Yours or mine? Ownership and memory', *Consciousness and Cognition*, 17, 312–18.

49 Cunningham, S., et al. (2013), 'Exploring early self-referential memory effects through ownership', *British Journal of Developmental Psychology*, 31, 289–301.

50 Rogers, T. B., Kuiper, N. A. and Kirker, W. S. (1977), 'Self-reference and the encoding of personal information', *Journal of Personality and Social Psychology*, 35, 677–88.

51 Turk, D. J., et al. (2011), 'Mine and me: exploring the neural basis of object ownership', *Journal of Cognitive Neuroscience*, 11, 3657–68.

52 Zhu, Y., et al. (2007), 'Neural basis of cultural influence on self-representation', *NeuroImage*, 34, 1310–16.

53 Shavitt, S. and Cho, H. (2016), 'Culture and consumer behavior: the role of horizontal and vertical cultural factors', *Current Opinion in Psychology*, 8, 149–54.

54 Shavitt, S., Johnson, T. P. and Zhang, J. (2011), 'Horizontal and vertical cultural differences in the content of advertising appeals', *Journal of International Consumer Marketing*, 23, 297–310.

55 https://www.theguardian.com/books/2016/dec/11/undoing-project-michael-lewis-review-amos-tversky-daniel-kahneman-behavioural-psychology.

56 Kahneman, D. and Tversky, A. (1984), 'Choices, values, and frames', *American Psychologist*, 39, 341–50.

57 Kahneman, D. (2012), *Thinking, Fast and Slow*. London: Penguin.

58 Brickman, P., Coates, D. and Janoff-Bulman, R. (1978), 'Lottery winners and accident victims: is happiness relative?', *Journal of Personality and Social Psychology*, 36, 917–27.

59 Lindqvist, E., Östling, R. and Cecarini, D. (2018), *Long-run Effects of Lottery Wealth on Psychological Well-being*. Working Paper Series 1220, Research Institute of Industrial Economics.

60 Rosenfeld, P. J., Kennedy, G. and Giacalone, R. A. (1986), 'Decision making: a demonstration of the postdecision dissonance effect', *Journal of Social Psychology*, 126, 663–5.

61 Langer, E. (1975), 'The illusion of control', *Journal of Personality and Social Psychology*, 32, 311–28.

62 van de Ven, N. and Zeelenberg, M. (2011), 'Regret aversion and the reluctance to exchange lottery tickets', *Journal of Economic Psychology*, 32, 194–200.

63 Gilovich, T., Medvec, V. H. and Chen, S. (1995), 'Commission, omission, and dissonance reduction: coping with regret in the "Monty Hall" problem', *Personality and Social Psychology Bulletin*, 21, 185–90.

64 Hintze, A., et al. (2015), 'Risk sensitivity as an evolutionary adaptation', *Science Reports*, 5, 8242, doi:10.1038/srep08242.

65 Dunbar, R. (1993), 'Coevolution of neocortical size, group size and language in humans', *Behavorial and Brain Sciences*, 16, 681–735.

66 Cronqvist, H. and Siegel, S. (2014), 'The genetics of investment biases', *Journal of Financial Economics*, 113, 215–34.

67 Rangel, A., Camerer, C. and Montague, P. R. (2008), 'A framework for studying the neurobiology of value-based decision making', *Nature Review Neuroscience*, 9, 545–56.

68 Knutson, B. and Greer, S. M. (2008), 'Anticipatory affect: neural correlates and consequences for choice', *Philosophical Transactions of the Royal Society B: Biological Sciences*, 363, 3771–86.

69 DeWall, C. N., Chester, D. S. and White, D. S. (2015), 'Can acetaminophen reduce the pain of decision-making?', *Journal of Experimental Social Psychology*, 56, 117–20.

70 Knutson, B., et al. (2008), 'Neural antecedents of the endowment effect', *Neuron*, 58, 814–22.

7. LETTING GO

1 Kahneman, D. and Tversky, A. (1979), 'Prospect theory: an analysis of decision under risk', *Econometrica*, 47, 263–92.

2 Novemsky, N. and Kahneman, D. (2005), 'The boundaries of loss aversion', *Journal of Marketing Research*, 42, 119–28.

3 Kahneman, D., Knetsch, J. L. and Thaler, R. H. (1991), 'The endowment effect, loss aversion and status quo bias', *Journal of Economic Perspectives*, 5, 193–206.

4 Bramsen, J.-M. (2008), 'A Pseudo-Endowment Effect in Internet Auctions', MPRA Paper, University Library of Munich, Germany.

5 Wolf, J. R., Arkes, H. R. and Muhanna, W. (2008), 'The power of touch: an examination of the effect of duration of physical contact on the valuation of objects', *Judgment and Decision Making*, 3, 476–82.

6 Maddux, W. M., et al. (2010), 'For whom is parting with possessions more painful? Cultural differences in the endowment effect', *Psychological Science*, 21, 1910–17.

7 Harbaugh, W. T., Krause, K. and Vesterlund, L. (2001), 'Are adults better behaved than children? Age, experience, and the endowment effect', *Economics Letters*, 70, 175–81.

8 Hood, B., et al. (2016), 'Picture yourself: self-focus and the endowment effect in preschool children', *Cognition*, 152, 70–77.

9 Hartley, C. and Fisher, S. (2017), 'Mine is better than yours: investigating the ownership effect in children with autism spectrum disorder and typically developing children', *Cognition*, 172, 26–36.

10 Lee, A., Hobson, R. P. and Chiat, S. (1994), 'I, you, me, and autism: an experimental study', *Journal of Autism and Developmental Disorders*, 24, 155–76.

11 Lind, S. E. (2010), 'Memory and the self in autism: a review and theoretical framework', *Autism*, 14, 430–56.

12 Apicella, C. L., et al. (2014), 'Evolutionary origins of the endowment effect: evidence from hunter-gatherers', *American Economic Review*, 104, 1793–805.

13 List, J. A. (2011), 'Does market experience eliminate market anomalies? The case of exogenous market experience', *American Economic Review*, 101, 313–17.

14 Tong, L. C. P., et al. (2016), 'Trading experience modulates anterior insula to reduce the endowment effect', *Proceedings of the National Academy of Sciences*, 113, 9238–43.

15 http://edition.cnn.com/2008/US/11/28/black.friday.violence/index.html.

16 Seymour, B., et al. (2007), 'Differential encoding of losses and gains in the human striatum', *Journal of Neuroscience*, 27, 4826–31.

17 Knutson, B. and Cooper, J. C. (2009), 'The lure of the unknown', *Neuron*, 51, 280–81.

18 Olds, J. and Milner, P. (1954), 'Positive reinforcement produced by electrical stimulation of septal area and other regions of rat brain', *Journal of Comparative Physiological Psychology*, 47, 419–27.

19 Blum, K., et al. (2012), 'Sex, drugs, and rock 'n' roll: hypothesizing common mesolimbic activation as a function of reward gene polymorphisms', *Journal of Psychoactive Drugs*, 44, 38–55.

20 Moore, T. J., Glenmullen, J. and Mattison, D. R. (2014), 'Reports of pathological gambling, hypersexuality, and compulsive shopping associated with dopamine receptor agonist drugs', *Journal of the American Medical Association*, 174, 1930–33.

21 Knutson, B., et al. (2006), 'Neural predictors of purchases', *Neuron*, 53, 147–56.

22 Cath, D. C., et al. (2017), 'Age-specific prevalence of hoarding and obsessive-compulsive disorder: a population-based study', *American Journal of Geriatric Psychiatry*, 25, 245–55.

23 http://time.com/2880968/connecticut-hoarder-beverly-mitchell/.

24 http://www.mfb.vic.gov.au/Community-Safety/Home-Fire-Safety/Hoarding-a-lethal-fire-risk.html.

25 Samuels, J. F., et al. (2007), 'Hoarding in obsessive-compulsive disorder: results from the OCD collaborative genetics study', *Behaviour Research and Therapy*, 45, 673–86.

26 Cooke, J. (2017), *Understanding Hoarding*. London: Sheldon Press.

27 Tolin, D. F., et al. (2012), 'Neural mechanisms of decision making in hoarding disorder', *Archives of General Psychiatry*, 69, 832–41.

28 Christopoulos, G. I., et al. (2009), 'Neural correlates of value, risk, and risk aversion contributing to decision making under risk', *Journal of Neuroscience*, 29, 12574–83.

29 Votinov, M., et al. (2010), 'The neural correlates of endowment effect without economic transaction', *Neuroscience Research*, 68, 59–65.

30 http://www.investinganswers.com/personal-finance/homes-mortgages/8-insane-ways-people-destroyed-their-foreclosed-homes-4603.

31 Garcia-Moreno, C., et al. (2005), *WHO Multicountry Study on Women's Health and Domestic Violence against Women: Initial Results on Prevalence, Health Outcomes and Women's Responses*. Geneva: World Health Organization.

32 Yardley, E., Wilson, D. and Lynes, A. (2013), 'A taxonomy of male British family annihilators, 1980–2012', *The Howard Journal of Crime and Justice*, 53, 117–40.

33 Nadler, J. and Diamond, S. S. (2008), 'Eminent domain and the psychology of property rights: proposed use, subjective attachment, and taker identity', *Journal of Empirical Legal Studies*, 5, 713–49.

34 https://www.theglobeandmail.com/real-estate/vancouver/meet-the-wealthy-immigrants-at-the-centre-of-vancouvers-housingdebate/article31212036/.

35 http://www.propertyportalwatch.com/juwei-com-survey-finds-chinese-buyers-prefer-new-homes/.

36 Quote in Revkin, Andrew C. (2016), 'In Italy's earthquake zone, love of place trumps safety', *New York Times*, 25 August, http://dotearth. blogs.nytimes.com/2016/08/25/in-italys-earthquake-zone-love-of-place-trumps-safety/.

37 Rozin, P. and Wolf, S. (2008), 'Attachment to land: the case of the land of Israel for American and Israeli Jews and the role of contagion', *Judgment and Decision Making*, 3, 325–34.

38 Dittmar, H., et al. (2014), 'The relationship between materialism and personal well-being: a meta-analysis', *Journal of Personality and Social Psychology*, 107, 879–924.

EPILOGUE

1 Csikszentmihalyi, M. (1982), 'The Symbolic Function of Possessions: Towards a Psychology of Materialism'. Paper presented at the 90th Annual Convention of the American Psychological Association, Washington, DC, quoted in Belk, R. (1988), 'Possessions and the extended self', *Journal of Consumer Research*, 15, 139–68.

2 https://www.facebook.com/WokeFolks/videos/10149900853080007/.

3 Schopenhauer, A. (1851), *Parerga und Paralipomena*. Berlin.

4 Ackerman, D., MacInnis, D. and Folkes, F. (2000), 'Social comparisons of possessions: when it feels good and when it feels bad', *Advances
   in Consumer Research*, 27, 173–8.

5 Belk, R. (2011), 'Benign envy', *Academy of Marketing Sciences Review*,
   1, 117–34.

6 Wolcott, R. C. (2018), 'How automation will change work, purpose and
   meaning', *Harvard Business Review*, January, https://hbr.org/2018/01/
   how-automation-will-change-work-purpose-and-meaning.

7 https://www.rita.dot.gov/bts/sites/rita.dot.gov.bts/files/publications/trans
   portation_economic_trends/ch4/index.html.

Index